AUDITING CASES

Frank A. Buckless

Mark S. Beasley

Steven M. Glover

Douglas F. Prawitt

Prentice Hall
Upper Saddle River, New Jersey 07458

#435373726

Acquisitions Editor: Annie Todd
Editorial Assistant: Fran Toepfer
Editor-in-Chief: P. J. Boardman
Marketing Manager: Beth Toland
Production Editor: Lynne Breitfeller
Permissions Coordinator: Monica Stipinov
Manufacturing Buyer: Lynne Breitfeller
Manufacturing Supervisor: Gail Steier de Acevedo
Manufacturing Manager: Vincent Scelta
Design Manager: Patricia Smythe
Cover Design: Michael J. Fruhbeis
Cover Illustration/Photo: George Schill
Composition: Omegatype Typography, Inc.

Prentice-Hall International (UK) Limited, London
Prentice-Hall of Australia Pty. Limited, Sydney
Prentice-Hall Canada, Inc., Toronto
Prentice-Hall Hispanoamericana, S.A., Mexico
Prentice-Hall of India Private Limited, New Delhi
Prentice-Hall of Japan, Inc., Tokyo
Simon & Schuster Asia Pte, Ltd., Singapore
Editora Prentice-Hall do Brasil, Ltda., Rio De Janeiro

Printed in the United States of America

10 9 8 7 6 5 4 3 2 1

Contents

Contents

Preface

In recent years many accounting practitioners and academics have requested accounting educators to increase the emphasis on the development of students' critical thinking, communication, and interpersonal relationship skills. Development of these types of skills requires a shift from passive involvement to active involvement of students in the learning process. Unfortunately, current course materials provided by many publishers are not readily adaptable to this more active learning environment. The objective of writing this casebook was to develop course materials that would provide students hands-on exposure to realistic cases involving all aspects of the audit process.

This casebook contains a collection of 28 auditing cases that address most major activities performed during the conduct of an audit from client acceptance to issuance of an audit report. Many of the cases are based on actual companies, some of which were engaged in financial reporting fraud. Several cases involve students working with realistic audit evidence and preparing and evaluating audit working papers. A couple of the cases expose students to assurance and other value added services.

The cases included in this book are suitable for both undergraduate and graduate students. At the undergraduate level, the cases provide students with active learning experiences that reinforce key audit concepts addressed by the instructor and textbook. At the graduate level, the cases provide students with active learning experiences that expand the depth of their audit knowledge. Use of the casebook will provide undergraduate and graduate students with opportunities to develop critical thinking, communication and interpersonal relationships skills.

The casebook provides a wide variety of cases to facilitate different learning and teaching styles. For example, several of the cases can be used either as in-class exercises or out-of-class assignments. The instructor resource manual accompanying the casebook clearly illustrates the different instructional approaches available for each case (e.g., examples of cooperative/active learning activities and identification of which cases are useful for brief in-class exercises and/or out-of-class individual or group assignments) and efficiently prepares the instructor for leading interactive discussions.

ACKNOWLEDGMENTS

We would like to thank our families for their understanding and support while writing this casebook. We would also like to thank our reviewers:

Dr. James Carroll	Georgian Court College
John E. Delaney	Southwestern University
Jerrell W. Habegger	Susquehana University
Brian Shapiro	University of Minnesota

Jacksonville Jaguars: Evaluating IT Benefits and Risks and Identifying Assurance Services Opportunities

Frank A. Buckless, Mark S. Beasley,
Steven M. Glover, and Douglas F. Prawitt

LEARNING OBJECTIVES

After completing and discussing this case, you should be able to

- Identify benefits to businesses from implementing information technologies
- Recognize risks that are associated with the use of information technology (IT)
- Determine how CPAs can provide assurance about processes designed to reduce risks created when new IT systems are introduced
- Understand ways CPAs can identify new assurance services opportunities
- Prepare a formal business memorandum

INTRODUCTION—PART A

The Jacksonville Jaguars National Football League (NFL) team is taking advantage of electronic commerce tools in the sale of stadium snacks and souvenirs. At Alltel Stadium where the Jaguars play their home games, football fans can use Spot Cards to purchase soft drinks, beer, popcorn, and Jaguar souvenirs rather than fumble for cash and change when making their purchases.[1]

Not only does the Spot Card offer benefits to fans in the stadium, but the use of electronic commerce offers advantages for snack and souvenir vendors by providing better information for monitoring their businesses. Although electronic commerce offers improvements for the fans and vendors, those who rely on the Spot Card to process sales

---

[1]Many of the facts about the Spot Card system are *based on* an article titled "Jacksonville Jaguars Fans Score Big with Smart Cards" by Maura McEnaney that appeared in *EC World,* January 1998, pp. 24–27.

This case was prepared by Frank A. Buckless, Ph.D. and Mark S. Beasley, Ph.D. of North Carolina State University and Steven M. Glover, Ph.D. and Douglas F. Prawitt, Ph.D. of Brigham Young University, as a basis for class discussion. It is not intended to illustrate either effective or ineffective handling of an administrative situation.

need assurance that the technology and related information produced is accurate and reliable.

CPAs are in a position to leverage their independence and their information accumulation and evaluation skills, among other abilities, to provide assurance to those relying on electronic commerce. The use of the Spot Card at Alltel Stadium offers opportunities for CPAs to provide valuable assurance, particularly to stadium management and vendors who must rely on this IT to do business.

BACKGROUND ABOUT THE JAGUAR'S SPOT CARD

The implementation of the Spot Card at the stadium in Jacksonville represents one of the first uses of that type of electronic commerce in a major sports stadium. The stadium contracted with First Union Bank, based in Charlotte, North Carolina, to develop and implement the Spot Card system. First Union contracted with Diebold Incorporated of Canton, Ohio, which manufactures card-based transaction systems, to develop the Spot Card system.

Customers purchase Spot Cards in various denominations such as $20, $50, and $100. ATM-like machines in the stadium allow fans to transfer funds from their bank or credit card onto an electronic chip on the Spot Card. Fans also can buy cards with cash. Other terminals also are located in various First Union branches around Jacksonville. Card readers located throughout the stadium allow fans to check the balances remaining on their cards.

Fans purchasing snacks and souvenirs present their Spot Card to vendors at concession and souvenir stands, who calculate sales amounts and swipe the cards through point-of-sale (POS) machines. Software tracks each transaction for vendors. Before the transaction is complete, fans review the amount to be deducted and punch the "Yes" key on the POS machine. At that point, the POS device deducts the purchase amount from the chip-embedded balance on the fan's Spot Card. These cards can also be used at battery-operated POS computers carried by vendors who roam the stadium stands selling merchandise during the game.

The POS machines capture information about each transaction. The system records the card number, location code, and the date and time of the transaction, as well as the items sold. That information is later summarized for vendors.

Once the game is over, vendors link their POS machines to a network that allows the transfer of data stored on each POS machine to a computer located in the stadium counting room. After all the data are downloaded to that computer, the information is then transmitted to a host computer at First Union Bank in Jacksonville. The host computer uses the data transmitted to settle that day's sales with each vendor in the stadium. The host computer produces various reports, which provide vendors detailed information to track sales volume for specific products in specific sections of the stadium.

First Union Bank receives a fee from every Spot Card transaction, and the bank collects whatever remains on an unused Spot Card at the end of two years. First Union also sells player-signature Spot Cards with pictures of selected Jaguar players on the front for an additional fee.

Other stadiums around the country, such as the Charlotte Panthers' stadium in North Carolina, have started to use similar technologies. As fans grow more accustomed to the use of transaction cards like the Spot Card, there will undoubtedly be expanded opportunities for using the cards to pay for stadium parking or merchandise and promotions outside stadiums.

OPPORTUNITIES FOR CPAS TO PROVIDE ASSURANCE

The American Institute of Certified Public Accountants' (AICPA) Special Committee on Assurance Services recently developed new CPA "assurance services" opportunities. These new services are designed to allow CPAs to provide assurance about the reliability and relevance of information decision-makers use to run their businesses.

Certain forms of assurance services have always been performed by CPAs. For example, auditors of historical financial statements provide assurance about whether those financial statements are in conformity with generally accepted accounting principles (GAAP). Continuous changes in IT will provide new opportunities for CPAs to provide assurance regarding the accuracy, reliability, and relevance of information produced by these technologies. Organizations will have greater need for assurance on systems and controls as IT continues to play a larger role in business.

One of the opportunities proposed for CPAs by the AICPA's Special Committee on Assurance Services relates to IT Systems Reliability Assurance. In these engagements, CPAs can provide users with assurance that an IT system has been properly designed and produces reliable data. In doing so, CPAs might test the integrity of an information system by analyzing sample IT output for accuracy. Assurance providers can also provide valuable services to help organizations determine whether systems are secure and whether adequate contingency plans are in place in the event of system failure or disaster.

As First Union and its competitors attempt to market Spot Card technologies to other stadiums and businesses, there may be opportunities for CPAs to provide assurance that the processes related to this technology produce accurate and reliable information. Providers, such as First Union, can then use the assurance to better market their products.

REQUIRED—PART A

1. To become more familiar with emerging assurance services opportunities, review the Assurance Services site at the AICPA's Web page (www.aicpa.org). The Assurance Services Site Map provides a great overview of the information contained in this site. Search this web site to complete the following exercises:

    a. Summarize in your own words the definition of assurance services

    b. Describe the 10 major themes the Special Committee on Assurances Services used to develop the new assurance service opportunities

    c. Read the Executive Summary under the "Future of the Financial Statement Audit," and then describe the "old paradigm" and "new paradigm" for providing assurance

    d. Identify the "Megatrends" the Special Committee on Assurance Services noted as affecting the demand for assurance services

    e. Describe briefly each of the six examples of assurance service opportunities developed by the Special Committee on Assurance Services

2. The use of electronic commerce offers tremendous advantages. What benefits does the use of Spot Cards offer to Jaguar stadium snack and souvenir vendors? What are the benefits for the fans in the stadium? What are the benefits to First Union?

3. Although the Spot Card offers several benefits, the use of IT to process snack and souvenir transactions does create new risks. Identify risks for the vendors, customers, and the bank.

4. What processes or controls could the stadium and First Union implement to help reduce these risks?

5. How might CPAs be able to structure an assurance services engagement to assure stadium vendors that information processed through the Spot Card system is reliable? What kind of information could the CPA examine and evaluate in order to assure stadium vendors that they can reasonably rely on the Spot Card system to conduct business?

INTRODUCTION—PART B

After completing Part A of this assignment, your instructor may ask you to complete Part B. Do not proceed to Part B unless requested to do so by your instructor.

BACKGROUND

Congratulations!!! You were recently promoted to audit manager. Your strong work ethic and, of course, your excellent college training have propelled your career to new heights.

One of the challenges of your new role is that you are now held accountable (i.e., raises, bonuses, the partnership!) for bringing in new business. You have been regularly reading the financial business press (i.e., newspapers, business magazines) to see if you can identify new service opportunities.

The managing partner came to you today and asked if you know of any companies that recently introduced new IT that could lead to consulting or assurance services opportunities. He is particularly interested in identifying opportunities to provide some form of assurance about risks related to newly implemented IT. After you indicated you are actually working on a couple of ideas, he was excited to hear more. He asked you to prepare a memorandum outlining your answers to address the following issues:

REQUIRED—PART B

1. Please describe a situation in which a company recently introduced new IT into their business operations. You should look for a real world example from the business press. Look for a business that recently increased its reliance on IT. The Spot Card technology used at the Jacksonville Jaguars stadium is a good example. Please attach a copy of the article you use to prepare your memorandum.

2. Please describe the new technology and how it is used. Provide enough information for the partner to understand the technology without having to go back to the attached article.

3. Explain why the company introduced the technology. Highlight the benefits to various constituents affected by the technology. The benefits related to the technology are probably easily identified and may even be discussed in the related article. However, the article does not likely address risks that are introduced. Please provide a thorough discussion of the risks to all parties affected by the new technology.

4. Given the risks identified, describe whether there are any related assurance services and discuss who would likely buy these services. Describe information risks about which your firm intends to provide assurance. Your memo will serve as the basis for the formal business proposal that will be sent to the potential client. Please be sure to briefly outline in your memo what assurance services are because the potential client may not have heard the terms. Make sure you explain the term "assurance services" in your own words so that the potential client has a better idea of exactly what services you propose to provide.

5. In describing the nature of the assurance services that you plan to provide, please highlight the types of evidence you would want to gather as a basis for providing the assurance. For example, you might consider evaluating the contingency plan describing how the company would deal with breakdowns in technology hardware or software or the communication infrastructure. In this example, you would want to specifically describe what types of information you would look for in that plan.

Your partner is very busy and does not want your memo to exceed four single-spaced pages. Again, be sure to attach the related article(s) to your memo. Strive to step out of the typical accountant's box and be creative!!! You'll be expected to do so in the real world.

A Day in the Life of Brent Dorsey: Staff Auditor Professional Pressures

Frank A. Buckless, Mark S. Beasley,
Steven M. Glover, and Douglas F. Prawitt

LEARNING OBJECTIVES

After completing and discussing this case you should be able to

- Understand some of the pressures faced by young professionals in the workplace
- Generate and evaluate alternative courses of action to resolve a difficult workplace issue
- Understand more fully the implications of "eating time" and "premature sign-off"
- More fully appreciate the need to balance professional and personal demands

INTRODUCTION

Brent Dorsey graduated eight months ago with a master's degree in accounting. After graduating, Brent began working with a large accounting firm in Portland. He is now on his second audit engagement—a company called Northwest Steel Producers. Working day-to-day with Brent on the audit are two other staff auditors, Scott Olsen and Megan Mills, along with the senior auditor, John Peters. Scott and Megan are both second-year staff accountants and are anticipating a promotion to senior in the next year.

John Peters has been with the firm for about five years and has been a senior-level auditor for almost three years. Following this busy season, the partners and managers will sit down and decide which seniors to promote to managers. The rumor around the office is that only four or five of the seven eligible seniors in the office will be promoted in the Portland office. Those not promoted in Portland will most likely be asked to transfer to other offices within the firm that need new managers. Some may even be "counseled out" of the firm. John has done a reasonably good job in the audits he's been

This case was prepared by Frank A. Buckless, Ph.D. and Mark S. Beasley, Ph.D. of North Carolina State University and Steven M. Glover, Ph.D. and Douglas F. Prawitt, Ph.D. of Brigham Young University, as a basis for class discussion. It is not intended to illustrate either effective or ineffective handling of an administrative situation.

in charge of, yet he feels he is "on the bubble" as far as the promotion in Portland goes. He has recently received several performance evaluations that have criticized him for letting his jobs get "out of control" (i.e., over budget and beyond deadline). He believes his performance on the Northwest Steel Producers audit could make a difference in his chances to stay in Portland. John and his wife are from the Portland area and neither one is ready for a transfer.

Northwest Steel is one of the office's biggest clients. The firm has been auditing Northwest for the past 13 years. Because of the client's reporting deadline, the Northwest Steel audit is notorious for tight deadlines and long hours.

BACKGROUND

With a final click on his laptop, Brent finished his audit work associated with Northwest's largest cash account. It was 5:45 p.m. on a Friday evening, and Brent was looking forward to a much-needed day off to spend some time with his wife, Katherine, who had a demanding job as a young attorney. They both understood that the degree of tension they had been feeling at home was probably due primarily to their stressful careers, and they felt a need to discuss their relationship in an attempt to "clear the air." It seemed there had been precious little time for any serious discussions these past few weeks.

Brent started saving files so he could shut down his computer when the door of the small conference room he was using as an office opened a crack. Brent's briefcase partially blocked the door. "Door's open," Brent called out. "Just push a little harder." The door opened wider and Scott Olsen poked his head in. By the expression on Scott's face, Brent had a feeling the news wasn't going to be good. "Hi Scott, what's up?" asked Brent, trying to be upbeat.

"John wants the audit team together for a meeting in 15 minutes," Scott said as he pushed his shoulders through the doorway.

Brent glanced quickly at his watch. "It's almost 6:00! What's he doing calling a meeting at this time of the day?"

"I don't know. He just called from his cell phone and said that he was on his way and that it was important that we all meet with him as soon as possible. But I have a feeling it's going to mean more work," Scott said as he pulled himself back out the doorway. "I've got to run down a couple of things before the meeting, so I'll see you there." Scott disappeared just as quickly as he had appeared.

Brent picked up the phone and called Katherine, who had just arrived home from work. "Hi Kate. John just called an emergency meeting. I'm going to be late again."

"Brent, this is getting ridiculous. Just because those people don't have a life doesn't mean we can't. I picked up a couple videos and some take-out on the way home. Just leave John a note that you had plans with your wife and come home."

"Katherine, you know I would rather be home with you than in another meeting, but at this stage in my career I don't think blowing off an urgent meeting would be the wise thing to do. I'll get home as soon as I can. Should I invite John over to watch the videos with us?"

"Very funny. Actually, maybe you should bring him along so I can try to talk some sense into him. Our lives seem so crazy. I don't know how much more of this I can take. I see the city bus driver more than I see you."

"It'll get better, Katherine. Once we get through with the Northwest audit, things will lighten up. But for now, this is a good opportunity for me to prove I'm a team player and that I can work as hard as the next guy. I've already seen how important a reputation is in this firm. I've done pretty well so far, and that's why they put me on this audit. If I can prove myself, at some point I'll have more control over my day-to-day schedule. It is just really important that I build a good foundation for my career."

"I know, but I worry that it will never stop. There will always be another client, another promotion. If we don't establish a good pattern now, when will we? Anyway, you do what you've got to do. I'll put your dinner in the fridge, and I'll tell you how the video was." A cold "click" sounded in Brent's ear.

Brent slowly put the receiver back on the hook and stared at the small picture he kept in his briefcase. The picture was taken on Brent and Katherine's wedding day almost ten months ago. They were now expecting their first child, due in another five months. Brent acknowledged he had been working a lot lately, but he felt a strong need to prove himself in the firm. He felt challenged and fulfilled by his work, and he felt that some sacrifice now would open up more opportunities in the future. Then he could spend more time with his family. Speaking of family, why did this baby have to come along now, of all times? He and Katherine had wanted children, but not quite this soon. They would soon be facing the difficult issues that come with balancing two careers *and* a family.

With a start he realized nearly 15 minutes had passed, and the meeting was about to begin. Jumping up, he grabbed his planner and ran out the door, knocking his briefcase to the floor. When he arrived at the other conference room that John was using as his on-site office, Scott and Megan were already there. Just as Brent nodded to Scott and Megan, both looking glum, John came into the room.

"Sorry to call a meeting so late, but we have something very important to talk over," John said. "So far on this audit we are more than 30 hours over budget." He slumped into his chair. We absolutely have to make some of this time up. We need to come in pretty close to budget on this audit, and we've absolutely got to get it wrapped up in time for the client's scheduled earnings release at the end of next week." John shuffled through some papers on the table. He finally came to the one he was looking for. "I've been looking over the budgeted hours for the remaining segments of the audit. One of the remaining areas is accounts payable. That segment's got a budget of 42 hours. But I'd like to see it completed in no more than 35 hours. We're running out of chances to bring in this audit close to budget. Do a good job, but I really think it should take 35 hours max to do payables and I'd like it wrapped up by Monday afternoon." Megan and Scott exchanged a glance.

John stood up and paced around the room. "I know I said I thought we'd be able to take Saturday off. But this is an important engagement and we need to deliver. We all stand to gain on our performance evaluations if we come in looking good on this audit. So let's keep our heads down a few more days. I need your help on this guys." John stopped pacing and put his hands on his hips. "Scott, I want you and Brent to start on payables first thing in the morning. Megan, you make sure you get receivables tied down by the time you go home tomorrow. You're still on track for coming in under budget on receivables, aren't you?" John stared until Megan nodded hesitantly. "Good. Well, that's it. I'll see you all tomorrow morning." John gathered up his things and walked out of the room, looking like he had the world on his shoulders.

"Great! There goes the weekend," said Megan as soon as John was out of sight. "Yeah, my wife and I had big plans, too," muttered Scott, glancing down at the stack of folders on his lap. Just then, Scott's pager went off. "Now what?" said Scott as he started for the door. Then he mumbled through a wry smile, "Maybe my house is on fire. At least then maybe I could take the rest of the weekend off."

WHAT ARE THE ALTERNATIVES?

Brent sat slumping in his chair, wondering how on earth he and Scott were going to finish accounts payable in 35 hours. Rumor had it that last year's team may have "eaten time" to get some parts of last year's audit done within budget, and this year's budget was even lower than last years' *reported* time. Brent looked up at Megan, who sat in her chair looking bleary-eyed. "How on earth are Scott and I going to get payables tied down in 35 hours, Meg?"

"We've been auditing this firm for years, so you'd think by now we would know how long it takes to audit accounts payable, wouldn't you? Last year it took almost 50 hours. I don't know why we insist on lowering the budget every year," said Megan. "I worked on payables last year and there weren't any problems with them at all. Or the year before, for that matter. In fact, I don't think there has ever been a problem with payables in all the years we've been auditing Northwest. I say if they want to cut the budget they should change the audit plan. Last year we pulled thirty invoices. Maybe this year we only need to pull twenty. That would save a few hours. Maybe that's what you and Scott should do. Why invest the extra time when you know there aren't going to be any problems anyway?"

"I see what you mean. Can *we* make that decision?" Brent asked.

"I don't see why not. They want us to finish on time and to work another Saturday. What do they expect?" responded Megan.

Brent walked slowly back to his conference room, thinking about what Megan had said. Northwest's people had mostly gone home almost an hour ago. At this time of the evening only the custodial crews were in action. As he reached his office, he saw Scott coming down the hall.

"Hey Scott, got a minute?"

"Yeah, what's up Brent?"

"I'm wondering what we're going to do to come in so far under budget on payables."

"Well, I've found that in times like this, you just have to work until it's done. If we put in a long day tomorrow, we should be about halfway through. Then we can get in here early Monday and get going again. My wife and I were thinking about going to the coast for the weekend but now it's going to be me, you, and piles of invoices, P. O.s, and receiving reports. Romantic, huh?" Scott waved a handful of papers at Brent. "And, frankly, given this audit program, not only will we not get payables done in 35 hours, who knows if we can get them done in less than 40 or 45."

"What's John going to say when we come in *over* 35 hours?"

"Nah, you're not getting it. I just work as much as I need to, to get the work done. Then I report that it took me the budgeted amount of hours—in this case 35, I guess. As long as the work gets done and we look good on our performance evals, I figure a few hours won't kill me. I just figure I'm donating a few extra hours to the firm. Plus, the way John is stressing out lately, it is not worth even *thinking* about coming in over his 35 hours. Well, I've got to get some hotel reservations cancelled and get home and tell my wife how great the *next* trip is going to be. I'll see you first thing tomorrow morning to get started on those lovely payables."

Brent stepped into conference room and sat down. He wanted to do the right thing for himself, the client, the firm, and all involved. Megan's and Scott's ideas kept going around in his mind. His old auditing professor's sermons about an auditor's duty to the public seemed so long ago and so far removed. "Are there other alternatives?" he asked himself. "On the other hand, maybe I'm being too idealistic." He glanced at the clock and decided he'd better head for home and warm up his dinner. By the time he fought the rush hour traffic, it was going to be late enough as it was. He gathered up his things and headed out the door and into the parking lot.

On his way home Brent began to think of all the issues he had been putting off. Katherine hadn't been feeling well lately and he had planned on stopping off to get her a little gift to cheer her up. Suddenly the car made that funny noise again, and Brent remembered for the twentieth time that he needed to get it into the shop before it died completely. Then he thought of his long-abandoned exercise program. "Yeah, right, exercise," thought Brent. "Maybe I'll start doing jumping jacks and lifting weights at the office, between audit memos." On top of the long hours and mounting pressures at work, Katherine was insisting that Brent help more around the house and spend more time with her, and he had to admit it was only fair. The traffic didn't bother Brent as much as usual. He had a lot to think about.

REQUIREMENTS

1. What alternatives are available to Brent in regards to the audit of payables? What are the pros and cons of each alternative?

2. What consequences for Brent, the auditing firm, and others involved, may arise out of "eating time," as Scott suggested? Similarly, what consequences for Brent, the auditing firm, and others involved, may arise out of not completing audit procedures, as Megan suggested?

3. In your opinion, which of Brent's alternative courses of action would provide the best outcome and why? What should Brent do? How would you handle the ethical issues involved in this situation?

4. What could John Peters and the other auditors do to better handle the demands of career and family life?

Nathan Johnson's Rental Car Reimbursement Solving Ethical Dilemmas: Should He Pocket the Cash?

Frank A. Buckless, Mark S. Beasley,
Steven M. Glover, and Douglas F. Prawitt

LEARNING OBJECTIVES

After completing and discussing this case you should be able to

- Understand ethical considerations that can arise during recruiting and in practice
- Reason through alternative courses of action when dealing with these issues

BACKGROUND

Nathan recently interviewed with one of the accounting firms in the city where he wants to live. The firm agreed to cover the expense of a rental car that he used to travel from his university to the firm's office. The rental car agency required that Nathan pay for the car with his credit card and have the firm reimburse Nathan for the expense rather than have the firm pay the expense directly. At the end of his trip Nathan was supposed to pay the bill and then send the receipt to the firm for reimbursement.

As Nathan prepares to send in the receipt, he notices that the car rental agency has overbilled him by $40. Nathan calls the accounting firm to explain that his reimbursement request will be delayed because he has been overbilled. During his phone conversation with the human resources (HR) manager, Nathan says he will call the rental agency to have his bill corrected and will send the firm a copy for reimbursement when the revised bill arrives. The HR manager tells Nathan not to bother correcting the overbilling; she requests that he simply send in the current receipt and the firm will reimburse him for the entire amount. The HR manager is not concerned about paying the higher bill—apparently it does not meet the firm's "materiality threshold."

This case was prepared by Frank A. Buckless, Ph.D. and Mark S. Beasley, Ph.D. of North Carolina State University and Steven M. Glover, Ph.D. and Douglas F. Prawitt, Ph.D. of Brigham Young University, as a basis for class discussion. It is not intended to illustrate either effective or ineffective handling of an administrative situation.

Before deciding whether to send in the incorrect bill, Nathan calls the rental car agency to see why he was overbilled. The agent is quite rude, essentially telling Nathan to "get lost." Now Nathan is determined to get the money back, and after several long-distance phone calls and considerable hassle, the rental car company agrees to credit his card to correct the $40 overbilling. The credit will show up on Nathan's next credit card statement.

The recruiter, however, has already told Nathan that the accounting firm will pay the higher amount and has requested that he forget about the error and send the bill in for reimbursement. Being a bright, aspiring business professional, Nathan immediately realizes he could have the rental agency credit his card for the $40, but send the current receipt to the accounting firm to get reimbursed for the amount he originally paid. Essentially he would walk away from the deal with $40 in his pocket, less the cost of his long-distance phone calls to correct the error. Given the hour he spent fighting with the rental company, a little reimbursement for his trouble does not sound too bad to Nathan.

REQUIREMENTS

1. Given that the firm did not have any problem paying the higher bill, would Nathan's planned course of action be ethical? Why or why not?

2. What other courses of action might be available to Nathan? Which do you think would be the best action for him to take?

The Anonymous Caller: Recognizing It's a Fraud and Evaluating What to Do

Frank A. Buckless, Mark S. Beasley,
Steven M. Glover, and Douglas F. Prawitt

LEARNING OBJECTIVES

After completing and discussing this case you should be able to

- Appreciate real-world pressures for meeting financial expectations
- Distinguish financial statement fraud from aggressive accounting
- Identify alternative actions when confronted with suspected financial statement fraud
- Develop arguments to resist or prevent inappropriate accounting techniques

BACKGROUND

It was 9:30 A.M. on a Monday morning when the call came through. "Hi Dr. Mitchell, do you have a minute?"

"Sure," the professor replied.

"I am one of your former students, but if you don't mind, I would prefer to remain anonymous. I think it is best for both of us if I not reveal my name or company to you. I am concerned that the senior executives of the company where I serve as controller just provided our local bank fraudulently misstated financial statements. I need some fast advice about what to do. Currently, I am on my car phone and need help evaluating my next step before I head to my office this morning. May I briefly describe what's going on and get some input from you?" she asked.

"Go ahead, let me see if there is some way I can help," responded Dr. Mitchell.

"I am the controller of a small start-up company that I joined three and one-half months ago. On Friday of last week, the company's chief executive officer (CEO), the

This case was prepared by Frank A. Buckless, Ph.D. and Mark S. Beasley, Ph.D. of North Carolina State University and Steven M. Glover, Ph.D. and Douglas F. Prawitt, Ph.D. of Brigham Young University, as a basis for class discussion. It is not intended to illustrate either effective or ineffective handling of an administrative situation.

vice president of operations, and the chief financial officer (CFO) met with representatives of the bank that funds the company's line of credit. One of the purposes of the meeting was to provide our most recent quarterly financial statements. The company is experiencing a severe cash shortage, and the bank recently halted funding the line of credit until we could present our most recent operating results. It was at that meeting, just three days ago, that our senior executive team knowingly submitted financial statements to the bank that overstated sales and receivables accounts."

"Earlier on Friday, prior to the bank meeting, I vehemently refused to sign the commitment letter required by the bank because of my concerns about the inclusion of sales transactions to customers on account that I knew did not meet revenue recognition criteria specified by GAAP. I explained to the CEO and CFO that I believed including those transactions in the quarterly results would constitute fraud. They continued to insist that the financial statements needed to reflect the transactions, because without them, the bank would not continue funding the line of credit. They accused me of living in an "ivory tower" and emphasized that companies booked these kinds of transactions all the time. Although they acted like they appreciated my desires for perfection and exactness, they made me feel like it was my lack of experience in the real world that kept me from having a more practical perspective to a common business practice. Unfortunately, none of the senior executives have accounting-related backgrounds. I am the top-level accounting person at the company."

"Over the weekend I had time to think about the situation, and now I am even more convinced that this is clearly fraud. My CEO and CFO have been arm-twisting the accounting staff to book sales transactions before sales occur. As a matter of fact, the customers haven't placed any kind of orders with our company and no goods have been shipped to them. The CEO and CFO noted that booking these kinds of credit sales transactions is a common business practice, even if it isn't technically compliant with GAAP, given that the transactions represent sales expected in the very near future, perhaps even next week."

"As it turns out, the CEO even instructed the accounts payable clerk, while I was out of the office for a couple of days, to record entries the CEO had handwritten on a piece of paper. The accounts payable clerk has never worked with sales and receivables. The CEO told the clerk, who works part-time while finishing his accounting degree at your university, to not mention the entries to me unless I specifically asked. In that event, the clerk was supposed to tell me that the entries related to new sales generated by the CEO and that all was under control. Fortunately, the student clerk is currently taking your auditing course, where financial statement fraud is a topic, and he was uncomfortable with what had transpired. He immediately updated me on the day I returned about what had happened. These bizarre entries make up almost half of our first quarter's sales. Of course, given that these are quarterly financial statements, they are unaudited. Our external auditor has not performed any kind of interim review of them."

"Do you think this is limited to just one quarter?" Dr. Mitchell asked."

"I think so," the caller replied. "As I mentioned, I joined the company three and a half months ago. One of my first tasks involved closing out the prior fiscal year and assisting the external auditors with the year-end audit. As best I can tell, these unusual activities began just recently given our poor results in the first quarter of this year. Our company is a start-up enterprise that has been operating at a net loss for a while. Just last week, the bank stopped clearing checks drawn off the company account. They weren't necessarily bouncing them, but they were not funding the line of credit until the first quarter results were presented on Friday. Interestingly, the bank immediately started funding the line late Friday and, I understand based on phone calls with my staff this morning, the bank is continuing to fund the line this morning. I really think the earnings misstatements first occurred this quarter and that the prior year audited financial statements are not misstated. Unfortunately, I had to sign a bank commitment letter only two weeks after joining the company. That commitment letter related to funding the loan right at the close of the last fiscal year. So, my signature is on file at the bank related to prior-year financial results. But, given the current events, I refused to sign the documents delivered to the bank on Friday. One of my accounting clerks resigned last week due to similar concerns. Our vice president of human resources (HR) discussed the resignation with me after learning about the clerk's concern during a final exit interview. I might add, however, that the HR vice president is the wife of the CEO."

"Anyway, I'm just not sure what responsibilities I have to disclose the earnings misstatements to outside parties. I am considering all sorts of options and thought I would see what advice you could offer. What do you think I should do, Dr. Mitchell?"

REQUIREMENTS

1. What would you recommend to the caller if you were Dr. Mitchell? What are the risks of continuing to work with the company? What are the risks of resigning immediately? Could the state board of accountancy be a source of advice?

2. What responsibility, if any, does the caller have to report this situation directly to the bank involved? Before you respond, think about the risks present if the caller does inform the bank and it later turns out that the caller's assessment of the situation was inaccurate and, in fact, there was no fraud.

3. What other parties should be notified in addition to the bank? What concerns do you have about notifying the external auditors?

4. Do you think situations like this (i.e., aggressive accounting or even financial statement fraud) are common practice? What pressures or factors will executives use to encourage accounting managers and staff to go along? What arguments can you use to resist those pressures? How does one determine whether a company is aggressively reporting, but still in the guidelines of GAAP, versus fraudulently reporting financial information?

Phar-Mor, Inc.:
Accounting Fraud, Litigation,
and Auditor Liability

Frank A. Buckless, Mark S. Beasley,
Steven M. Glover, and Douglas F. Prawitt

LEARNING OBJECTIVES

After completing and discussing this case you should be able to

- Identify factors contributing to an environment conducive to accounting fraud
- Understand what factors may inappropriately influence the client-auditor relationship and auditor independence
- Understand auditor legal-liability issues related to suits brought by plaintiffs under both statutory and common law

INTRODUCTION

In December 1995, the flamboyant entrepreneur Michael "Mickey" Monus, formerly president and chief operating officer (COO) of the deep-discount retail chain Phar-Mor, Inc., was sentenced to 19 years and seven months in prison. Monus was convicted for the accounting fraud that inflated Phar-Mor's shareholder equity by $500 million, resulted in more than $1 billion in losses, and caused the bankruptcy of the twenty-eighth largest private company in the United States. The massive accounting fraud went largely undetected for nearly six years. Several members of top management confessed to, and were convicted of, financial-statement fraud. Former members of Phar-Mor management were collectively fined more than $1 million, and two former Phar-Mor management employees received prison sentences. Phar-Mor's management, as well as Phar-Mor creditors and investors, subsequently brought suit against Phar-Mor's independent auditors, Coopers & Lybrand LLP (Coopers), alleging Coopers was reckless in performing its audits. At the time the suits were filed, Coopers faced claims in excess of $1 billion. Even though there were never allegations that the auditors knowingly participated

This case was prepared by Frank A. Buckless, Ph.D. and Mark S. Beasley, Ph.D. of North Carolina State University and Steven M. Glover, Ph.D. and Douglas F. Prawitt, Ph.D. of Brigham Young University, as a basis for class discussion. It is not intended to illustrate either effective or ineffective handling of an administrative situation.

in the Phar-Mor fraud, on February 14, 1996, a jury found Coopers liable under both state and federal laws. Ultimately, Coopers settled the claims for an undisclosed amount.

PHAR-MOR STORES[1]

Between 1985 and 1992, Phar-Mor grew from 15 stores to 310 stores in 32 states, posting sales of more than $3 billion. By seemingly all standards, Phar-Mor was a rising star touted by some retail experts as the next Wal-Mart. In fact, Sam Walton once announced that the only company he feared at all in the expansion of Wal-Mart was Phar-Mor.

Mickey Monus, Phar-Mor's president, COO and founder, was a local hero in his hometown of Youngstown, Ohio. As demonstration of his loyalty, Monus put Phar-Mor's headquarters in a deserted department store in downtown Youngstown. Monus—known as shy and introverted to friends, cold and aloof to others—became quite flashy as Phar-Mor grew. Before the fall of his Phar-Mor empire, Monus was known for buying his friends expensive gifts, and he was building an extravagant personal residence, complete with an indoor basketball court. He was also an initial equity investor in the Colorado Rockies major league baseball franchise. This affiliation with the Colorado Rockies and other high-profile sporting events sponsored by Phar-Mor fed Monus' love for the high life and fast action. He frequently flew to Las Vegas, where a suite was always available for him at Caesar's Palace. Mickey would often impress his traveling companions by giving them thousands of dollars to gamble.

Phar-Mor was a deep-discount retail chain selling a variety of household products and prescription drugs at substantially lower prices than other discount stores. The key to the low prices was "power buying," the phrase Monus used to describe his strategy of loading up on products when suppliers were offering rock-bottom prices. The strategy of deep-discount retailing is to beat the other guys' prices, thereby attracting cost-conscious consumers. Phar-Mor's prices were so low that competitors wondered how Phar-Mor could do it. Monus' strategy was to undersell Wal-Mart in each market where the two retailers directly competed.

Unfortunately, Phar-Mor's prices were so low that Phar-Mor began losing money. Unwilling to allow these shortfalls to damage Phar-Mor's appearance of success, Monus and his team began to engage in creative accounting so that Phar-Mor never reported these losses in its financial statements. Federal fraud examiners discerned later that 1987 was the last year Phar-Mor actually made a profit.

Investors, relying upon these erroneous financial statements, saw Phar-Mor as an opportunity to cash in on the retailing craze. Among the big investors were Westinghouse Credit Corp., Sears Roebuck & Co., mall developer Edward J. de Bartolo, and the prestigious Lazard Freres & Co. Corporate Partners Investment Fund. Prosecutors say banks and investors put $1.14 billion into Phar-Mor based on the phony records.

The fraud was ultimately uncovered when a travel agent received a Phar-Mor check signed by Monus paying for expenses that were unrelated to Phar-Mor. The agent showed the check to her landlord, who happened to be a Phar-Mor investor, and he contacted CEO David Shapira. On August 4, 1992, David Shapira announced to the business community that Phar-Mor had discovered a massive fraud perpetrated primarily by Michael Monus, former president and COO, and Patrick Finn, former CFO. In order to hide Phar-Mor's cash flow problems, attract investors, and make the company

---

[1]Unless otherwise noted, the facts and statements included in this case are based on actual trial transcripts.

look profitable, Monus and Finn altered Phar-Mor's accounting records to understate costs of goods sold and overstate inventory and income. In addition to the financial statement fraud, internal investigations by the company estimated an embezzlement in excess of $10 million.[2]

Phar-Mor's executives had cooked the books and the magnitude of the collusive management fraud was almost inconceivable. The fraud was carefully carried out over several years by persons at many organizational layers, including the president and COO, CFO, vice president of marketing, director of accounting, controller, and a host of others.

Many factors facilitated the Phar-Mor fraud. The following list outlines seven key factors contributing to the fraud and the ability to cover it up for so long.

1. **The lack of adequate management information systems (MIS).** According to the federal fraud examiner's report, Phar-Mor's MIS was inadequate on many levels. At one point, a Phar-Mor vice president raised concerns about the company's MIS systems and organized a committee to address the problem. However, senior officials involved in the scheme to defraud Phar-Mor dismissed the vice president's concerns and ordered the committee disbanded.

2. **Poor internal controls.** For example, Phar-Mor's accounting department was able to bypass normal accounts payable controls by maintaining a supply of blank checks on two different bank accounts and using them to make disbursements. Only those involved in the fraud were authorized to approve use of these checks.

3. **The hands-off management style of David Shapira, CEO.** For example, in at least two instances Shapira was made aware of potential problems with Monus' behavior and Phar-Mor financial information. In both cases Shapira chose to distance himself from the knowledge.

4. **Inadequate internal audit function.** Ironically, Michael Monus was appointed a member of the audit committee. When the internal auditor reported that he wanted to investigate certain payroll irregularities associated with some of the Phar-Mor related parties, the CFO forestalled these activities and then eliminated the internal audit function altogether.

5. **Collusion among upper management.** At least six members of Phar-Mor's upper management, as well as other employees in the accounting department, were involved in the fraud.

6. **Phar-Mor's knowledge of audit procedures and objectives.** Phar-Mor's fraud team was made up of several former auditors, including at least one former auditor who had worked for Coopers on the Phar-Mor audit. The fraud team indicated that one reason they were successful in hiding the fraud from the auditors was because they knew what the auditors were looking for.

7. **Related parties.** Coopers & Lybrand, in a countersuit, stated that Shapira and Monus set up a web of companies to do business with Phar-Mor. Coopers contended that the companies formed by Shapira and Monus received millions in payments from Phar-Mor. The federal fraud examiner's report confirms Coopers' allegations. The complexity of the related parties involved with Phar-Mor made detection of improprieties and fraudulent activity difficult. During its investigation, the federal fraud examiner identified 91 related parties.

---

[2]Stern, Gabriella, "Phar-Mor Vendors Halt Deliveries; More Layoffs Made," *The Wall Street Journal,* August 10, 1992.

ALLEGATIONS AGAINST COOPERS

Attorneys representing creditors and investors pointed out that every year from 1987 to 1992, Coopers & Lybrand acted as Phar-Mor's auditor and declared the retailer's books in order. At the same time, Coopers repeatedly expressed concerns in its annual audit reports and letters to management that Phar-Mor was engaged in hard-to-reconcile accounting practices and called for improvements. Coopers identified Phar-Mor in its audit planning documents as a "high risk" audit, and their auditors documented that Phar-Mor appeared to be systematically exaggerating its accounts receivables and inventory, its primary assets. Phar-Mor's bankruptcy examiner would later note that the retailer said its inventory jumped from $11 million in 1989 to $36 million in 1990 to a whopping $153 million in 1991.

Creditors suggested that the audit partner's judgment was clouded by his desire to sell additional services to Phar-Mor and other related parties. Such "cross-selling" is not uncommon, and it is not against professional standards; however, the creditors claimed Coopers put extraordinary pressure on its auditors to get more business. The audit partner was said to be hungry for new business because he had been passed over for additional profit sharing for failing to sell enough of the firm's services. The following year, the audit partner began acquiring clients connected to Mickey Monus and eventually sold more than $900,000 worth of services to 23 persons who were either Monus' relatives or friends.

INVESTORS AND CREDITORS—WHAT COURSE OF ACTION TO TAKE?

After the fraud was uncovered, investors and creditors sued Phar-Mor and individual executives from both companies. These lawsuits were settled for undisclosed terms. Although many of the investors were large corporations like Sears and Westinghouse, representatives from these companies were quick to point out that their stockholders, many of whom were pension funds and individual investors, were the ultimate losers. These investors claimed they were willing to accept the business risk associated with Phar-Mor; however, they did not feel they should have had to bear the information risk associated with fraudulent financial statements. One course of action was to sue Phar-Mor's external auditors, Coopers & Lybrand. However, although the investors and creditors were provided with copies of the audited financial statements, they did not have a written agreement with the auditor outlining the auditor's duty of care. As is common with many audits, the only written contract was between Coopers and Phar-Mor.

Thirty-eight investors and creditors filed suit against Coopers, under Section 10(b) of the Federal Securities Exchange Act of 1934 and under Pennsylvania state common law. All but eight plaintiffs settled their claims with Coopers without going to trial. However, the remaining plaintiffs chose to take their cases to a jury trial.

COURTROOM STRATEGIES

The Defense Attorneys for Coopers continually impressed upon the jury that this was a massive fraud perpetrated by Phar-Mor's management. They clearly illustrated the fraud was a collusive effort by multiple individuals within the upper management at Phar-Mor who continually worked to hide evidence from the auditors. The auditors were portrayed as victims of a fraud team at Phar-Mor that would, and did, do whatever it took to cover up the fraud. After the verdict was rendered against the auditors, Coopers' attorney Robert J. Sisk (chairman of New York's Hughes Hubbard & Reed) said,

> "The jury [rightly] saw that a corporate fraud had been committed, but it mistakenly blamed the outside auditor for not uncovering something no one but the perpetrators could have known about." He added, "It's a first…that effectively turns outside auditors into insurers against crooked management."

The Plaintiffs   The plaintiffs opened their case by acknowledging the incidence of fraud does not, by itself, prove there was an audit failure. Moreover, they did not allege that Coopers knowingly participated in the Phar-Mor fraud; nor did they allege Coopers was liable because they did not find the fraud. Rather, plaintiffs alleged Coopers made misrepresentations in their audit opinions. The following quotes from plaintiff attorneys' statements to the jury illustrate the plaintiffs' strategy:

> …[W]e're not going to try to prove in this case what happened at Coopers & Lybrand. That's not our burden. We don't know what happened. We do know that we invested in Phar-Mor on the basis of the financials of Phar-Mor, with the clean opinions of Coopers & Lybrand. We've now lost our investment, and it's a very simple case. We just want our money back…. [I]f Coopers can demonstrate to you that they performed a generally accepted auditing standards (GAAS) audit in the relevant time periods, then you should find for them. But if you find based upon the testimony of our experts and our witnesses that Coopers never, ever conducted a GAAS audit…then I submit you should ultimately find for [plaintiffs]. (Ed Klett, attorney for Westinghouse)

> So the question, ladies and gentlemen, is not whether Coopers could have discovered the fraud. The question is whether Coopers falsely and misleadingly stated that it conducted a GAAS audit and falsely and misleadingly told [plaintiffs] that Phar-Mor's worthless financial statements were fairly presented. And the answer to that question is yes. (Sarah Wolff, attorney for Sears)

Throughout the five-month trial, the plaintiffs continually emphasized the following facts in an effort to have the jury believe the auditors were motivated to overlook any problems that might have been apparent to a diligent auditor:

- The fraud went on for a period of six years, and, therefore, should have become apparent to a diligent auditor.
- Coopers was aware that Phar-Mor's internal accountants never provided the auditors with requested documents or data without first carefully reviewing them.
- Greg Finnerty, the Coopers partner in-charge of the Phar-Mor audit, had previously been criticized for exceeding audit budgets and, therefore, was under pressure to carefully control audit costs.
- Mickey Monus, Phar-Mor's president, was viewed by Finnerty as a constant source of new business.

The areas where the plaintiffs alleged the auditors were reckless and did not perform an audit in accordance with GAAS centered around accounting for inventory and corresponding effects on both the balance sheet and income statement. The plaintiffs' allegations centered on the five major issues detailed below.

EARLY WARNING SIGNS—THE TAMCO SETTLEMENT

The Fact Pattern In 1988, internal gross profit reports at Phar-Mor indicated serious deterioration in margins. Phar-Mor was facing an unexpected $5 million pretax loss. It was determined, with the assistance of a specialist from Coopers, that the drop in margins was due mainly to inventory shortages from one of Phar-Mor's primary suppliers, Tamco. Tamco, a subsidiary of Giant Eagle, Phar-Mor's principal shareholder, had been shipping partial orders but billing Phar-Mor for full orders. Unfortunately, Tamco's records were so poor they could not calculate the amount of the shortage. Likewise, Phar-Mor had no way to determine the exact amount of the shortage because during this time period Phar-Mor was not logging in shipments from Tamco.

A Phar-Mor accountant performed the only formal analysis of the shortage, which he estimated to be $4 million. However, negotiations between Phar-Mor and Tamco (along with its parent company Giant Eagle) resulted in a $7 million settlement. Phar-Mor recorded the $7 million as a reduction to purchases, resulting in a pretax profit of approximately $2 million in 1988. Because Tamco and Phar-Mor were both subsidiaries of Giant Eagle, the settlement was disclosed in a related-party footnote to the financial statements.

Trial evidence indicates the final settlement amount was determined, in part, by looking at Phar-Mor's profitability in prior years. After the settlement, Phar-Mor's gross margin was nearly identical to the prior year. After the fraud was uncovered, it was determined there were signals that Phar-Mor's profitability had slipped in 1988.

Plaintiff Allegations The plaintiffs claimed the settlement was a disguised capital contribution and thus simply a vehicle to artificially inflate Phar-Mor's earnings. The plaintiffs alleged Coopers acted recklessly by not obtaining sufficient persuasive evidence to support this highly material transaction. The following excerpts are from testimony given (in a deposition) by Pat Finn, former CFO of Phar-Mor, and Charles Drott, an expert witness for the plaintiffs:

> There was really no way to support the amount of the settlement. We did a number of tests, but based on our in-house review, we didn't think that we could support $7 million. Mickey [Monus] did an excellent job of negotiating with David [Shapira] and he got us $7 million. (Pat Finn, former CFO of Phar-Mor)

> What Mr. Finn is basically describing is that, although there may well have been some shortages, that what Phar-Mor was really doing was entering into a transaction which would enable them to manipulate its profit to overcome losses, to hide losses. So, essentially what he's describing is fraudulent financial reporting.… [T]he Coopers & Lybrand workpapers contain no independent verification, nor was there any attempt by Coopers & Lybrand to determine the actual amount of the shortages. It simply just was not done. (Charles Drott, expert witness for the plaintiffs)

Plaintiffs also alleged the footnote documenting the receipt and the accounting treatment of the settlement was misleading. Although the footnote disclosed the nature and amount of the related-party transaction, the plaintiffs argued the footnote should have more clearly indicated the uncertainty in the settlement estimate. And plaintiffs felt the footnote should have explicitly stated that without the settlement, Phar-Mor would have shown a loss.

Defense Response A copy of the analysis conducted by the Phar-Mor accountant indicating a $4 million shortage was included in Coopers' workpapers. However,

Coopers considered the analysis very crude and included it only as support for the existence of a shortage, not the dollar amount. Although the workpapers contained relatively little documentation specifically supporting a $7 million settlement, Coopers, who audited all three companies party to the negotiation, did perform a number of procedures to satisfy themselves of the propriety of the settlement. After the internal investigation pointed to Tamco, Phar-Mor began to maintain a log of Tamco shipments. Coopers tracked the results of the log and in every subsequent Tamco shipment shortages were found. Coopers also contacted another company that had received Tamco shipments during this time period and learned that retailer was also experiencing shortages from Tamco.

Coopers experts examined Tamco's operations and confirmed the shortages were due to a new computer inventory system at Tamco. Greg Finnerty, Coopers' partner in charge of the audit, explained the auditors' position as follows:

> ...[I]t's a related-party transaction, and we don't have the responsibility to validate the amount. The responsibilities in accordance with GAAS standards are twofold. One, in any related-party transaction, is to understand the business purpose of the transaction; and two, to agree to the disclosure of the transaction...[W]e understood the business transaction, and the disclosure was adequate. It talked about the $7 million transaction; and we saw a check, not just an intercompany account. We did a lot of those transactions, so we fulfilled our two responsibilities that are the standards for related-party transactions. I was not in that settlement session, nor should I have been. That was between the two related parties. When the discussions were over with, I talked to both parties separately, myself, and talked to them about the settlement, the reasonableness of that settlement. I, in fact, asked David Shapira—and I specifically recall asking David Shapira—of the $7 million, is that all merchandise or is there any sense that you are—you or the board of directors of Giant Eagle—passing additional capital into Phar-Mor through this transaction? And I was given absolute assurance that he was satisfied that the $7 million was a reasonable number; and, in fact, he indicated that this was a number much lower than what Phar-Mor thought it should have been. So it seemed to me that there was a reasonable negotiation that went on between these parties. (Greg Finnerty, engagement partner for the Phar-Mor audit)

Regarding the footnote disclosure, Coopers pointed out the footnote was typical of related-party footnotes, and that it was rather obvious that without the $7 million settlement, Phar-Mor would have reported a loss. Evidence also showed that, prior to the release of the financial statements, Phar-Mor met with investors and creditors to cover the terms and significance of the settlement. Finally, to this day, none of the parties involved—not Tamco, Phar-Mor, or Giant Eagle—have suggested the settlement was part of the fraud. Further testimony in the trial suggested the Tamco settlement was not an issue of concern with investors and creditors until their attorneys made it an issue years later in the litigation.

THE PRICE TEST

The Fact Pattern   Inventory at Phar-Mor increased rapidly from $11 million in 1989 to $36 million in 1990 to $153 million in 1991. Phar-Mor's inventory system did not include a perpetual inventory record. Therefore, Phar-Mor used the retail method for valuing inventory. Phar-Mor contracted with an outside firm to physically count and provide the retail price of each item in inventory twice per year. Phar-Mor would then apply a cost complement to determine the cost of inventory. Phar-Mor's initial strategy was to mark all merchandise up 20%, resulting in a gross margin of 16.7% and a cost complement of 83.3%. However, to be competitive, Phar-Mor lowered the margins on certain "price sensitive" items to get customers in the door. As a result, Phar-Mor's overall budgeted gross margin fell to 15.5%, resulting in a cost complement of 84.5%.

Coopers identified inventory valuation as a high risk area in their workpapers. As a detailed test of Phar-Mor's inventory costing, Coopers annually attended the physical inventory at four stores and selected from 25 to 30 items per store to perform price testing. Sample items were determined by the attending auditor in a haphazard fashion. Purchase invoices were examined for the items selected and an overall gross margin for the sample was determined. In the years 1988 through 1991, Coopers' sample gross margins averaged from 16.1% to 17.7%. Coopers explained the difference between the expected 15.5% gross margin and the sample gross margin resulted because the sample taken did not include many price sensitive items, and, therefore, the sample gross margin was higher than Phar-Mor's overall margin. Coopers concluded the difference noted was reasonable and consistent with their expectations.

After the fraud was uncovered, it was determined that Phar-Mor's actual margins were really much lower than the budgeted 15.5%, because the price sensitive items made up a relatively large percentage of sales. When Phar-Mor's management saw the fiscal 1989 gross profit reports were coming in below historical levels, they started changing the gross margin reports because they feared Giant Eagle would want back some of the $7 million paid in Tamco settlement money. Management continued to alter the gross profit reports from that time until the fraud was uncovered

Plaintiffs' Allegations The plaintiffs argued that had Coopers employed a more extensive and representative price test, they would have known what Phar-Mor's gross margins actually were, no matter what the fraud team was doing to the gross profit reports. Plaintiffs alleged the way the auditors conducted their price test and the way they interpreted the results were woefully inadequate and unreliable due to the sample size and acknowledged lack of representativeness.

> ...[T]he attitudes of the people involved in this were simply that even though there was clear recognition in the workpapers that this test was so flawed that it was virtually worthless, did not produce anything to them that they could use in their audit, yet they still concluded year after year that everything was reasonable, and that's—that defies my imagination. I don't understand how that conclusion can come from their own recognition of that, the test was so severely flawed. Also, they gave consideration to doing a better price test, but in fact never made any attempt to do so because in each of the four years they did the same exact kind of test, year after year after year, even though they knew the test produced unreliable results. (Charles Drott, expert witness for the plaintiffs)

The plaintiffs also pointed to Coopers' workpapers, in which the auditors had indicated that even a one-half percent misstatement in gross margin would result in a material misstatement. Plaintiffs argued the auditors recklessly ignored the sample results indicating a material misstatement.

The plaintiffs also argued the gross profit schedules could not be used to independently test the cost complement because the calculated profit margin and ending inventory were functions of the standard cost complement that was applied to the retail inventory balance derived from the physical inventory.

So, what we have here is a daisy chain…the price test is the basis for the gross margin test. The price test is reasonable because the gross margins are reasonable. But, the only reason the gross margins are reasonable is because they are based on the price test. It keeps ping-ponging back and forth. And the problem is, none of this was tested. And when it was tested…the price tests [and] the cost complement did not meet Coopers' expectations. It was not what it was supposed to be. (Sarah Wolff, attorney for Sears)

Defense Response Coopers explained to the jury that the price test was simply a reasonableness test intended to provide limited assurance that Phar-Mor was properly applying its methodology for pricing and costing inventory.

…[I]n the context of all our inventory testing and testing the gross profit, which is a continuous testing of the pricing philosophy, we felt it was adequate testing for our purposes…[T]he price test is just one element of what we did to confirm our understanding and the representation of management as to their pricing philosophy. The primary test of all that is the continuation of taking the physical inventories that they did throughout the year, reconciling that through the compilation and determining the gross profit. If [Phar-Mor is] receiving the gross profit that [they] expected, that is the truest indication and the most valid indication that the pricing philosophy is, in fact, working. It was a valid test, it still is a valid test after reviewing it time and time again. And the staff person suggesting we drop it was just not…right. And throughout the whole time that we audited Phar-Mor, we continued to do the price test. It was a valid test, and it still is. (Greg Finnerty, engagement partner for the Phar-Mor audit)

Further, Coopers pointed out that differences are expected in reasonableness tests and those differences do not represent actual misstatements. It was obvious to Coopers that while Phar-Mor's costing method was applying one standard cost factor, Phar-Mor was applying a variety of pricing strategies. Coopers' price tests on the individual items selected resulted in a wide range of gross margins from items sold below cost to margins of 30% or higher.

Coopers also pointed out that they performed a number of other procedures that compensated for the weaknesses in the price tests. The primary testing was performed on Phar-Mor's gross profit reports. For a sample of gross profit schedules, Coopers recalculated percentages and traced inventory balances back to the physical inventory report submitted by the independent count firm. This was an important procedure for Coopers because, if the margins were consistent, this indicated that the controls over purchases and sales were operating properly. In addition to these procedures, the control environment over purchases and inventory was documented, and certain controls were tested. Individual store and overall company inventory levels and gross margins were compared to prior years. Analytics, such as inventory turnover and days in inventory, were also examined.

INVENTORY COMPILATIONS

The Fact Pattern After the outside inventory service submitted a report of their physical count, Phar-Mor accountants would prepare an inventory compilation packet. The package included the physical counts, retail pricing, Phar-Mor's calculations of inventory at cost, and cost of goods sold. Based on the compilation, a series of journal entries were prepared and recorded in the operating general ledger to adjust inventory per books to the physical count. Each year, the auditors randomly selected one compilation packet for extensive testing and 14 other packets for limited testing. The auditors reviewed journal entries for reasonableness for all 15 packets.

The postfraud examination determined that many of Phar-Mor's inventory compilation packets contained fraudulent journal entries. The entries were often large in even dollar amounts, did not have journal entry numbers, had no explanation or supporting documentation, and contained suspicious account names like "Accounts Receivable Inventory Contra" or "Cookies." Phar-Mor's fraud team used these entries to inflate inventory and earnings. Based on the physical count and results of the compilation, an appropriate entry was made to reduce (credit) inventory. However, rather than record the offsetting debit to cost of goods sold, a debit entry was recorded to a "bucket" account. The bucket accounts accumulated the fraudulent entries during the year. At year-end, to avoid auditor detection, the bucket accounts were emptied by allocating a portion back to the individual stores as inventory or some other asset.

Plaintiffs' Allegations The plaintiffs alleged that some of the compilations reviewed by the auditors contained fraudulent entries. Plaintiffs' experts claimed Coopers should have noticed these unusual entries.

> Coopers' audit work in this inventory compilation area, because of its failure to investigate all of these fraudulent entries which were obvious, suspicious entries on their face, their failure to do this is a failure, in my opinion, that is reckless professional conduct, meaning that it is an extreme departure from the standard of care. They had the entries in front of them, and they chose to do nothing whatsoever to investigate. Had they done so, they would have found the fraud right then and there. (Charles Drott, expert witness for the plaintiffs)

Defense Response Coopers was able to prove with their workpapers that none of the compilations selected by the auditors for extensive review over the years contained fraudulent entries. Although Coopers did retain an entire copy of the extensively tested compilation packet in their workpapers, they noted only key information from the packets on which they performed limited testing.

In preparation for the trial, the packets that had been subjected to only limited testing were pulled from Phar-Mor's files, many of them containing fraudulent journal entries. However, there was evidence suggesting these compilations may have been altered after Coopers reviewed them. For instance, in many cases even the key information Coopers had noted in their workpapers no longer agreed to the file copies. Mark Kirsten, a Coopers audit manager who was the staff and senior auditor on the Phar-Mor engagement, testified why he believes the compilations retrieved from Phar-Mor's files were altered after Coopers performed their audit work:

> I never saw this entry or any other fraudulent entries. When we got these packages, we got them from John Anderson who was part of this fraud. And I refuse to agree that John Anderson walked into my audit room, and we are pouring over these for a couple days at a time, and says, here, if you happen to turn to the third page, you are going to find a fraudulent entry that has no support. That's unimaginable...we know there is a fraud. That's why we are here. I know I did my job. My job was to review the packages. These packages went through extensive reviews. So, I am saying when you show me a package that has on one page something that...is fraud, I can't imagine that

I saw that. We didn't see these packages for ten seconds during the audit. We spent days with these. I am a staff accountant who is doing my job, and I am pouring through these and asking questions. We don't audit in a box. (Mark Kirsten, engagement senior for the Phar-Mor audit)

GENERAL LEDGER

The Fact Pattern   A monthly operating general ledger (GL) was prepared and printed for each store and for corporate headquarters. The plaintiffs argued that not only could the fraud have been uncovered by examining the journal entries proposed on the inventory compilations, but through scanning the GL. Post-fraud reviews of the GLs revealed the fraudulent entries from the compilation reports were posted directly to the GLs. The GLs contained other fraudulent entries as well. Because the fraud team was aware that zero-balance accounts typically draw little attention from the auditor, they recorded numerous "blow-out" entries in the last monthly corporate GL to empty the bucket accounts that had accumulated the fraud during the year. The bucket accounts were emptied by allocating a portion, usually in equal dollar amounts, back to the stores as inventory or other assets. These entries were typically very large. For example, in 1991, there was an entry labeled "Accrued Inventory" for $9,999,999.99. Also, in 1991, there was an entry labeled "Alloc Inv" (Allocate Inventory) for $139 million.

Plaintiffs' Allegations   The plaintiffs pointed out that scanning the GL, which was a recognized procedure in Coopers' audit manual and training materials, would certainly and easily have uncovered the fraud. Further, plaintiffs pointed to Coopers' inventory audit program for Phar-Mor that included procedures requiring the examination of large and unusual entries. The following comments from plaintiff attorney Sarah Wolff to the jury illustrates the plaintiffs' allegations.

> I want to talk about the issue of general ledger.... All we ask you to do in this issue is, don't listen to what the lawyers have told you...what we ask you to do is look at Coopers' own words. Look at Coopers' training materials. The auditor must also review for large or unusual nonstandard adjustments to inventory accounts. Read Coopers & Lybrand's own audit program for this particular engagement that has steps nine and steps eleven that say look for fourth quarter large and unusual adjustments. Those are their words, ladies and gentlemen. That's their audit program, and you have seen witness after witness run from those words. (Sarah Wolff, attorney for Sears)

Although a witness for the plaintiffs agreed it would not have been practical to carefully scan all the operating GLs, (which would have been a pile of computer paper 300 hundred feet tall), they felt it was reckless, and a failure to comply with GAAS, to not carefully scan at least the last month of the corporate office GL.

The plaintiffs repeatedly played a video clip of one of the chief perpetrators of the Phar-Mor fraud, the former CFO, saying that if Coopers had asked for the backup to any one of the fraudulent journal entries, "It [the fraud] would have been all over."

Defense Response   Coopers' audit program did have a step to obtain selected nonstandard adjusting journal entries so that any large and unusual items could be further examined. The step was signed off by staff auditors without further explanation. Coopers witnesses testified that the fact that the step was signed off indicated that either the step was performed or was considered not necessary. Trial testimony indicated

Coopers auditors asked Phar-Mor accountants if there were any large and unusual adjusting entries and the auditors were told there were none. Coopers pointed out it is normal for the client to provide the auditor with an audit packet including lead schedules that agree to the GL and tie to the financial statements. None of the lead schedules contained fraudulent or "bucket" accounts. When it was suggested by plaintiff attorneys that if the auditors had reviewed the operating general ledgers, there would have been a high probability that they would have discovered the fraud, the partner responded:

> No. I would say that it wouldn't be a high probability of that because we are doing a GAAS audit. A GAAS audit requires us to do the procedures that we did. There is no requirement in GAAS—none of my partners or I have ever followed a procedure that says you review operating general ledgers line by line, or whatever, unless you are doing a fraud audit. In the course of doing our GAAS audit, we would look to the general ledgers to the extent necessary in order to do our work on the account balances. We don't audit all the various ways that the balances are arrived at.... We don't look at day-to-day activity. This is not what we do as accountants, not only at Phar-Mor, but in every audit we do. We look at the ending balances and audit the ending balances. (Greg Finnerty, engagement partner for the Phar-Mor audit)

Although Coopers was aware of the operating GLs, they worked primarily with the consolidated GL, which combined all the operating GLs and included only ending balances and not transaction detail. In the consolidated GL, the "bucket" or fraud accounts were either completely absent or had zero balances. To counter the plaintiffs' video clip of the CFO saying the auditors never asked for backup to the blowout entries, the defense played their own video clip of this same CFO (who was a former Big Six auditor), testifying he and his fraud team went to great lengths to prepare for the audit. On this same video clip, the former CFO also testified that if Coopers had asked for the closing journal entry binder, he would have removed the journal entries that emptied the fraud bucket before giving it to the auditors. Members of the fraud team also testified that had Coopers changed their approach to more carefully scrutinize the operating GLs, they would have changed their approach to cover up the fraud.

ROLL FORWARD

The Fact Pattern Because the physical inventories were completed during the fiscal year, it was necessary to roll forward or account for the inventory purchase and sales transactions between the inventory count date and the balance sheet date. Coopers' roll-forward examinations always revealed there was a large increase in the ending book inventory balance. Phar-Mor explained to the auditors that the "spike" was due to two factors. First, inventory levels at the physical count date were always lower than normal because a store would reduce inventory shipments in the weeks prior to the physical inventory to prepare for the physical count. Second, because the fiscal year-end was June 30, there was always a buildup of inventory to handle the big Fourth of July holiday demand. The drop-off in inventory just after year-end was attributed mainly to the large amounts of inventory sold over July 4th. Although the client's explanation did account for a portion of the spike, investigations performed subsequent to the discovery of the fraud indicate that a large portion of the spike was due to the fraud.

Plaintiffs' Allegations   Plaintiffs claimed the spike was a big red flag that Coopers recklessly overlooked.

> And what this is simply showing is that the increase is a sharp spike upward at fiscal year-end. Interestingly, also, is that subsequent to the fiscal year, just a short time thereafter—the inventory levels drop off. Now, that is a very interesting red flag as to why would that be. If I were an auditor, I'd certainly want to know why the inventories increase sharply, reaching its crest right at the fiscal year-end date. In other words, when the financial statements were prepared, and why they drop off again after fiscal year-end, just two weeks later, as a matter of fact, and go down that much. It's what I call the spike. Clearly the spike, in my opinion, was caused in large part by the actual fraud at Phar-Mor, because if you recall, these fraudulent entries, these blow-out entries that I described, were these very large journal entries that were adding false inventory to each of the stores, and it was done at fiscal yearend; so if you're adding—and we're talking like entries as high as $139 million of false inventory being added in one journal entry to these stores. When you have that, being false inventory, added to the stores at fiscal yearend, that's obviously going to spike up the books at yearend. And then subsequent to yearend, many of these entries are what we call reversed or taken out of the stores, which would cause some of that spike, if not all of it, to come down. (Charles Drott, expert witness for the plaintiffs)

The plaintiffs also argued that auditing texts and an AICPA practice guide describe tests of controls and tests of detail that must be performed for the interim period. In addition, plaintiffs pointed to a procedure described as scrutinizing the books of original entry to identify unusual transactions during the roll-forward period.

Defense Response   When asked if the spike would cause an experienced retail auditor to have suspicions about inventory at Phar-Mor, the audit partner responded:

> Well, no, it wouldn't. But, let me give you an example. At Christmastime, it's the same concept. There is a tremendous spike in inventory of retailers at Christmastime, and then after that, after Christmas, sales go down. That is, you are going to see a natural decline in the inventory levels of a retailer after Christmas. So, it so happens in this analysis, this has to do with the yearend of Phar-Mor, June 30. (Greg Finnerty, engagement partner for the Phar-Mor audit)

Given that this sort of spike was not unusual, Coopers expected the inventory roll-forward comparisons to result in differences. Coopers explained the difference noted in their reasonableness test comparing year-end inventory and the previous physical inventory was within their expectations and differences in reasonableness tests do not represent known, actual misstatements.

Coopers elected not to test specific purchases or sales transactions during the roll-forward period. Rather, they relied on their tests of the gross profit schedules both before and after year-end, which suggested the controls over purchases and sales were functioning properly. Coopers contended that if any large or unusual journal entries were recorded after the last physical count and before year-end, they should affect the gross profit of the general ledger, which was one of the comparisons made on the gross profit reports. Unfortunately, the fraud team was falsifying the gross profit reports.

VERDICT

On February 14, 1996, a jury found Coopers liable. After the verdict, plaintiff attorney Sarah Wolff indicated this case could prove to be the model for getting a jury to find a respected accounting firm behaved recklessly. Ultimately Coopers settled the claims for an undisclosed amount.

POSTFRAUD PHAR-MOR

Discovery of the fraud resulted in immediate layoffs of more than 16,000 people and the closure of 200 stores. In September 1995, after more than three years of turmoil, Phar-Mor emerged from Chapter 11 bankruptcy. Phar-Mor's CEO at that time, Robert Half, was optimistic about the company's future: "You can make money in this business. It's our job to prove it."[3]

Today, Phar-Mor operates 106 stores in 19 states and its common stock trades on the NASDAQ under the symbol PMOR. Ironically on the day Phar-Mor opened its 106th store, March 6, 1998, Mickey Monus was back in court to hear another jury's decision. Monus was charged with obstruction of justice after his first trial, in 1994, ended in a hung jury. One of Monus' friends did plead guilty to offering a $50,000 bribe to a juror. Monus, still serving prison time connected with the corporate fraud, denied any knowledge of the offer and cried when a U.S. District Court jury acquitted him on the jury tampering charges.

REQUIREMENTS

1. Some of the members of Phar-Mor's financial management team were former auditors for Coopers & Lybrand. (a) Why would a company want to hire a member of its external audit team? (b) If the client has hired former auditors, would this affect the independence of the existing external auditors? (c) What are the implications with respect to the Code of Professional Conduct if a client offers an auditor a job while an audit engagement is ongoing? (d) Is it appropriate for auditors to trust executives of a client?

2. (a) What factors in the auditor-client relationship can put the client in a more powerful position than the auditor? (b) What measures has and/or can the profession take to reduce the potential consequences of this power imbalance?

3. (a) Assuming you were an equity investor, would you pursue legal action against the auditor? Assuming the answer is yes, what would be the basis of your claim? (b) Define negligence as it is used in legal cases involving independent auditors. (c) What is the primary difference between negligence and fraud; between fraud and recklessness?

4. Coopers & Lybrand was sued under both federal statutory and state common law. The judge ruled that under Pennsylvania law the plaintiffs were not primary beneficiaries. Pennsylvania follows the legal precedent inherent in the Ultramares Case. (a) In jurisdictions following the Ultramares doctrine, under

---

[3] "Our Destiny Is in Our Hands," *Drug Store News,* October 9, 1995, p. 3.

what conditions can auditors be held liable under common law to third parties who are not primary beneficiaries? (b) How do jurisdictions that follow the legal precedent inherent in the Rusch Factors case differ from jurisdictions following Ultramares?

5. Coopers was also sued under the Securities Exchange Act of 1934. The burden of proof is not the same under the Securities Acts of 1933 and 1934. Identify the important differences and discuss the primary objective behind the differences in the laws (1933 and 1934) as they relate to auditor liability?

6. A December 1992 *Wall Street Journal* article, "Inventory Chicanery Tempts More Firms, Fools More Auditors," cited the rise in inventory fraud as one of the biggest single reasons for the proliferation of accounting scandals. (a) Name two other high-profile cases in which companies have committed fraud by misstating inventory. (b) What makes the intentional misstatement of inventory difficult to detect? How was Phar-Mor successful in fooling Coopers & Lybrand for several years with overstated inventory? (c) To help prevent or detect the overstatement of inventory, what are some audit procedures that could be effectively employed?

7. (a) The auditors considered Phar-Mor to be an inherently "high risk" client. List several factors at Phar-Mor that would have contributed to a high inherent-risk assessment. (b) Should auditors have equal responsibility to detect errors and irregularities? (c) Which conditions, attitudes, and motivations at Phar-Mor that created an environment conducive for fraud could have been identified as red flags by the external auditors?

The Runners Shop:
Litigation Support Review of Audit
Working Papers for Notes Payable

Frank A Buckless, Mark S. Beasley,
Steven M. Glover, and Douglas F. Prawitt

LEARNING OBJECTIVES

After completing and discussing this case you should be able to

- Read working papers prepared by audit staff to support management assertions related to Notes Payable
- Identify deficiencies with the preparation of the Notes Payable working papers
- Highlight implications of the auditors not properly documenting the work performed in the working papers

INTRODUCTION

The Runners Shop (TRS) was a family-owned business that was founded 17 years ago by Robert and Andrea Johnson. In July of 200Y, TRS found itself experiencing a severe cash shortage that forced it to file for bankruptcy protection. Prior to shutting down its operations, TRS was engaged in the retail sale of athletic footwear and related products for runners. TRS's 200X audited financial statements reported net sales of $2,217,292 and a net loss of $50,980. Consistent with prior years, sales were strongest in the second and fourth calendar-year quarters, with the first calendar-year quarter substantially weaker than the rest.

The company's basic strategy was to provide superior customer service over competing sporting goods and mass merchandiser retail stores. The company attempted to provide superior service by hiring college-age runners as sales staff and then training them on shoes/strategies that would correct common running ailments. This strategy helped TRS develop a very loyal customer base for its first store located in Charlottesville, Virginia. Sales at the Charlottesville store were so strong that Robert and Andrea

This case was prepared by Frank A. Buckless, Ph.D. and Mark S. Beasley, Ph.D. of North Carolina State University and Steven M. Glover, Ph.D. and Douglas F. Prawitt, Ph.D. of Brigham Young University, as a basis for class discussion. It is not intended to illustrate either effective or ineffective handling of an administrative situation.

decided to expand into three other markets: Richmond, Virginia; College Park, Maryland; and Cary, North Carolina.

Unfortunately, the expansion effort did not go as well as Robert and Andrea had anticipated. They expected that the first three years of operations for the new locations would be difficult, but after that point they would experience significant improvement in operations. The expected performance improvement did not materialize and after four years of operations the expansion stores were still running at a loss. In July 200Y, Robert and Andrea, with almost all of their personal assets exhausted, realized they could no longer hang on and filed for bankruptcy protection.

BACKGROUND INFORMATION ABOUT THE LAWSUIT

The plaintiffs in the lawsuit were First Commercial Bank and National Bank and Trust. First Commercial Bank provided a short-term line of credit that allowed TRS to borrow up to $100,000 to cover cash disbursements for merchandise purchases prior to peak sales periods. This loan agreement did require TRS to pay off its outstanding balance the last business day of every July. National Bank and Trust provided an installment loan to TRS when it expanded from one to four locations. This loan agreement required TRS to remit monthly interest and principal payments. Both lenders required TRS to have its annual financial statements audited as a condition of the loan agreements.

Unfortunately, as a result of the bankruptcy both lending institutions lost the outstanding principal balances owed them by TRS. The two lending institutions jointly filed a lawsuit against the firm that audited TRS's financial statements: Green and Brown, LLP. The lawsuit alleges that the audit firm did not perform the audit in accordance with generally accepted auditing standards and as a result the two banks were unable to recover their outstanding loan balances. The law firms representing the defendant (Green and Brown, LLP) and the plaintiffs (First Commercial Bank and National Bank and Trust) are now conducting discovery procedures. The objectives of the discovery process are to ensure that all evidence is equally available to all parties and to facilitate settlement of the case.

BACKGROUND INFORMATION ABOUT THE AUDIT

Green and Brown, LLP, had audited the financial statements of TRS for the last 10 years. The audit report issued for the 200X and 200W financial statements was as follows:

Independent Auditor's Report

To Robert and Andrea Johnson, President and Treasurer of The Runners Shop

We have audited the accompanying balance sheets of The Runners Shop as of December 31, 200X and 200W, and the related statements of income, retained earnings, and cash flows for the years then ended. These financial statements are the responsibility of the company's management. Our responsibility is to express an opinion on these statements based on our audits.

We conducted our audits in accordance with generally accepted auditing standards. Those standards require that we plan and perform the audit to obtain reasonable assurance about whether the financial statements are free of material misstatement. An audit includes examining, on a test basis, evidence supporting the amounts and disclosures in the financial statements. An audit includes assessing the accounting principles used and significant estimates made by management, as well as evaluating the overall financial statement presentation. We believe that our audits provide a reasonable basis for our opinion.

In our opinion, the financial statements referred to above present fairly, in all material respects, the financial position of The Runners Shop as of December 31, 200X and 200W, and the results of its operations and its cash flows for the years then ended in conformity with generally accepted accounting principles.

Green and Brown, LLP

Audittown, USA
March 5, 200Y

The audit staff for the 200X audit of TRS's financial statements consisted of four individuals: Pete Letterman, audit partner; Carol Maddox, audit manager; Mary Lewis, audit senior; and Joe Manaker, staff auditor. All of these individuals also worked on the previous year's audits of TRS. Enclosed is the audit program and working papers related to TRS's Notes Payable. Joe performed the audit work in this area and Mary reviewed his work.

REQUIREMENTS

You are working for the litigation support firm hired to identify deficiencies with the audit work performed by Green and Brown, LLP. Your assignment is to identify deficiencies with the audit work performed by the audit firm related to TRS's Notes Payable. The purpose of reviewing this section of the working papers is to demonstrate a pattern of careless behavior on the part of the auditors to build a case of auditor negligence.

The audit work performed by the audit firm related to TRS's Notes Payable is documented in the enclosed working papers. Green and Brown, LLP's guidelines for the preparation of working papers have also been provided for your information. Deficiencies you identify should be listed on the enclosed schedule.

GREEN AND BROWN, LLP
FIRM GUIDELINES—AUDIT WORKING PAPERS

Provided below are firm guidelines related to the preparation of working papers:

- *Title*—each schedule/document included in the working papers should indicate the client name, description of content, and year-end financial statement date.
- *Source of schedule/document*—schedules/documents prepared by the client should be clearly indicated.
- *Work performed*—each schedule/document should include the initials of audit staff who performed work related to the schedule/document, as well as the date the work was completed.
- *Indexing*—each schedule/document should be indexed to facilitate filing and referencing between documents.
- *Cross-referencing*—information on a schedule/document shared or used on another schedule/document should be cross-referenced by indicating on both schedules/documents the index (as close to the information) of the other schedule/document.
- *Tickmark (footnote) explanations*—should be included on each schedule/document to indicate the work performed.

Approved December 7, 199Q

The Runners Shop
Financing and Investing Cycle—Short- and
Long-term Debt Audit Program
Year Ended: December 31, 200X

Audit Procedures	Initial	Date	W/P Ref.
1. Confirm terms and balances of Notes Payable with lenders.	JM	12/31/0X	FI 114-1 FI 114-2
2. Obtain the client-prepared lead schedule for short- and long-term debt.	JM	1/14/0Y	FI 110
A. Crossfoot the lead schedule.	JM	1/14/0Y	FI 110
B. Agree the prior-year balances to prior-year working papers.	JM	1/14/0Y	FI 110
C. Agree the current-year balances to the general ledger and trial balance.	JM	1/14/0Y	FI 110
3. Obtain the client-prepared supporting schedule(s) for Notes Payable.	JM	1/14/0Y	FI 111
A. Foot and crossfoot the schedule(s).	JM	1/14/0Y	FI 111
B. Agree the prior-year balances to prior-year working papers.	JM	1/14/0Y	FI 111
C. Agree the current-year balances to the general ledger and trial balance.	JM	1/14/0Y	FI 111
D. Agree the reported balances to the lead schedule.	JM	1/14/0Y	FI 111
E. Agree terms and year-end balances with the confirmations.	JM	1/14/0Y	FI 111 FI 114
F. Recompute the current and long-term portion of notes using the loan agreement.	JM	1/14/0Y	FI 111
G. Review the cash receipts journal and schedule of fixed-asset additions to determine that all debt is properly included on the schedule.	A	1/14/0Y	N/A
H. Review bank cash confirmations to determine that all debt is properly included on the schedule.	JM	1/14/0Y	FI 111
4. Recompute year-end accrued interest for each outstanding loan based on the last date interest was paid.	JM	1/14/0Y	FI 112
5. Test the reasonableness of interest expense by multiplying the average outstanding balance by the appropriate interest rate.	JM	1/14/0Y	FI 113
6. Review the provisions of the loan agreements to determine if there are any violations.	JM	1/14/0Y	FI 111
7. Conclude to the fair presentation of Notes Payable.	JM	1/14/0Y	FI 110

Buckless / Beasley / Glover / Prawitt

Reference: ___FI 110___
Prepared by: ___JM___
Date: ___1/14/0Y___
Reviewed by: ___ML___

The Runners Shop
Financing and Investing Cycle—Short- and Long-Term Debt Lead Schedule
For the Year Ended December 31, 200X

Account Name and Description	12/31/0W Balance	12/31/0X Balance	Adjustments	12/31/0X Adjusted Balance	
Accrued Interest	$747.67	$1,344.71	—	$1,344.71	*cf*
	FI112, PWP	*FI112, GL*	—		
Notes Payable—Short-term	$51,803.40	$65,676.52	—	$65,676.52	*cf*
	PWP	*FI111, GL*	—		
Notes Payable—Long-term	$66,053.47	$48,836.95	—	$48,836.95	*cf*
	PWP	*FI111, GL*	—		
Interest Expense	$14,669.79	$14,199.73	—	$14,199.73	*cf*
	FI113, PWP	*FI113, GL*			

$117,856.87
FI111, Σ

Tickmark Legend

PWP – *Agreed to prior-year working papers without exception.*

GL – *Agreed to 12/31/200X general ledger and trial balance without exception.*

cf – *Crossfooted amount without exception.*

Σ – *The Short- and Long-term Notes Payable balances were summed together by the auditor.*

Reference: _FI 111_
Prepared by: _JM_
Date: _1/14/0Y_
Reviewed by: _____

The Runners Shop
Financing and Investing Cycle—Notes Payable Schedule
For the Year Ended December 31, 200X

Lender	Loan Terms	12/31/0W Balance	Additions	Reductions	12/31/0X Balance	Current Portion	Non-Current Portion	
First Commercial Bank✓	10% ✓ $100,000 short-term line of credit, ✓interest due on last day of each month, outstanding balance due on last day of July, no collateral.✓	$43,090.00 *PWP*	$149,360.00	$143,990.00	$48,460.00✓ *cf*	$48,460.00 *rc*	$0	Σ
National Bank and Trust✓	12%✓ installment note,✓ principal and interest due on first day of each month, no collateral.✓	$74,766.87 *PWP*	$0	$8,713.40	$66,053.47✓ *cf*	$17,216.52	$48,836.95	Σ
Total		$117,856.87	$149,360.00	$152,703.40	$114,513.47	$65,676.52	$48,836.95	Σ
		FI110,PWP, f	*f*	*f*	*f*	*FI110, GL, f*	*FI110, GL, f*	

Tickmark Legend

PWP – *Agreed to prior-year working papers without exception.*

GL – *Agreed to 12/31/200X general ledger and trial balance without exception.*

f – *Footed amount without exception.*

cf – *Crossfooted amount without exception.*

✓ – *Agreed to confirmation without exception.*

rc – *Recomputed based on the terms of the note without exception.*

Σ – *The current and non-current balances were summed and agreed to the total balance without exception.*

Notes

A) *Per review of the bank confirmations, no debt is excluded from this schedule.*

B) *Per review of the two loan agreements, TRS is only in violation of the covenant with National Bank and Trust that prohibits loans to officers. Robert Johnson has had a small $5,000 loan from TRS for the last two years. The bank does not seem to care.*

Reference: _____FI 112_____
Prepared by: __JM_____
Date: ___1/14/0Y_____
Reviewed by: _ML_____

The Runners Shop
Financing and Investing Cycle—Accrued Interest Schedule
For the Year Ended December 31, 200X

Lender	12/31/0W Balance	12/31/0X Balance	Last Interest Payment
First Commercial Bank	$0 *PWP*	$0	12/31/0X
National Bank and Trust	$747.67 *PWP*	$1,434.71	12/01/0X
Total Accrued Interest	$747.67	$1,434.71	

PWP, FI110, f   *GL, FI110, f*

Tickmark Legend

PWP – Agreed to prior-year working papers without exception.

GL – Agreed to 12/31/200X general ledger and trial balance without exception.

f – Footed by auditor.

Reference: ___FI 113___
Prepared by:___JM_____
Date: ___1/14/0Y_____
Reviewed by: __ML_____

The Runners Shop
Financing and Investing Cycle—Interest Expense Schedule
For the Year Ended December 31, 200X

Lender	12/31/0W Interest Expense	12/31/0X Interest Expense
First Commercial Bank	$5,185.97 PWP	$5,696.61
National Bank and Trust	$9,483.82 PWP	$8,503.12
Total Interest Expense	$14,669.79	$14,199.73
	PWP, FI110, f	GL, FI110, f

Interest Expense Analytical Procedure

$$(43,090 + 48,460)/2 \times 10\% = 4,577.50 \;\; c$$
$$(74,766.87 + 69,053.47)/2 \times 12\% = 8,629.22 \;\; c$$
$$\text{Estimated Interest Expense} = \underline{13,206.72}$$
$$f$$

Tickmark Legend

PWP – _Agreed to prior-year working papers without exception._

GL – _Agreed to 12/31/200X general ledger and trial balance without exception._

f – _Footed by auditor._

c – _Computed by auditor._

Notes:

The difference between the actual and estimated interest expense of $993.01 ($14,199.73 – $13,206.72) results from the fact that the outstanding balance for the short-term line of credit varies substantially from month to month consistent with the company's sales activity. The estimated amount is not materially different from the actual amount, therefore, no further work is needed.

The Runners Shop
Barracks Road
Charlottesville, VA

December 31, 200X

Mr. Charles M. Banker
First Commercial Bank
Banktown, USA 11111-1111

Dear Mr. Banker:

In connection with an audit of the financial statements of The Runners Shop as of December 31, 200X, and for the year then ended, we have advised our independent auditors of the information listed below, which we believe is a complete and accurate description of our line of credit from your institution as of the close of business on December 31, 200X. Although we do not request nor expect you to conduct a comprehensive, detailed search of your records, if during the process of completing this confirmation additional information about other lines of credit from your financial institution comes to your attention, please include such information below.

- The company has available at the financial institution a line of credit totaling $100,000. The current terms of the line of credit are contained in the agreement letter dated November 15, 199P. The related debt outstanding at the close of business on December 31, 200X, was $48,460.

- The amount of the unused line of credit, subject to the terms of the related agreement letter, at December 31, 200X, was $51,540.

- The interest rate at the close of business on December 31, 200X, was 10%.

- There are no requirements for compensating balances in connection with this line of credit.

- The line of credit does not support commercial paper or any other borrowing arrangement.

Please confirm whether the information about lines of credit presented above is correct by signing below and returning this letter directly to our independent auditors, Green and Brown, LLP, 1 Hill Street, Audittown, USA 22222-2222.

Sincerely,

Robert Johnson

Robert Johnson
President, The Runners Shop

Dear Green and Brown, LLP:

The above information regarding the line-of-credit arrangement agrees with the records of this financial institution. Although we have not conducted a comprehensive, detailed search of our records, no information about other lines of credit came to our attention. [Note exceptions below or in attached letter.]

_____

No exceptions.

_____

_____

First Commercial Bank

By: _Charles M. Banker, Vice President, Loans_____   _January 10, 200Y_____
     (Officer and Title)   (Date)

STANDARD FORM TO CONFIRM ACCOUNT
BALANCE INFORMATION WITH FINANCIAL INSTITUTIONS

Financial
Institution's
Name and
Address

[National Bank and Trust
100 Main Street
Credittown, USA 33333-333

]

[   ]

The Runners Shop
_____
CUSTOMER NAME

We have provided to our accountants the following information as of the close of the business on December 31, 20 0X. regarding our deposit and loan balances. Please confirm the accuracy of the information, noting any exceptions to the information provided. If the balances have been left blank, please complete this form by furnishing the balance in the appropriate space below.* Although we do not request nor expect you to conduct a comprehensive, detailed search of your records, if during the process of completing this confirmation additional information about other deposit and loan accounts we may have with you comes to your attention, please include such information below. Please use the enclosed envelope to return the form directly to our accountants.

1. At the close of business on the date listed above, our records indicated the following deposit balance(s):

ACCOUNT NAME	ACCOUNT NO.	INTEREST RATE	BALANCE*
None			

2. We were directly liable to the financial institution for loans at the close of business on the date listed above as follows:

ACCOUNT NO./ DESCRIPTION	BALANCE*	DATE DUE	INTEREST RATE	DATE THROUGH WHICH INTEREST IS PAID	DESCRIPTION OF COLLATERAL
086-738950/ Installment Note	$66,053.47	Monthly Installments Matures 02/01/AD	12%	12/01/0X	None

_____
Robert Johnson
(Customer's Authorized Signature)

_____
12/31/0X
(Date)

The information presented above by the customer is in agreement with our records. Although we have not conducted a comprehensive, detailed search of our records, no other deposit or loan accounts have come to our attention except as noted below.

_____
Brian G. Lender
(Financial Instituition Authorized Signature)

_____
01/11/0Y

_____
Vice President of Loans
(Title)

EXCEPTIONS AND OR COMMENTS
No exceptions.

Please return this form directly to our accountants:

Brown and Green, LLP
1 Hill Street
Audittown, USA 22222-2222

*Ordinarily, balances are intentionally left blank if they are not available at the time the form is prepared.

Approved 1990 by American Bankers Association, American Institute of Certified Public Accountants, and Bank Administration Institute. Additional forms available from AICPA— Order Department, P.O. Box 1003, NY NY 10108-1003

D451 5951

Prepared by: _____
Date Prepared: _____

The Runners Shop
Audit Review Sheet
For 12/31/200X Audit

#	Description of Deficiency
1)	*No indication that schedule FI110 was prepared by the client.*
2)	*No conclusion was noted on schedule FI110 regarding the fair presentation of Notes*
	Payable (audit step 7).

Prepared by: _____
Date Prepared: _____

The Runners Shop
Audit Review Sheet
For 12/31/200X Audit

#	Description of Deficiency

Prepared by: _____
Date Prepared: _____

The Runners Shop
Audit Review Sheet
For 12/31/200X Audit

#	Description of Deficiency

Ocean Manufacturing, Inc.: The New-Client Acceptance Decision

Frank A. Buckless, Mark S. Beasley,
Steven M. Glover, and Douglas F. Prawitt

LEARNING OBJECTIVES

After completing and discussing this case you should be able to

- Understand the types of information relevant to evaluating a prospective audit client
- List some of the steps an auditor should take in deciding whether to accept a prospective client
- Identify and evaluate factors important in the decision to accept or reject a prospective client
- Understand the process of making and justifying a recommendation regarding client acceptance

INTRODUCTION

The accounting firm of Barnes and Fischer, LLP, is a medium-sized, national CPA firm. The partnership, formed in 1954, now has more than 6,000 professionals on the payroll. The firm mainly provides auditing and tax services, but it has recently had success in building the information-systems-consulting side of the business.

It is mid-January 200X, and you are a newly promoted audit manager in an office of Barnes and Fischer, located in the Pacific Northwest. You have been a senior auditor for the past three years of your five years with Barnes and Fischer. Your first assignment as audit manager is to assist an audit partner on a client acceptance decision. The partner explains to you that the prospective client, Ocean Manufacturing, Inc. is a medium-sized manufacturer of small home appliances. The partner recently met the company's president at a local chamber of commerce meeting. He indicated that, after some difficult negotiations, the company has decided to terminate its relationship with its current auditor. The president explained that the main reason for the switch is to establish a

This case was prepared by Frank A. Buckless, Ph.D. and Mark S. Beasley, Ph.D. of North Carolina State University and Steven M. Glover, Ph.D. and Douglas F. Prawitt, Ph.D. of Brigham Young University, as a basis for class discussion. It is not intended to illustrate either effective or ineffective handling of an administrative situation.

relationship with a more nationally known CPA firm because the company plans to make an initial public offering (IPO) of its common stock within the next few years. Ocean's annual financial statements have been audited each of the past 12 years in order to comply with debt covenants and to receive favorable interest rates on the company's existing line of credit. Because the company's December 31 fiscal year-end has already passed, time is of the essence for the company to contract with a new auditor to get the audit under way.

The partner is intrigued with the idea of having a client in the home appliance industry, especially one with the favorable market position and growth potential of Ocean Manufacturing. Although there are several small home appliance manufacturers in the area, your office has never had a client in the industry. Most of Barnes and Fischer's current audit clients are in the healthcare services industry. Thus, the partner feels the engagement presents an excellent opportunity for Barnes and Fischer to enter a new market. On the other hand, knowing the risks involved, the partner, Jane Hunter, wants to make sure the client acceptance decision is carefully considered.

BACKGROUND ABOUT OCEAN MANUFACTURING, INC.

Ocean Manufacturing, Inc. manufactures small- to medium-sized home appliances. Although Ocean's common stock is not publicly traded, the company is planning an IPO in the next few years in hopes that they will be able to trade the stock on the NASDAQ. You have been assigned to gather information in order to make a recommendation on whether your firm should accept Ocean Manufacturing as a client.

Ocean wants to hire your firm to issue an opinion on their December 31, 200W, financial statements and has expressed interest in obtaining help in getting their recently installed information technology (IT) system in better shape. They also want your firm's advice and guidance on getting everything in order for the upcoming IPO. During the initial meeting with Ocean's management, the following information was obtained about the industry and the company.

The Home Appliances Industry   Over the past several years, the domestic home appliances industry has been growing at a steady, moderate pace. The industry consists of a wide variety of manufacturers (domestic and foreign) who sell to a large number of wholesale and retail outlets. Though responsive to technological improvements, product marketability is linked to growth in the housing market. Retail outlets are served by both wholesale and manufacturer representatives.

Ocean Manufacturing, Inc.   Ocean's unaudited December 31, 200W, financial statements report total assets of $76 million, sales revenues of $145 million, and net profit of $3.4 million. In the past, the company has not attempted to expand aggressively or develop new product lines. Rather, it has concentrated on maintaining a steady growth rate by providing reliable products within a moderate to low price range. However, Ocean hopes to use the capital from the upcoming IPO to aggressively expand from a regional to a national market. Ocean primarily sells its products in small quantities to individually owned appliance stores. Over the last few years the company has begun to supply larger quantities to three national retail chains. Two of these larger retailers started buying Ocean's products about two years ago. In order to handle the increased sales, Ocean significantly expanded its manufacturing capacity. The company's products include items like toasters, blenders, and trash compactors.

Though shaken by recent management turnover and ongoing difficulties with the company's new accounting system, management feels that Ocean is in a position to grow considerably. They note that earnings have increased substantially each year over the past three years and that Ocean's products have received increasing acceptance in the small appliance marketplace. Three years ago the company received a qualified audit opinion relating to revenues and receivables. Ocean has changed auditors three times during the past 12 years.

Management   In October 200W, the company experienced significant management turnover when both the vice president of operations and the controller resigned to take jobs in other cities. The reason for their leaving was disclosed by management as being related to "personal issues." A new vice president, Jack Zachery, was hired in November, and the new controller joined early last month. Jack is an MBA with almost 12 years of experience in the industry. Theodore Jones, the new controller, has little relevant experience and seems frustrated with the company's new IT system. The company president, Andrew Cole, has a BBA and, as the founder, has worked at all levels of the business. Mr. Zachery, who is principally in charge of the company's procurement and manufacturing functions, meets weekly with Mr. Cole, as does Frank Stevens, who has served as vice president over finance for the past eight years.

Accounting and Control Systems   The company switched to a new, integrated central accounting system early last year. This new system maintains integrated inventory, accounts receivable, accounts payable, payroll, and general ledger software modules. The transition to the new system throughout last year was handled mainly by the former controller. Unfortunately, the transition to this system was not well managed, and the company is still working to modify it to better meet company needs, to retrain the accounting staff, and to adapt the company's accounting controls to better complement the system.

Problems still exist in inventory tracking and cost accumulation, receivables billing and aging, payroll tax deductions, payables, and balance sheet account classifications. The company stopped parallel processing the old accounting system in April 200X. During several brief periods throughout last year, conventional audit trails were not kept intact due to system failures and errors made by untrained personnel.

The company's accounting staff and management are frustrated with the situation because, among other problems, internal management budget reports, inventory status reports, and receivables billings are often late and inaccurate, and several shipping deadlines have been missed.

Your office has never audited a company with the specific IT system in place at Ocean. However, your local office's IT team is fairly confident they will be able to diagnose Ocean's control weaknesses and help Ocean overcome current difficulties.

Accounts Receivable, Cash, and Inventories   The sales/receivables system handles a volume ranging from 2,900 to 3,400 transactions per month, including sales and payments on account for about 1,200 active credit customers. The six largest customers currently account for about 15% of accounts receivable, whereas the remainder of the accounts range from $1,500 to $32,000, with an average balance around $8,000.

Finished goods inventories are organized and well protected, but in-process inventories appear somewhat less organized. The company uses a complicated hybrid form of process-costing to accumulate inventory costs and to account for interdepartmental in-process inventory transfers for its four major product lines.

Predecessor Auditor   When you approached Frank Stevens, Ocean's V.P. of finance, to request permission to speak with the previous auditor, he seemed hesitant to discuss much about the prior audit firm. He explained that, in his opinion, the previous auditor did not understand Ocean's business environment very well and was not technically competent to help the company with its new IT system. He further indicated that the predecessor auditor and Ocean's management had disagreed on minor accounting issues during the prior year's audit. In Mr. Stevens' opinion, the disagreement was primarily due to the auditor's lack of understanding of Ocean's business and industry environment. According to Mr. Stevens, the previous auditor felt that because of the accounting issues, he would be unable to issue a clean opinion on the financial statements. In order to receive an unqualified opinion, Ocean had to record certain adjustments to revenues and receivables. Mr. Stevens noted that Ocean's management feels confident that your firm's personnel possess better business judgment skills and have the knowledge and ability to understand and help improve Ocean's IT system. Mr. Stevens also indicated that Ocean wants to switch auditors at this time to prepare for the upcoming IPO, noting that companies often switch to larger accounting firms with national reputations in preparation for going public. Your firm has been highly recommended to him by a friend who is an administrator of a hospital audited by Barnes and Fischer. After some discussion between Mr. Stevens and Mr. Cole, Ocean's president, you are granted permission to contact the previous auditor.

During your visit with the previous auditor, he indicated that the problems his firm had with Ocean primarily related to (1) the complexities and problems with Ocean's new IT system and (2) management's tendency to aggressively reflect year-end accruals and revenue in order to meet creditors' requirements. The auditor also disclosed that the dissolution of the relationship with Ocean was a mutual agreement between the two parties and that his firm's relationship with management had been somewhat difficult almost from the beginning. Apparently the final straw that broke the relationship involved a disagreement over the fee for the upcoming audit.

Client Background Check A check on the background of Ocean's management revealed that five years ago Ocean's V.P. of finance was charged with a misdemeanor involving illegal gambling on local college football games. According to the news reports, charges were later dropped in return for Mr. Stevens' agreeing to pay a fine of $500 and perform 100 hours of community service. The background check revealed no other legal or ethical problems with any other Ocean executives.

Independence Review As part of Barnes and Fischer's quality control program, every three months each employee of Barnes and Fischer is required to file with the firm an updated disclosure of their personal stock investments. You ask a staff auditor to review the disclosures as part of the process of considering Ocean as a potential client. She reports to you that there appears to be no stock ownership issue except that a partner in Barnes and Fischer's Salt Lake City office owns shares in a venture capital fund that in turn holds investments in Ocean common stock. The venture capital fund holds 50,000 shares of Ocean stock, currently valued at approximately $18 a share. This investment represents just over a half of one percent of the value of the fund's total holdings. The partner's total investment in the mutual fund is currently valued at about $56,000.

Financial Statements You acquired the past three years' financial statements from Ocean, including the unaudited statements for the most recent year ended December 31, 200W. This financial information is provided on the pages that follow. The partner who will be in charge of the Ocean engagement wants you to look them over to see what information you can draw from them, paying particular attention to items that might be helpful in determining whether or not to accept Ocean as a new audit client.

REQUIREMENTS

1. The client acceptance process can be quite complex. Identify five procedures an auditor should perform in determining whether to accept a client. Which of these five are required by auditing standards?

2. Using Ocean's financial information, calculate relevant preliminary analytical procedures to obtain a better understanding of the prospective client and to determine how Ocean is doing financially. Compare Ocean's ratios to the industry ratios provided. Identify any major differences.

3. What nonfinancial matters should be considered before accepting Ocean as a client? How important are these issues to the client acceptance decision? Why?

4. a. Ocean wants Barnes and Fischer to aid in developing and improving their IT system. What are the advantages and disadvantages of having the same CPA firm provide both auditing and consulting services? Given current AICPA independence rules, will Barnes and Fischer be able to help Ocean with their IT system and still provide a financial statement audit?

    b. As indicated in the case, one of the partners in another office has invested in a venture capital fund that owns shares of Ocean common stock. Would this situation constitute a violation of independence according to the AICPA *Code of Professional Conduct*? Why or why not?

5. a. Prepare a memo to the partner making a recommendation as to whether Barnes and Fischer should or should not accept Ocean Manufacturing, Inc. as an audit client. Carefully justify your position in light of the information in the case. Include consideration of reasons both for and against acceptance and be sure to address both financial and nonfinancial issues to justify your recommendation.

    b. Prepare a separate memo to the partner briefly listing and discussing the five or six most important factors or risk areas that will likely affect how the audit is conducted if the Ocean engagement is accepted. Be sure to indicate specific ways in which the audit firm should tailor its approach based on the factors you identify.

Ocean Manufacturing, Inc.
Balance Sheets as of December 31, 200U–200W
(In Thousands)

ASSETS

	(Unaudited) 200W	200V	200U
CURRENT ASSETS			
Cash	$ 3,008	$ 2,171	$ 1,692
Accounts receivable (net of allowance)	12,434	7,936	6,621
Raw & in-process inventories	11,907	10,487	10,685
Finished goods inventories	3,853	4,843	7,687
Other current assets	1,286	1,627	1,235
Total Current Assets	32,488	27,064	27,920
PROPERTY, PLANT, & EQUIPMENT	53,173	46,664	39,170
Less accumulated depreciation	11,199	9,009	7,050
Net PP&E	41,974	37,655	32,120
OTHER ASSETS			
Deferred income taxes	714	547	339
Other noncurrent assets	1,216	1,555	735
Total Other Assets	1,930	2,102	1,074
TOTAL ASSETS	$76,392	$66,821	$61,114

LIABILITIES AND SHAREHOLDERS' EQUITY

	200W	200V	200U
CURRENT LIABILITIES			
Accounts payable and accrued expenses	$12,284	$ 9,652	$12,309
Current portion of long-term debt	3,535	3,054	2,899
Income tax payable	865	565	295
Other current liabilities	872	847	988
Total Current Liabilities	17,556	14,118	16,491
LONG-TERM DEBT	20,000	17,234	11,675
TOTAL LIABILITIES	37,556	31,352	28,166
SHAREHOLDERS' EQUITY			
Common stock (10,000,000 shares auth.)	10,675	10,675	10,675
Additional paid-in capital	5,388	5,388	5,388
Retained earnings	22,773	19,406	16,885
Total Shareholders' Equity	38,836	35,469	32,948
TOTAL LIABILITIES AND EQUITY	$76,392	$66,821	$61,114

Ocean Manufacturing, Inc.
Statement of Earnings for Years Ended December 31, 200U–200W
(In Thousands)

	(Unaudited) 200W	200V	200U
Sales	$145,313	$104,026	$92,835
Cost of sales	95,906	69,177	63,870
Gross profit	49,407	34,849	28,965
Operating expenses:	41,414	28,607	24,601
Operating income	7,993	6,242	4,364
Interest expense	1,700	1,474	699
Provision for income taxes	2,821	2,247	1,595
Net Earnings	$ 3,472	$ 2,521	$ 2,070

Ocean Manufacturing, Inc.
Statement of Retained Earnings
(In Thousands)

	(Unaudited) 200W	200V	200U
Balance, beginning of year	$19,406	$16,885	$14,815
Cash dividends paid	(105)	0	0
Net earnings for year	3,472	2,521	2,070
Balance, end of year	$22,773	$19,406	$16,885

Industry Ratios for Comparison

	200W	200V
Return on Equity (ROE)	22.10%	28.50%
Return on Assets (ROA)	7.20%	8.80%
Assets to Equity	3.59	3.06
Accounts Receivable Turnover	8.14	7.57
Average Collection Period	44.84	48.21
Inventory Turnover	8.8	7.5
Days in Inventory	41.48	47.67
Debt in Equity	2.58	2.06
Times Interest Earned	1.5	2.2
Current Ratio	1.2	1.3
Profit Margin	9.80%	10.00%

Comptronix Corporation: Identifying Inherent Risk and Control Risk Factors

Frank A. Buckless, Mark S. Beasley,
Steven M. Glover, and Douglas F. Prawitt

LEARNING OBJECTIVES

After completing and discussing this case you should be able to

- Understand how managers can fraudulently manipulate financial statements
- Recognize key inherent risk factors that increase the potential for financial reporting fraud
- Recognize key control risk factors that increase the potential for financial reporting fraud
- Understand the importance of effective corporate governance for overseeing the actions of top executives

INTRODUCTION

All appeared well at Comptronix Corporation, a Guntersville, Alabama, electronics company, until word hit the streets November 25, 1992, that there had been a fraud. When reports surfaced that three of the company's top executives had inflated company earnings for the past three years, the company's stock price plummeted 72% in one day, closing at $6\frac{1}{8}$ a share, down from the previous day's closing at $22 a share.[1]

The Securities and Exchange Commission's (SEC) subsequent investigation determined that Comptronix's chief executive officer (CEO), chief operating officer (COO), and controller/treasurer colluded to overstate assets and profits by recording fictitious transactions. The three executives overrode existing internal controls so that others at Comptronix would not discover the scheme. All this unraveled when the executives

---

[1]Source: "Company's profit data were false," *The New York Times*, November 26, 1992, D-1.

This case was prepared by Frank A. Buckless, Ph.D. and Mark S. Beasley, Ph.D. of North Carolina State University and Steven M. Glover, Ph.D. and Douglas F. Prawitt, Ph.D. of Brigham Young University, as a basis for class discussion. It is not intended to illustrate either effective or ineffective handling of an administrative situation.

surprisingly confessed to the company's board that they had improperly valued assets, overstated sales, and understated expenses. The three were immediately suspended from their duties.

Within days, class action lawsuits were filed against the company and the three executives. Immediately, the company's board of directors formed a special committee to investigate the alleged financial reporting fraud, an interim executive team stepped in to take charge, and Arthur Andersen, LLP was hired to conduct a detailed fraud investigation.

Residents of the small Alabama town were stunned. How could a fraud occur so close to home? Were there any signs of trouble that were ignored?

BACKGROUND ABOUT COMPTRONIX CORPORATION

Comptronix based its principal operations in Guntersville, a town of approximately 7,000 residents located about 35 miles southeast of Huntsville, Alabama. The company provided contract manufacturing services to original equipment manufacturers in the electronics industry. Their primary product was circuit boards for personal computers and medical equipment. Neighboring Huntsville's heavy presence in the electronics industry provided Comptronix a local base of customers for its circuit boards. In addition to the Alabama facility, the company also maintained manufacturing facilities in San Jose, California, and Colorado Springs, Colorado. In total, Comptronix employed about 1,800 people at the three locations and was one of the largest employers in Guntersville.

The company was formed in the early 1980s by individuals who met while working in the electronics industry in Huntsville. Three of those founders became senior officers of the company. William J. Hebding became Comptronix's chairman and CEO, Allen L. Shifflet became Comptronix's president and COO, and J. Paul Medlin served as the controller and treasurer. Prior to creating Comptronix, all three men worked at SCI Systems, a booming electronics maker. Mr. Hebding joined SCI Systems in the mid-1970s to assist the chief financial officer (CFO). While in that role, he met Mr. Shifflet, the SCI Systems operations manager. Later, when Mr. Hebding became SCI Systems' CFO, he hired Mr. Medlin to assist him. Along with a few other individuals working at SCI Systems, these three men formed Comptronix in late 1983 and early 1984.[2]

The local townspeople in Guntersville were excited to attract the startup company to the local area. The city enticed Comptronix by providing it with an empty knitting mill in town. As additional incentive, a local bank offered Comptronix an attractive credit arrangement. Comptronix in turn appointed the local banker to its board of directors. Town business leaders were excited to have new employment opportunities and looked forward to a boost to the local economy.

The early years were difficult, with Comptronix suffering losses through 1986. Local enthusiasm for the company attracted investments from venture capitalists. One of those investors included a partner in the Massey Burch Investment Group, a venture capital firm located in Nashville, Tennessee, just more than 100 miles to the north. The infusion of venture capital allowed Comptronix to generate strong sales and profit growth during 1987 and 1988. Based on this strong performance, senior management

---

[2]Source: "Comptronix fall from grace: Clues were there, Alabama locals saw lavish spending, feud," *The Atlanta Journal and Constitution*, December 5, 1992, D:1.

took the company's stock public in 1989, initially selling Comptronix stock at $5 a share in the over-the-counter markets.[3]

THE ACCOUNTING SCHEME[4]

According to the SEC's investigation, the fraud began soon after the company went public in 1989 and was directed by top company executives. Mr. Hebding as chairman and CEO, Mr. Shifflett as president and COO, and Mr. Medlin as controller and treasurer used their positions of power and influence to manipulate the financial statements issued from early 1989 through November 1992.

They began their fraud scheme by manipulating the quarterly statements filed with the SEC during 1989. They misstated those statements by inappropriately transferring certain costs from cost of goods sold into inventory accounts. This technique allowed them to overstate inventory and understate quarterly costs of goods sold, which in turn overstated gross margin and net income for the period. The three executives made monthly manual journal entries, with the largest adjustments occurring just at quarter's end. Some allege that the fraud was motivated by the loss of a key customer in 1989 to the three executives' former employer, SCI.

The executives were successful in manipulating quarterly financial statements partially because their quarterly filings were unaudited. However, as fiscal year 1989 came to a close, the executives grew wary that the company's external auditors might discover the fraud when auditing the December 31, 1989, year-end financial statements. To hide the manipulations from their auditors, they devised a plan to cover up the inappropriate transfer of costs. They decided to remove the transferred costs from the inventory account just before year-end, because they feared the auditors would closely examine the inventory account as of December 31, 1989, as part of their year-end testing. Thus, they transferred the costs back to cost of goods sold. However, for each transfer back to cost of goods sold, the fraud team booked a fictitious sale of products and a related fictitious accounts receivable. That, in turn, overstated revenues and receivables.

The net effect of these activities was that interim financial statements included understated cost of goods sold and overstated inventories, while the annual financial statements contained overstated sales and receivables. Once they had tasted success in their manipulations of year-end sales and receivables, they later began recording fictitious quarterly sales in a similar fashion.

To convince the auditors that the fictitious sales and receivables were legitimate, the three company executives recorded cash payments on the bogus customer accounts due Comptronix. In order to do this, they developed a relatively complex fraud scheme. First, they recorded fictitious purchases of equipment on account. That, in turn, overstated equipment and accounts payable. Then, Hebding, the chairman and CEO, and Medlin, the controller and treasurer, cut checks to the bogus accounts payable vendors associated with the fake purchases of equipment. But they did not mail the checks. Rather, they deposited them in Comptronix's disbursement checking account and recorded the phony payments as debits against the bogus accounts payable and credits against the bogus receivables. This accounting scheme allowed the company to eliminate the bogus payables and receivables, while still retaining the fictitious sales and equipment on the income statement and balance sheet, respectively.

---

[3]Source: See footnote 2.

[4]Source: Accounting and Auditing Enforcement Release No. 543, Commerce Clearing House, Inc., Chicago.

This scheme continued more than four years, stretching from the beginning of 1989 to November 1992, when the three executives confessed to their manipulations. The SEC investigation noted that the Form 10-K filings for the years ended December 31, 1989, 1990, and 1991 were materially misstated as follows:

	1989	1990	1991
Sales (in 000's)			
Reported Sales	$42,420	$70,229	$102,026
Restated Sales	37,275	63,444	88,754
Overstatement of Sales	5,145	6,785	13,272
Percentage Overstatement	13.8%	10.7%	14.9%
Net Income (in 000's)			
Reported Net Income	$ 1,470	$ 3,028	$ 5,071
Restated Net Income	(3,524)	(3,647)	(3,225)
Overstatement of Net Income	4,994	6,675	8,296
Earnings Per Share (EPS)			
Reported EPS	$ .19	$ .35	$ .51
Restated EPS (loss)	(.47)	(.43)	(.34)
Overstatement of EPS	.66	.78	.85
Property, Plant, & Equipment (in 000's)			
Reported PP&E	$18,804	$26,627	$ 38,720
Restated Sales	13,856	15,846	20,303
Overstatement of PP&E	4,948	10,781	18,417
Percentage Overstatement	35.7%	68.0%	90.7%
Stockholders' Equity (in 000's)			
Reported Stockholders' Equity	$19,145	$22,237	$ 39,676
Restated Stockholders' Equity	14,151	10,568	18,778
Overstatement of Stockholders' Equity	4,994	11,669	20,898
Percentage Overstatement	35.3%	110.4%	111.3%

The executives' fraud scheme helped the company avoid reporting net losses in each of the three years, with the amount of the fraud increasing in each of the three years affected.[5] The fraud scheme also inflated the balance sheet by overstating property, plant, and equipment and stockholders' equity. By the end of 1991, property, plant, and equipment was overstated by more than 90%, with stockholders' equity overstated by 111%.

THE COMPANY'S INTERNAL CONTROLS[6]

The three executives were able to perpetrate the fraud by bypassing the existing accounting system. They avoided making the standard entries in the sales and pur-

---

[5]Information about fiscal year 1992 was not reported because the fraud was disclosed before that fiscal year ended.

[6]Source: See footnote 4.

chases journals as required by the existing internal control, and recorded the fictitious entries manually. Other employees were excluded from the manipulations to minimize the likelihood of the fraud being discovered.

According to the SEC's summary of the investigation, Comptronix employees normally created a fairly extensive paper trail for equipment purchases, including purchase orders and receiving reports. However, none of these documents were created for the bogus purchases. Approval for cash disbursements was typically granted once the related purchase order, receiving report, and vendor invoice were matched. Unfortunately, Mr. Shifflett or Mr. Medlin could approve payments based solely on an invoice. As a result, the fraud team was able to bypass internal controls over cash disbursements. They simply showed a fictitious vendor invoice to an accounts payable clerk, who in turn prepared a check for the amount indicated on the invoice.

Internal controls were also insufficient to detect the manipulation of sales and accounts receivable. Typically, a shipping department clerk would enter the customer order number and the quantity to be shipped to the customer into the computerized accounting system. The accounting system then automatically produced a shipping document and a sales invoice. The merchandise was shipped to the customer, along with the invoice and shipping document. Once again, Mr. Medlin, as controller and treasurer, had the ability to access the shipping department system. This allowed him to enter bogus sales into the accounting system. He then made sure to destroy all shipping documents and sales invoices generated by the accounting system to keep them from being mailed to the related customers. The subsequent posting of bogus payments on the customers' accounts were posted personally by Mr. Medlin to the cash receipts journal and accounts receivable subsidiary ledger.

The fraud scheme was obviously directed from the top ranks of the organization. Like most companies, the senior executives at Comptronix directed company operations on a day-to-day basis, with only periodic oversight from the company's board of directors.

The March 1992 proxy statement to shareholders noted that the Comptronix board of directors consisted of seven individuals, including Mr. Hebding, who served as board chairman. Of those seven individuals serving on the board, two individuals, Mr. Hebding, chairman and CEO, and Mr. Shifflett, president and COO, represented management on the board. Thus, 28.6% of the board consisted of inside directors. The remaining five directors were not employed by Comptronix. However, two of those five directors had close affiliations with management. One served as the company's outside general legal counsel and the other served as vice president of manufacturing for a significant customer of Comptronix. Directors with these kinds of close affiliations with company management are frequently referred to as "gray" directors due to their perceived lack of objectivity. The three remaining "outside" directors had no apparent affiliations with company management. One of the remaining outside directors was a partner in the venture capital firm that owned 574,978 shares (5.3%) of Comptronix's common stock. That director was previously a partner in a Nashville law firm and was currently serving on two other corporate boards. A second outside director was the vice chairman and CEO of the local bank originally loaning money to the company. He also served as chairman of the board of another local bank in a nearby town. The third outside director was president of an international components supplier based in Taiwan. All of the board members had served on the Comptronix board since 1984, except for the venture capital partner who joined the board in 1988 and the president of the key customer, who joined the board in 1990.

Each director received an annual retainer of $3,000 plus a fee of $750 for each meeting attended. The company also granted each director an option to purchase 5,000 shares of common stock at an exercise price that equaled the market price of the stock on the date that the option was granted.

The board met four times during 1991. The board had an audit committee that was charged with recommending outside auditors, reviewing the scope of the audit engagement, consulting with the external auditors, reviewing the results of the audit examination, and acting as a liaison between the board and the internal auditors. The audit committee was also charged with reviewing various company policies, including those related to accounting and internal control matters. Two outside directors and one gray director made up the three-member audit committee. One of those members was an attorney, and the other two served as presidents and CEOs of the companies where they were employed. There was no indication of whether any of these individuals had accounting or financial reporting backgrounds. The audit committee met two times during 1991.

MANAGEMENT BACKGROUND

The March 1992 proxy statement provided the following background information about the three executives allegedly committing the fraud: Mr. Hebding, Mr. Shifflett, and Mr. Medlin.

William J. Hebding served as the Comptronix chairman and CEO. He was responsible for sales and marketing, finance, and general management of the company. He also served as a director from 1984 until 1992 when the fraud was disclosed. He was the single largest shareholder of Comptronix common stock by beneficially owning 6.7% (720,438 shares) of Comptronix common stock as of March 2, 1992. Before joining Comptronix, Mr. Hebding worked for SCI Systems Inc., from 1974 until October 1983. He held the title of treasurer and CFO at SCI from December 1976 to October 1983. In October 1983, Mr. Hebding left SCI to form Comptronix. He graduated from the University of North Alabama with a degree in accounting and was a certified public accountant. Mr. Hebding's 1991 cash compensation totaled $187,996.

Allen L. Shifflett served as the Comptronix's president and COO, and he was responsible for manufacturing, engineering, and programs operations. He also served as a director from 1984 until 1992 when the fraud unfolded. He owned 4% (433,496 shares) of Comptronix common stock as of March 2, 1992. Like Mr. Hebding, he joined the company after previously being employed at SCI, as a plant manager and manufacturing manager from October 1981 until April 1984, when he left to help form Comptronix. Mr. Shifflett obtained his B.S. degree in industrial engineering from Virginia Polytechnic Institute. Mr. Shifflett's 1991 cash compensation totaled $162,996.

Paul Medlin served as Comptronix controller and treasurer. He also previously worked at SCI, as Mr. Hebding's assistant after graduating from the University of Alabama. Mr. Medlin did not serve on the Comptronix board. The 1992 proxy noted that the board of directors approved a company loan to him for $79,250 on November 1, 1989, to provide funds for him to repurchase certain shares of common stock. The loan, which was repaid on May 7, 1991, bore interest at an annual rate equal to one percentage point in excess of the interest rate designated by the company's bank as that bank's "Index Rate." The 1992 proxy did not disclose Mr. Medlin's 1991 cash compensation.

The company had employment agreements with Mr. Hebding and Mr. Shifflett, which expired April 1992. Those agreements provided that if the company terminated employment with them prior to the expiration of the agreement for any reason other than cause or disability, they would each receive their base salary for the remaining term of the agreement. If terminated for cause or disability, each would receive their base salary for one year following the date of such termination.

The company had an Employee Stock Incentive Plan and an Employee Stock Option Plan that the compensation committee of the board of directors administered. The committee made awards to key employees at its discretion. The compensation committee consisted of three nonemployee directors. One of these directors was an attorney who served as Comptronix's outside counsel on certain legal matters. Another served as an officer of a significant customer of Comptronix. The third member of the committee was a partner in the venture capital firm providing capital for Comptronix.

The SEC's investigation noted that during the period of the fraud, the three men each sold thousands of shares of Comptronix common stock. Their knowledge of material, nonpublic information about Comptronix's actual financial position allowed them to avoid trading losses in excess of $500,000 for Mr. Hebding and Mr. Shifflett, and more than $90,000 for Mr. Medlin. Each also received bonuses: $198,000 for Mr. Hebding, $148,000 for Mr. Shifflett, and $46,075 for Mr. Medlin. These bonuses were granted during the fraud years as a reward for the supposed strong financial performance.

After the fraud was revealed, newspaper accounts reported that red flags had been present. *The New York Times* reported that Mr. Hebding and Mr. Shifflett created reputations in the local community that contrasted with their conservative professional reputations. Mr. Hebding purchased a home worth more than $1 million, often described as a mansion with two boathouses, a pool, a wrought-iron fence with electric gate, and a red Jaguar in the driveway. *The Atlanta Journal and Constitution* reported that Mr. Hebding's marriage had failed, and that he had led an active bachelor's life that led to some problems in town. He also had a major dispute with another company founder who was serving as executive vice president. That individual was suddenly fired from Comptronix in 1989. Later it was revealed that he was allegedly demoted and fired for trying to investigate possible wrongdoing at Comptronix.[7]

Mr. Shifflett, too, had divorced and remarried. He and his second wife purchased an expensive scenic lot in an exclusive country club community in a neighboring town. Mr. Shifflett reportedly had acquired extensive real estate holdings in recent years.[8]

Others were shocked, noting that they were the last to be suspected of any kind of fraud. In the end, it was unclear why the three stunned the board with news of the fraud. There was some speculation that an ongoing IRS tax audit triggered their disclosure of the shenanigans.

EPILOGUE

After the fraud was revealed, all three men were suspended and the board appointed an interim CEO and an interim president to take over the reins. The SEC's investigation led to charges being filed against all three for violating the antifraud provisions of the Securities Act of 1933 and the Securities and Exchange Act of 1934, in addition to other violations of those securities acts. None of the men admitted or denied the allegations against them. However, all three men agreed to avoid any future violations of the securities acts.

---

[7]Source: "A Comptronix founder, in 1989 suit, says he flagged misdeeds," *The Wall Street Journal,* December 7, 1992, A:3.

[8]Sources: See footnote 2 and "In town, neighbors saw it coming," *The New York Times,* December 4, 1992, D:1.

They also consented to being permanently prohibited from serving as officers or directors of any public company. The SEC ordered them to pay back trading losses avoided and bonuses paid to them by Comptronix during the fraud period, and it directed Mr. Hebding and Mr. Shifflett to pay civil penalties of $100,000 and $50,000, respectively. The SEC did not impose civil penalties against Mr. Medlin due to his inability to pay.

The company struggled financially. It sold its San Jose operations in 1994 and eventually filed for Chapter 11 bankruptcy protection in August 1996. Chapter 11 allowed the company to continue operating while developing a restructuring plan. In September 1996, the company announced that it sold substantially all of its assets to a California-based leading electronics manufacturer. As a result of the sale, the secured creditors of Comptronix were fully repaid; however, the unsecured creditors received less than 10 cents on the dollar.

REQUIREMENTS

1. Professional auditing standards present the audit risk model, which is used to determine the nature, timing, and extent of audit procedures. Describe the components of the model and discuss how changes in each component affect the auditor's need for evidence.

2. One of the components of the audit risk model is inherent risk. Describe typical factors that auditors evaluate when assessing inherent risk. With the benefit of hindsight, what inherent risk factors were present during the audits of the 1989 through 1992 Comptronix financial statements?

3. Another component of the audit risk model is control risk. Describe the five components of internal control. What characteristics of Comptronix's internal control increased control risk for the audits of the 1989–1992 year-end financial statements?

4. The board of directors, and its audit committee, can be an effective corporate governance mechanism. Discuss the pros and cons of allowing inside directors to serve on the board. Describe typical responsibilities of audit committees. What strengths or weaknesses were present related to Comptronix's board of directors and audit committee?

5. Public companies must file quarterly financial statements in Form 10-Qs. Professional standards allow CPAs to perform timely reviews of those statements. Briefly describe the key requirements of SAS No. 71, *Interim Financial Statements*. Why wouldn't all companies engage their auditors to perform SAS No. 71 reviews?

6. Do you think Comptronix's executive team was inherently dishonest from the beginning? How is it possible for otherwise honest people to become involved in frauds like the one at Comptronix?

Flash Technologies, Inc.: Risk Analysis and Resolution of Client Issues

Frank A. Buckless, Mark S. Beasley, Steven M. Glover, and Douglas F. Prawitt

LEARNING OBJECTIVES

After completing and discussing this case you should be able to

- Identify and understand the implications of key inherent and business risks associated with a new client
- Appreciate the degree of professional judgment involved in analyzing risk related to the audit of a rapidly growing company in a high technology industry
- Understand how to address client accounting and disclosure concerns
- Write a report containing your risk analysis and response to client concerns

INTRODUCTION

Flash Technologies, Inc. has recently engaged your firm to perform the annual audit for the year ending December 31, 2000. Flash has determined that their current auditors, Adams & Adams LLP, cannot provide the international support that Flash now requires with their increased investment in Korea and Canada. Partners from your firm have discussed the prior audits with the engagement partner at Adams & Adams, and everything seems to be in order. Your firm also met with executives at Flash in December 1999, and a verbal (but informal) agreement was reached regarding fees, timing, scope, etc. Your firm has decided that additional analyses are needed before finalizing the details of the engagement (assume that it is January 2001). On the following pages you will find (1) two memos from the audit manager of your firm to the planning files regarding background information and three questions/concerns the client would like the firm to address, (2) industry articles, (3) industry ratios, and (4) the draft annual report for fiscal year 2000 that Flash has prepared.

This case was prepared by Frank A. Buckless, Ph.D. and Mark S. Beasley, Ph.D. of North Carolina State University and Steven M. Glover, Ph.D. and Douglas F. Prawitt, Ph.D. of Brigham Young University, as a basis for class discussion. It is not intended to illustrate either effective or ineffective handling of an administrative situation.

REQUIREMENTS

1. Provide written recommendations in response to the issues the client has identified (see the "Client Issues" audit memo).

2. Perform a risk analysis and document your findings in a written report. A report like this would be used as a foundation document for engagement planning and client meetings. Using only the information provided in the case (e.g., memos, annual report, and articles), describe the key business risks Flash faces and the key audit risks posed to your audit firm by Flash. (Please focus primarily on factors that will influence acceptable audit risk and inherent risk.) In describing the key inherent risks, please be sure to discuss why a factor represents a risk, and then briefly discuss what implications that particular risk will have on the audit. Auditors are required to specifically assess the risk of material misstatement whether caused by error or fraud. The following AICPA Professional Standards may be useful references for your risk analysis: AU 311, "Planning and Supervision," AU 312, "Audit Risk and Materiality in Conducting an Audit," and AU 316, "Consideration of Fraud in a Financial Statement Audit." To help you identify critical risk factors, you may also wish to perform analytical procedures based on the company's financial data and general industry ratios.

Your firm demands polished, concise, professional analyses and writing. Be thorough, but get to the issues without unnecessary verbiage. In describing your analyses and conclusions, please consider relatively short, "punchy" or to-the-point sentences. Paragraphs will probably not contain more than about five sentences. You may want to organize your risk analysis around categories like General Areas of Risk (e.g., foreign ventures, etc.), Industry Risks, and Specific Financial Statement Risks (e.g., significant or unusual increases in ending balances). Please use headings appropriately and consider using bullet point listings. Exhibits should be referred to in the body of the report and should not include unnecessary detail. Your instructor will provide further guidance on the length and format of the report.

Flash Technologies, Inc.
Memo to the Planning File by Audit Manager—General Information
12/31/00

General Background Information—Emanuel "Manny" Schwimez, is the CEO and chairman of the board of Flash. Mr. Schwimez is originally from Tel Aviv. He has an impressive resume, including a master's degree from the London School of Economics and many years of executive-level experience. He has led several high technology companies in the U.S. and abroad since the late 1960's. In 1987 he became president of Seatac Inc., a start-up company in Seattle, WA, which manufactured and sold font cartridges for printers. In 1989 Seatac agreed to merge with Boston Printing of Massachusetts. In 1990 the combined company was incorporated in Massachusetts as Flash Technologies, Inc. and began developing and commercializing font cartridges for laser printers. Headquarters for the company are in Binex, MA. Beginning in 1996, the company began to shift its emphasis from font cartridges to the growing PC card market. A PC card is a rugged, lightweight, credit card-sized device inserted into a dedicated slot in a broad range of electronic equipment that contain microprocessors, such as portable computers, telecommunications equipment, manufacturing equipment, and vehicle diagnostic systems. Although Flash Technologies, Inc. is still a relatively small player in the industry, it has enjoyed impressive success. The company's stock price has grown 300% during the last 3 years. In 1998 Flash's stock graduated to the New York Stock Exchange. The stock recommendation from analysts following Flash's stock is currently "strong buy." However, I did some market research and noticed short positions in Flash stock have increased during November and December.

While I was researching the stock, I visited the Yahoo! (Internet) Message Board about Flash. The message board is a place where interested parties can discuss the future prospects of the company and share information about it with others. The message board is not connected in any way with the company, and any messages are solely the opinion and responsibility of the poster. Most of the posts on the message board are positive and suggest investors are bullish on Flash stock. However, there were a few posts from someone who goes by "Mr. Truth" that were very negative with respect to Mr. Schwimez. Mr. Truth calls Schwimez a "pathological liar" and referred to alleged wrong doings by Mr. Schwimez in the 1960s when he was a journalist for an Israeli newspaper and in the 1970s when Schwimez was an executive with a Swiss company in Geneva. To this point, our local background checks for Mr. Schwimez (e.g., local bankers, attorneys, business associates, vendors, etc.) have been positive. I mentioned the negative allegations to the chief financial officer, Jane Murphy, and she indicated that she had also heard similar allegations. She indicated that Mr. Schwimez is an aggressive, successful businessman and that because of his particular style of business not everyone likes Mr. Schwimez. Ms. Murphy believes the allegations are baseless and are simply the result of envy and jealousy. Although the CFO is probably correct, we may want to conduct a more thorough background check on Mr. Schwimez.

New Product—In the fourth quarter of 2000, Flash began shipping a new product "Flash 2000." It is a miniature memory card for notebook computers. Sales for fiscal year 2000 amounted to about $2 million. The company is attempting to keep the details of this card relatively quiet for a few more months for competitive reasons. Due to design advances developed by Flash's research and development team, these new cards have an extremely low cost (less than $20). However, they are currently selling for about $300. To date, all sales of Flash 2000 have been made to one customer, CCB Computers, which is located in New Hampshire. Mr. Schwimez indicated that CCB and Flash have an excellent working relationship. The president of CCB, Andrew Jolsen, is a long-time associate of Mr. Schwimez. Mr. Jolsen will be joining Flash's Board of Directors within the next few months.

Plant Tour—After the December 23rd meeting with Flash, I visited the Massachusetts manufacturing facility just outside Binex. This is one of the original manufacturing facilities and thus is not as "leading edge" as Flash's other manufacturing facilities around the world. I was somewhat surprised at how much of the product is still assembled manually. I saw a lot of people pounding PC Card cases together with rubber mallets. Nonetheless, I was generally impressed with the organization and efficiency of the facility. It appeared employees were well trained. In one assembly line, I was particularly interested in the inspection team over product quality. They were examining the welds on the flash card casings. I watched the process for several minutes (and several hundred flash cards) noting no faulty product during that time. I examined a casing that was in the "reject" bin due to a failed weld. When a weld did fail, the inspection team member indicated most of the time the casing could be rewelded without any spoilage. I noticed all the reject casings were empty (no electronics inside). An inspection team member told me that after the casings are inspected and rejected, the "insides" are removed for cleaning and then carefully reprocessed in a static-free environment.

In the employee dining area I overheard some disgruntled employees talking about the pressure they were getting to ship customer items. When I inquired further I was informed that Mr. Schwimez had just decided to send out large holiday baskets of fruit and candy to show the company's appreciation to valued customers. Because of the rush to get the baskets in the overnight mail, Mr. Schwimez asked the shipping department to take care of the packing and shipping. Employees indicated that what Mr. Schwimez wants, he gets.

Major Contract—Mr. Schwimez informed me that Flash is close to sealing a deal with AT&T for a satellite tracking system for truck fleets that could be worth up to $300 million. He is very excited about the deal and believes it will really put Flash Technologies "on the map." He indicated that when the formal announcement is made is should boost the stock price even higher. Because the deal is so close to completion, he has been disclosing the information to institutional investors. Industry publications have mentioned the possibility of a big AT&T contract for such a tracking system, but AT&T has thus far declined comment and no agreement has been announced.

SEC Investigation—The CFO, Ms. Murphy, informed me that Flash has received informal notification from the SEC that they are performing a review of Flash's financial statement filings. The client has indicated that this is a routine process that is common for rapidly growing companies, particularly high technology companies. The CFO indicates that many high technology companies have recently received comment letters regarding their accounting for in-process R&D.

Flash Technologies, Inc.
Memo to the Planning File by Audit Manager—Client Issues
12/31/00

In our December 23rd meeting with Flash, management asked our firm to respond to the following questions/issues:

1. Management would like to know if footnote disclosure will be required for the Design Circuits, Inc. purchase that took place after year-end (the purchase is included in the management discussion of the draft annual report). We need to research subsequent-event auditing standards. If it appears disclosure will be required, the client would like us to draft the footnote disclosure. If we need to draft a footnote, we can refer to "Accounting Trends and Techniques" or the SEC's EDGAR database for footnote examples for subsequent events.

2. As Flash has enjoyed more success, they have noticed legal activity has increased. Although no formal lawsuits have been filed, they are aware of a potential lawsuit accusing Flash of patent infringement. It seems likely that the lawsuit will be filed before spring. Although management is confident they have sound legal footing for the design and manufacture of their Flash cards, they would like us to inform them of disclosure requirements.

3. Our firm has also been asked to comment on Flash's position in derivatives. The CFO, Jane Murphy, has indicated that the company will report gains on derivative contracts for 2000. It seems that in 2000 Flash purchased a call option allowing them to buy Korean currency (won) at a specified price. This option was purchased to hedge a firm commitment that Flash entered into with one of its Korean suppliers. During 2000, the market value of the option contract has increased; however, Flash won't actually take delivery of the goods until 2001. Currently the draft financials do not report the gain or disclose the company's derivative position. Ms. Murphy has explained to top management that, under the FASB's standard on accounting for derivatives, all derivative contracts are reported at market value. Therefore, the company will be able to report a gain on the option contract in the current year, and this will increase net income for the year. Other executives at Flash have heard a lot about accounting for derivatives, and they are concerned about inappropriately reporting the derivative position.

"THROW AWAY YOUR SCREWDRIVER—PLUG-IN CREDIT CARD-SIZED DEVICES HAVE A BIG ROLE TO PLAY IN ENHANCING PC FUNCTIONS/ PC CARDS; EASIER WAYS OF UPGRADING PCS ARE EMERGING"

By Jessica Mara
November 2, 1998, *Financial Times*

Personal computers may be becoming easier to use, but upgrading a PC—to add memory, an internal modem or perhaps a sound card circuit board—is still a daunting task. That is changing, however, as a new standard for plug-in add-on circuit cards continues to gain popularity. Unlike most of today's PC add-on circuit boards, PC cards (also known as PCMCIA cards) do not mean taking out a screwdriver.

The awkward moniker stands for Personal Computer Memory Card International Standard Association, the industry group that has agreed upon technical specifications for the way that these add-on cards connect to personal computers and interact with personal computer software. To make that easier to say, the name of the standard was changed late last year to PC card technology.

Apart from the original name, however, PC cards are simple to use. The credit card-sized devices are plugged into a socket on the outside of the PC, much like a standard floppy disk.

Originally defined as a standard for adding memory capacity or data storage capacity to a handheld or portable notebook PC, the PC card standard has now been expanded to include circuit cards with a broad range of functions for all manner of PCs. BIS Strategic Decisions, the U.S. market research group, predicts that within four years, 70 percent of desktop PCs will include PC card slots.

If this standard is widely accepted by desktop computer manufacturers, there would no longer be any need for users to open the lids of their computers to install circuit cards, flip DIP switches, or connect cables—a frustrating exercise that PC upgraders have faced since the early days of the Apple II. Before PC cards can achieve this kind of success, however, the PC industry as a whole will have to agree to support it on systems other than notebook and handheld computers, where it is already the de facto expansion standard. To date, that has not happened and sales of PC cards have not taken off as quickly as industry analysts expected.

The question of standardization has been a thorn in the side of the PCMCIA group for the last five years as the standard for PC cards has evolved—with the greater capability and power being added as the specification for the card allowed it to be ever thicker. If you want to buy a PC card, you will hear about Type I, II, III and IV card slots.

"PC card technology will continue to be an extremely strong technology, if not the strongest," said Andy Morris, Intel's VP/GM memory components division. "We're doing a pretty good job going out and talking with customers, letting them know how much they can expect next year. Everyone will get a lot more, but there will still be constraints. The rapid growth PC card technology has experienced this year will continue next." Having proven itself in more pedestrian applications such as PC BIOS and mass storage, this technology, commonly referred to as "flash," is poised for swift penetration into the digital cellular, digital camera and digital voice recording markets in the coming years, with its showing in the PCMCIA and small form factor PC card arena improving steadily.

"THE FUTURE OF DATA STORAGE IN PORTABLE SYSTEMS"

by Anna Jayne
January 30, 1999, *Portable Computing and Communicating*

The immense success of notebook computers speaks volumes about the demand for portability in computing systems. Notebook users want to write documents, share presentations, work on spreadsheets, download data and communicate with other users anywhere, at any time. With the availability of more user-friendly online information services, Windows 95 and associated applications, the challenge of fulfilling this need increases dramatically. Indeed, notebook computer users store almost as much software on their notebook systems as on their desktop PCs. And if this trend continues at a rate similar to the growth of desktop applications, it will tax the ability of many storage system vendors to provide adequate storage capacity to mobile users.

Flash Memory. According to analysts at CompTrend, Inc., worldwide market consumption of flash memory (PC) cards will have increased 190% between 1997 and 1998 to $521 million in sales. However, despite ongoing technological improvements, fundamental issues such as raw storage capacity and cost per megabyte continue to channel these products into markets and applications outside of the notebook computing realm. Barring some unforeseen technological development, PC cards will always be more expensive per megabyte than hard disk drives. Still, in applications where only a few megabytes of memory are needed, flash may actually be the less expensive option compared to rotating disk drives.

Smaller capacity PC card or "flash" devices may gain acceptance, for example, as "ruggedized floppy" storage devices for file transfer between portable and desktop systems. With operating shock loads of over 10Gs, solid state memory devices have clearly superior durability to rotating memory devices. In fact, in applications where durability is of extreme importance (including some military applications), flash memory devices are the preferred memory technology at any capacity. Because of the enormous potential for this market there may be opportunities for smaller niche players to be successful. However, before other companies' products can find widespread acceptance, they will have to overpower the already prodigious market lead developed by companies such as Intel and AMD, which manufacture PCMCIA-compliant PC cards.

INDUSTRY RATIOS		
	2000	**1999**
Current Ratio	1.50	
Quick Ratio	1.10	
Debt to Equity Ratio	28.00%	
Inventory Turnover	8.1%	
Profit Margin	14.60%	11.18%
Return on Total Assets	5.03%	

Flash Technologies, Inc.
Annual Report, Management Discussion of Financial Condition, Report of Independent Auditors, and Notes to Consolidated Financial Statements For the Year Ending December 31, 2000

Annual Report

OVERVIEW

Flash Technologies, Inc. (the "Company") designs, manufactures and markets an extensive line of PC cards. A PC card is a rugged, lightweight, credit card-sized device inserted into a dedicated slot in a broad range of electronic equipment that contain microprocessors, such as portable computers, telecommunications equipment, manufacturing equipment and vehicle diagnostic systems. The Company sells its PC cards primarily to original equipment manufacturers ("OEMs") for industrial and commercial applications. The Company's PC cards provide increased storage capacity, communications capabilities, and programmed software for specialized applications. These specialized applications include data acquisition and processing, navigation, information encryption, and security.

The OEM market served by the Company has rigorous demands for quality products, technical service and support, and rapid order turnaround. The Company provides its OEM customers with comprehensive PC card solutions, including in-house design, programming, engineering, manufacturing, and private labeling. The Company believes its ability to provide a full range of services, rapid order turnaround, and manufacturing flexibility to accommodate both large and small production runs provides a competitive advantage in servicing the OEM market. The Company sells into a broad range of markets, including: Communications (routers, wireless telephones, and local area networks); Transportation (navigation, vehicle diagnostics); Mobile Computing (handheld data collection terminals, notebook computers, personal digital assistants); and Medical (blood gas analysis systems, defibrillators, handheld glucometers). The Company has sold its products and services to more than 250 OEMs, including 3Com Corporation ("3Com"), Bay Networks, Inc. ("Bay Networks"), Lucent Technologies, Inc. ("Lucent Technologies"), Philips Electronics N. V. ("Philips"), Trimble Navigation Limited ("Trimble Navigation"), Digital Equipment Corporation ("Digital"), Sharp Electronics Corporation ("Sharp"), and Xerox Corporation ("Xerox").

The Company was incorporated and began operation in 1990 to develop and commercialize font cartridges for laser printers. Beginning in 1996, the Company began designing, manufacturing, and marketing cards that conformed to the specifications agreed upon by the Personal Computer Memory Card International Association ("PCMCIA") and became known as "PC cards," and gradually de-emphasized the marketing and sales of font cartridges in order to focus on the rapidly growing PC card market.

RECENT DEVELOPMENTS

In September 2000, the Company entered into an agreement to form Flash Technologies (Korea) Limited ("Flash Korea"), which will provide contract manufacturing services for third parties, as well as serve as an offshore manufacturer of the Company's PC cards. Under the agreement, the Company will acquire a 51% interest in Flash Korea in exchange for $1.25 million in cash. The remaining 49% will be held by an unaffiliated company. The Company expects Flash Korea to begin operations by May 2001. No assurance can be given that Flash Korea will commence operations on schedule, or that it will not experience significant and unforeseen expenses, costs, and delays.

In January 2001, the Company purchased a majority interest in Design Circuits, Inc. ("DCI"), a contract manufacturer of printed circuit boards and related products primarily for OEMs. DCI has a June 30 fiscal year-end. For the six months ended December 31, 2000, and the fiscal years ended June 30, 2000 and 1999, sales at DCI totaled approximately $7,000,000, $9,070,000 and $8,482,000, respectively, and net income (losses) totaled approximately ($509,000), ($1,418,000) and $171,000, respectively. The Company acquired approximately a 75% interest in DCI in exchange for approximately $3.2 million in cash and 125,000 shares of the Company's common stock (the "Common Stock"). The remaining 25% of DCI was acquired by outside investors for approximately $2.4 million.

The Company believes that DCI and Flash Korea may benefit from the Company's existing supply relationships and customer contacts. In addition, the Company believes that it may benefit from exposure to the products and customers of DCI and Flash Korea.

TECHNOLOGY AND INDUSTRY BACKGROUND

In recent years, digital computing and processing have expanded beyond the boundaries of desktop computer systems to include a broader array of electronic systems, such as mobile communication systems, communications switches, network switches, medical devices, navigation systems, cellular telephones, portable computers, digital cameras, and portable data collection terminals. PC card characteristics, such as shock and vibration tolerance, low power consumption, small size, and higher access speed, better meet the requirements of these emerging applications than do traditional hard drive and floppy disk storage solutions. In addition, PC cards can provide features, such as additional or specialized memory technologies, that previously resided on computer add-in boards or required external hardware devices. The Company believes that demand for PC cards will increase from increased adoption of PCMCIA standards by electronic equipment manufacturers, the inclusion of PC card slots on next-generation electronic devices, and the development of PC cards offering new applications. In addition, the Company believes that widening acceptance of Microsoft Corporation's handheld and mobile computer operating system, Windows CE, may stimulate demand for certain handheld computers and personal digital assistants ("PDAs") that use PC cards for storage and other applications.

PC cards may contain configurations of more than one type of memory, as well as communications software and related connection devices for facsimile/modems and local area networks. PC cards connect directly to an electrical device on a computer's main circuit board, which contains both the computer memory and the central processing unit ("CPU"). This direct connection results in more rapid retrieval of information than with hard drives and floppy disks, which must have data transferred to the main circuit board before it is available to the CPU. Additionally, unlike hard drives and floppy disks, PC cards generally do not have moving parts and, therefore, require less energy consumption and are generally more rugged. These advantages have become important as computing devices become smaller and more portable. Management believes that the introduction of flash SIMM Modules and miniature cards could complement the Company's extensive PC card product offerings and provide the Company's OEM customers with more alternatives to address data acquisition and processing needs.

The Company primarily targets OEM customers in the following four industries: Communication (routers, cellular data, local area networks); Transportation (fleet data recording, navigation, auto diagnostics); Medical (medical devices); and Mobile (handheld data collection terminals, notebooks, palmtops, personal digital assistants).

CUSTOMER SALES AND MARKETING

The Company targets industrial and commercial applications for PC cards in the communications, transportation, medical device, and mobile computing industries. The company has a direct sales force of 12 people with offices in Massachusetts, California, Canada, England, and Germany.

The Company's sales staff and engineers often work with OEM engineers to design and engineer PC cards to OEM requirements, which often leads to the Company providing custom-designed PC cards for specific applications. The Company also markets its products to corporate end-users directly and through value-added resellers. Corporate end-users purchase PC cards to provide additional memory and for communications applications for local area networks and data and facsimile/modems. In addition, they purchase specialty cards for terminal emulation, mixed signal converters and data encryption. The Company recently began to market PC cards to the United States government for data encryption and for use in conjunction with global positioning systems in military equipment and vehicles. Data encryption devices are used by federal agencies to ensure the security of confidential information.

MANUFACTURING

The Company's PC card manufacturing process includes programming, production, assembly, ultrasonic welding, cleaning, final assembly, labeling, and packaging. Nearly all of these operations are conducted at the Company's manufacturing facility in Binex, Massachusetts. The Company's manufacturing facility has generally operated on a two-shift, five-day-per-week basis.

Manufacturing Flexibility. The Company has designed its manufacturing facility to accommodate its customers' requirement for rapid order turnaround. The Company's manufacturing process may be converted to accommodate the production of different products with a minimum of down time.

In fiscal 2000, the Company subcontracted a small portion of its manufacturing to a Canadian electronic-assembly contract manufacturer with specialized manufacturing capabilities, which include wire bonding and ceramic printing. The Company believes its ability to subcontract a portion of its manufacturing will give it greater flexibility with respect to manufacturing capacity.

Product Quality and Testing Procedures. The Company continually seeks to improve product quality. The Company's zero-defect policy, implemented in April 1999, is designed to ensure that there are no defects in PC card products shipped from the Company's facility. In connection with this effort, the Company hired additional production and testing engineers and established additional quality control checks throughout its manufacturing process. In October 1999, the Company became a certified ISO 9001 manufacturer with respect to its Binex, Massachusetts, facility. Certification requires that the Company undergo an annual audit of certain policies and procedures.

Manufacturing Efficiency. The Company places a high priority on maintaining efficient operations. The Company is upgrading manual production lines to automated production lines in order to reduce cost and increase throughput. For example, the Company uses ultrasonic welders that encase the Company's PC cards more efficiently than manual labor and produce a more rugged card with better protection against electrostatic discharge.

SOURCES OF SUPPLY

The Company has, from time to time, experienced shortages in electronic components used to manufacture PC cards, specifically computer memory chips. The Company expects such supply shortages to continue, particularly for electronic components used in products targeted at high-growth market segments. These components may include flash and SRAM memory chips, many of which are subject to industry-wide allocation by chip suppliers.

The Company purchases certain key components from sole or single-source vendors for which alternative sources are not currently available. The Company does not maintain long-term supply agreements with any of its vendors. The inability to develop alternative sources for these single or sole-source components or to obtain sufficient quantities of components could result in delays or reductions in product shipments. The Company relies on certain sole-source suppliers to provide components used in certain of the Company's products. The Company seeks to maintain close working relationships with its suppliers to ensure timely and reliable delivery.

COMPETITION

The Company competes with manufacturers of PC cards and related products, including SanDisk Corporation and Smart Modular Technologies, Inc., as well as with electronic component manufacturers who also manufacture PC cards, including Mitsubishi Electronic Corporation, Intel Corporation, Epson of America, Inc., and Fujitsu Microelectronics, Inc. Certain of these competitors also supply the Company with raw materials, including electronic components that are from time to time subject to industry-wide allocation. Such competitors may have the ability to manufacture PC cards at lower costs than the Company as a result of their higher levels of integration.

The Company expects competition to increase in the future from existing competitors and from other companies that may enter the Company's existing or future markets with similar or alternative solutions that may be less costly or provide additional features. The Company believes that its ability to compete successfully depends on a number of factors, which include product quality and performance, order turnaround, the provision of competitive design capabilities, success in developing new applications for PC cards, adequate manufacturing capacity, efficiency of production, timing of new product introductions by the Company, its customers and its competitors, the number and nature of the Company's competitors in a given market, price, and general market and economic conditions. In addition, increased competitive pressure may lead to intensified price competition, resulting in lower prices and gross margins.

Management Discussion of Financial Condition

OVERVIEW

The Company was incorporated and began operation in 1990 to develop and commercialize font cartridges for laser printers. Beginning in fiscal 1996, when the Company began designing, manufacturing, and marketing PC cards, the Company gradually de-emphasized the marketing and sales of font cartridges in order to focus on the rapidly growing PC card market. As the Company effected this shift in focus, the Company's sales increased from $6.3 million in fiscal 1997 to $37.8 million in fiscal 2000. Net income has correspondingly increased from $442,000 in fiscal 1997 to $4.9 million in fiscal 2000.

The declining gross margin has been attributable to the shift in the Company's product mix from font cartridges to lower-margin PC cards and, more recently, to increases in the cost of certain electronic components used in the Company's PC cards. The cost of these components generally stabilized during the latter half of fiscal 2000. PC card sales may comprise a lower percentage of the Company's total sales in future periods due to the recent acquisition of DCI, a contract manufacturer, and the commencement of contract manufacturing operations at Flash Korea, expected in May 2001. The Company expects to realize lower gross margins associated with its future contract manufacturing services than those realized from the sale of its PC cards.

RESULTS OF OPERATIONS—Years Ended December 31, 2000 and 1999

Sales. Sales increased 204% to approximately $37.8 million in fiscal 2000 from approximately $12.4 million in fiscal 1999, primarily as a result of increased volume of sales of PC cards. Sales of PC cards as a percentage of total sales increased to approximately 98% in fiscal 2000 from approximately 86% in fiscal 1999. The growth in the Company's PC card sales resulted primarily from expansion of the PC card market, increased sales and marketing efforts by the Company, and the broadening of the Company's PC card product line. The increase in the Company's PC card sales was partially offset by a decrease in sales of font cartridges.

Gross Margin. Gross margin increased 153% to approximately $14.2 million in fiscal 2000 from approximately $5.6 million in fiscal 1999. As a percentage of sales, gross margin decreased to 37.5% in fiscal 2000 from 45.1% for fiscal 1999, primarily due to an increase in the cost of electronic components used in the Company's products and to the continuing shift in product mix from font cartridges to lower-margin PC cards.

General and Administrative Expenses. General and administrative expenses increased 36% to approximately $4.6 million in fiscal 2000 from approximately $3.4 million in fiscal 1999. The increase was due to expanded sales and marketing efforts, increased depreciation expense resulting primarily from the acquisition of additional manufacturing equipment, and to an increase in personnel. As a percentage of sales, general and administrative expenses decreased to 12.1% in fiscal 2000 from 27% for fiscal 1999, primarily due to the Company's increased sales. The Company intends to amortize the goodwill associated with its recent acquisition of a majority interest in DCI over a 10-year period. The annual amortization expense of this goodwill is expected to be approximately $940,000.

Research and Development Costs. Research and development costs increased 91% to approximately $1.4 million in fiscal 2000 from approximately $753,000 in fiscal 1999. As a percentage of sales, research and development costs were 3.8% in fiscal 2000, as compared to 6.1% for fiscal 1999. In addition to its research and development spending, the Company has invested in companies with technologies and capabilities complementary to those of the Company and has licensed proprietary technology from third parties. See "Business—Engineering and Product Development."

Income from Operations. Income from operations increased 448% to approximately $8.2 million in fiscal 2000 from approximately $1.5 million in fiscal 1999 primarily as a result of increased sales, which were partially offset by higher component costs and increases in general and administrative and research and development costs. As a percentage of sales, income from operations was 21.6% in fiscal 2000, as compared to 12% for fiscal 1999.

Net Interest Expense. Net interest expense was approximately $17,000 in fiscal 2000, compared to the net interest expense of $64,000 in fiscal 1999. Interest expense increased by approximately $296,000 due to increased borrowing under its credit agreement. This increase was offset by an increase in interest income of approximately $343,000 generated primarily by the proceeds received from the Company's public offering in March 2000.

Provision for Income Taxes. Provision for income taxes increased 488% to approximately $3.3 million in fiscal 2000 from approximately $556,000 in fiscal 1999. The effective tax rates were 40% and 38.9% for fiscal 2000 and 1999, respectively.

SIGNATURES

In accordance with Section 13 or 15(d) of the Securities Exchange Act of 1934, as amended, the registrant caused this report to be signed on its behalf by the undersigned, thereunto duly authorized.

Date: December 31, 2000

Manny Schwimez, Chief Executive Officer

Manny Schwimez, Chairperson of the Board, Chief Executive Officer, and Secretary

Ronald J. McDonald, President and Director

Jane M. Murphy, Chief Financial Officer (Principal financial and accounting officer), and Director

REPORT OF INDEPENDENT ACCOUNTANTS (*copy of prior year's report*)

To the Board of Directors and Stockholders of FLASH TECHNOLOGIES, INC.:

We have audited the accompanying consolidated balance sheets of Flash Technologies, Inc. as of December 31, 1999 and 1998, and the related consolidated statements of income, stockholders' equity and cash flows for each of the three years in the period ended December 31, 1999. These financial statements are the responsibility of the Company's management. Our responsibility is to express an opinion on these financial statements based on our audits.

We conducted our audits in accordance with generally accepted auditing standards. Those standards require that we plan and perform the audit to obtain reasonable assurance about whether the financial statements are free of material misstatement. An audit includes examining, on a test basis, evidence supporting the amounts and disclosures in the financial statements. An audit also includes assessing the accounting principles used and significant estimates made by management, as well as evaluating the overall financial statement presentation. We believe that our audits provide a reasonable basis for our opinion.

In our opinion, the financial statements referred to above present fairly, in all material respects, the consolidated financial position of Flash Technologies, Inc., as of December 31, 1999 and 1998, and the consolidated results of its operations and its cash flows for each of the three years in the period ended December 31, 1999, in conformity with generally accepted accounting principles.

Adams & Adams, AUDITOR. Boston, Massachusetts.

FLASH TECHNOLOGIES, INC.
Consolidated Balance Sheet

ASSETS	Unaudited Dec. 31, 2000	Dec. 31, 1999
Current assets:		
Cash and cash equivalents	$ 6,181,520	$ 970,446
Available-for-sale securities	4,932,763	—
Accounts receivable, net of allowance for doubtful accounts of $230,000 and $122,200 at Dec. 31, 2000 and 1999, respectively	12,592,231	3,932,170
Inventories	18,229,317	8,609,492
Current portion of notes receivable	3,680,750	767,758
Deferred income taxes	211,100	209,300
Other current assets	2,362,887	670,812
Total current assets	48,190,568	15,159,978
Equipment and leasehold improvements, net of accumulated depreciation and amortization of $822,011 and $299,355 at Dec. 31, 2000 and 1999, respectively	4,698,616	1,322,637
Notes receivable, less current portion	—	1,072,939
Investments	2,472,381	—
Other assets	170,392	266,658
Deferred income taxes	121,300	126,000
Intangible assets, net of accumulated amortization of $412,463 and $290,437 at Dec. 31, 2000 and 1999, respectively	128,918	250,944
	$ 55,782,175	$ 18,199,156

FLASH TECHNOLOGIES, INC. **DRAFT** FOR INTERNAL USE ONLY

LIABILITIES AND STOCKHOLDERS' EQUITY	Unaudited Dec. 31, 2000	Dec. 31, 1999
Current liabilities:		
Note payable	$ 4,683,876	$ 1,153,167
Current portion of long-term obligations under capital leases	336,058	102,645
Accounts payable and accrued expenses	3,494,693	3,570,519
Income taxes payable	614,036	591,265
Deferred revenue	—	175,000
Total current liabilities	9,128,663	5,592,596
Long-term obligations under capital leases	366,944	161,134
Deferred income taxes	241,600	—
Stockholders' equity:		
Common stock, $.01 par value; 15,000,000 shares authorized, 8,315,935 shares issued and outstanding at Dec. 31, 2000 and 5,591,288 shares issued and outstanding at Dec. 31, 1999	83,159	55,913
Additional paid-in capital	38,883,677	10,213,517
Retained earnings	7,078,132	2,175,996
Total stockholders' equity	46,044,968	12,445,426
Total liabilities and stockholders' equity	$ 55,782,175	$ 18,199,156

FLASH TECHNOLOGIES, INC.
Consolidated Income Statements

	Years Ended Dec. 31,		
	2000	1999	1998
	Unaudited		
Sales	$ 37,847,681	$ 12,445,015	$ 8,213,236
Cost of goods sold	23,636,299	6,832,927	4,523,186
Gross margin	14,211,382	5,612,088	3,690,050
General and administrative expenses	4,590,413	3,365,752	1,888,602
Research and development costs	1,433,765	752,654	567,248
Income from operations	8,187,204	1,493,682	1,234,200
Other income (expense):			
Interest income	352,606	9,944	8,159
Interest expense	(369,584)	(73,952)	(169,755)
Loss on sale of receivables to factor	—	—	(76,892)
Amortization of discount on bridge financing	—	—	(247,500)
	(16,978)	(64,008)	(485,988)
Income before income taxes	8,170,226	1,429,674	748,212
Provision for income taxes	3,268,090	555,958	284,320
Net income	$ 4,902,136	$ 873,716	$ 463,892
Earnings per share: Primary	$ 0.67	$ 0.16	$ 0.14
Weighted average shares outstanding: Primary	7,338,906	5,511,606	3,325,000

FLASH TECHNOLOGIES, INC.
Consolidated Statement of Cash Flows

	Years Ended Dec. 31,		
	2000	1999	1998
Cash flows from operating activities:	**Unaudited**		
Net income	$ 4,902,136	$ 873,716	$ 463,892
Adjustments to reconcile net income			
Depreciation and amortization	644,682	337,151	192,673
Provision for loss on accounts receivable	280,000	162,200	49,000
Discount on bridge financing	—	—	247,500
Compensation from option grants	19,875	52,650	—
Tax benefit related to stock option exercise	614,322	—	—
Deferred income taxes	244,500	(219,593)	(76,506)
Changes in operating assets and liabilities:			
Accounts receivable	(8,940,061)	(2,432,829)	(981,064)
Inventories	(9,619,825)	(5,238,039)	(1,115,211)
Notes receivable	759,947	(1,840,697)	—
Other assets	(1,595,809)	(564,033)	(58,726)
Accounts payable and accrued expenses	(75,826)	2,954,790	(974,411)
Income taxes payable	22,771	74,854	75,070
Deferred revenue	(175,000)	175,000	—
Net cash used for operating activities	(12,918,288)	(5,664,830)	(2,177,783)
Cash flows from investing activities:			
Capital expenditures	(3,898,635)	(862,396)	(525,438)
Purchase of available-for-sale securities	(8,913,741)	—	—
Proceeds from sale of available-for-sale securities	3,980,978	—	—
Notes receivable	(2,800,000)	—	—
Purchases of investments	(2,272,381)	—	—
Net cash used for investing activities	(13,903,779)	(862,396)	(525,438)
Cash flows from financing activities:			
Cash overdraft	—	—	(54,398)
Net borrowings under line of credit	3,530,709	1,153,167	—
Borrowings from sales leaseback of equipment	691,034	319,735	—
Payments on equipment financing	(251,811)	(55,956)	—
Net proceeds from exercise of stock options	698,671	149,550	—
Net proceeds from exercise of warrants and representatives' warrants	5,193,785	3,809,630	—
Net proceeds from public offerings	20,928,753	—	4,637,589
Net proceeds pursuant to the underwriters' overallotments	1,242,000	—	26,100
Net proceeds from private placement	—	1,140,476	—
Proceeds from bridge financing	—	—	550,000
Repayment of bridge financing	—	—	(550,000)
Payments on notes payable	—	—	(925,000)
Net cash provided by financing activities	32,033,141	6,516,602	3,684,291
Net increase (decrease) in cash	5,211,074	(10,624)	981,070
Cash and cash equivalents at beginning of the year	970,446	981,070	—
Cash and cash equivalents at end of the year	$ 6,181,520	$ 970,446	$ 981,070

Notes to Consolidated Financial Statements

SUMMARY OF SIGNIFICANT ACCOUNTING POLICIES

Basis of Presentation. The consolidated financial statements of Flash Technologies, Inc. (the "Company") include the accounts of the Company, all wholly-owned subsidiaries and majority-owned subsidiaries. Investments in companies in which ownership interests range from 20 percent to 50 percent, and the Company exercises significant influence over operating and financial policies, are accounted for using the equity method. Other investments are accounted for using the cost method. All significant intercompany balances and transactions have been eliminated.

Industry Segment. The Company operates in a single industry segment: the design, manufacture, and marketing of PC Cards used primarily by original equipment manufacturers for industrial and commercial applications. In September 2000, the Company entered into an agreement to acquire a 51% interest in a joint venture. The joint venture intends to manufacture PC Cards and provide contract manufacturing services.

Revenue Recognition. Revenue from product sales is recognized at time of shipment.

Warranty Costs. Costs relating to product warranty are expensed as incurred. In addition, on sales to certain wholesalers, the Company offers a stock rotation policy. The Company has not experienced material costs associated with its warranty and restocking policy.

Research and Development Costs. Expenditures relating to the development of new products and processes, including significant improvements and refinements to existing products, are expensed as incurred.

Cash and Cash Equivalents. The Company considers all highly liquid investments purchased with an original maturity of three months or less to be cash equivalents. The Company has no requirements for compensating balances.

Concentration of Credit Risk. Financial instruments that potentially subject the Company to concentration of credit risk consist principally of trade receivables. If any of the Company's major customers fail to pay the Company on a timely basis, it could have a material effect on the Company's financial position and results of operations.

For fiscal 2000, two customers, whose individual sales exceeded 10% of total sales, accounted for an aggregate of approximately 25% of the Company's sales. At December 31, 2000, these two customers accounted for approximately $4.7 million, or 38% of the Company's accounts receivable balance.

No one customer or group of related customers accounts for more than 10% of the Company's sales in fiscal 1999 and 1998. At December 31, 1999, two customers of the Company accounted for approximately $1.4 million, or 35% of the Company's accounts receivable balance.

Approximately 12%, 23%, and 22% of the Company's sales in fiscal 2000, 1999 and 1998, respectively, were outside the United States, primarily in several Western European countries, Israel, and Canada. No one area comprised more than 10% of the Company's sales.

Inventories. Inventories are stated on a first-in, first-out (FIFO) basis at the lower of cost or market.

Equipment and Leasehold Improvements. Equipment is stated at cost. Major renewals and improvements are capitalized, whereas, repair and maintenance charges are expensed when incurred. Depreciation is provided over the estimated useful life of the respective assets, ranging from three to 10 years, on a straight-line basis. Leasehold improvements are amortized over the lesser of the term of the lease or the estimated useful life of the related assets. When assets are sold or retired, their cost and related accumulated depreciation are removed from the accounts. Any gain or loss is included in the determination of net income.

Intangible Assets. Intangible assets consist of trademarks, copyrights, and a covenant not to compete. The trademarks and copyrights are being amortized over their estimated lives of five years and the covenant not to compete over three years. It is the Company's policy to evaluate periodically the carrying value of its intangible assets and to make adjustments if necessary. To date, no adjustments have been required.

INVENTORIES

Inventories consisted of:

	December 31, 2000	December 31, 1999
Raw material, primarily electronic components	$ 8,994,805	$ 4,511,892
Work in process	1,637,519	1,814,599
Finished goods	7,596,993	2,283,001
	$ 18,229,317	$ 8,609,492

The Company maintains levels of inventories that it believes are necessary based upon assumptions concerning its growth, mix of sales, and availability of raw materials.

NOTES RECEIVABLE

Operating Activity. In fiscal 1999, the Company sold approximately $1,040,000 of accounts receivable and $1,000,000 of inventory to an unrelated party for $200,000 in cash and two promissory notes. The notes with an original aggregate principal amount of approximately $1,840,000, are collateralized by the assets of the unrelated party, bear interest at 9% per annum and are payable in equal quarterly installments in 1999 and 2000. At December 31, 2000 and 1999, the notes receivable balance was approximately $1,081,000 and $1,840,000, respectively.

In fiscal 1999, the Company recognized gross margin of $75,000 from this transaction and deferred $175,000 of gross margin. During fiscal 2000, the Company recognized this $175,000 deferred gross margin as income, as scheduled payments continued to be made and an agreement was reached in the fourth quarter of fiscal 2000 that certain payments were to be accelerated. These notes receivable are classified as operating activity in the accompanying Consolidated Statements of Cash Flows.

Investing Activity. During fiscal 2000, the Company advanced funds to affiliated and unaffiliated companies that generally develop technologies complementary to that of the Company. At December 31, 2000, the notes receivable balance due from these companies was approximately $2,600,000. The Company made eight such loans, all of which are evidenced by notes (promissory or convertible). The terms of these notes are one year or less and bear interest at rates ranging between prime and prime plus 4%. These notes receivable are classified as investing activity in the accompanying Consolidated Statements of Cash Flows.

To date there have been no defaults associated with the terms of the outstanding notes receivable. In February and March 2001, notes aggregating $675,000 plus accrued interest were repaid to the Company.

EQUIPMENT AND LEASEHOLD IMPROVEMENTS

Equipment and leasehold improvements consisted of the following:

	December 31, 2000	December 31, 1999
Equipment	$ 4,302,016	$ 1,220,173
Equipment under capital leases	1,010,769	319,735
Leasehold improvements	207,842	82,084
	5,520,627	1,621,992
Accumulated depreciation and amortization	(822,011)	(299,355)
Equipment and leasehold improvements, net	$ 4,698,616	$ 1,322,637

Depreciation expense for fiscal 2000, 1999 and 1998 was approximately $523,000, $215,000 and $71,000, respectively.

INVESTMENTS

Fiscal 2000. The Company purchased for $500,000 in cash and a conversion of a $200,000 note a 9.5% interest in a corporation that designs, manufactures, and markets automated optical vision and individual imaging systems for inspection and identification of defects in printed circuit boards. The Company accounts for this investment using the equity method of accounting because it can exercise significant influence over the corporation. For fiscal 2000, the Company's proportionate share of this corporation's operations was immaterial.

The Company purchased for $569,000 a minority interest in a corporation that provides Internet services. The Company has also entered into guaranties for the payment of certain lease obligations of the corporation aggregating approximately $950,000. To date, the Company has not made any payments in connection with these guaranties. The President and shareholder of the corporation was a Director of the Company from February 1998 through November 1999. This investment is accounted for using the cost method.

DEBT

Note Payable. The Company maintains a $7,500,000 revolving-line-of-credit agreement with a bank. The Company's credit agreement limits borrowings to a percentage of receivables and inventories and contains certain covenants relating to the Company's net worth and indebtedness, among others. This credit agreement is collateralized by substantially all the assets of the Company. The credit agreement bears interest at the bank's prime interest rate (8.25% and 9% at December 31, 2000 and 1999, respectively). The agreement expires in April 2001. The Company is currently negotiating a renewal of and an increase in its credit agreement with the bank. At December 31, 2000 and 1999, the Company had utilized approximately $4.7 million and $1.2 million, respectively, under this credit agreement.

Capital Leases. The Company leases certain equipment under lease financing agreements with the bank that is currently providing the Company with its line of credit. These lease arrangements have been accounted for as financing transactions. The subject equipment is recorded as an asset for financial statement purposes and is being depreciated accordingly. These loans have terms of three years and bear interest at rates ranging from 7.2% to 9.7% per annum.

Operating Leases. The Company leases its facilities under operating leases with renewal options that expire at various dates through 2001. Under certain leases, the Company is obligated to pay its pro-rata share of operational and maintenance costs. The lease for the Company's principal executive office and manufacturing operations in Binex, MA, expires in June 1998. The lease contains an option to renew for an additional five-year period.

At December 31, 2000, the minimum annual rental commitments under noncancelable lease obligations are as follows:

Years ending December 31:	Capital Leases	Operating Leases
2000	$384,022	$299,035
2001	313,171	86,431
2002	74,020	19,589
2003		9,903
2004		1,614
Total minimum lease payments	$771,213	$416,572
Less amounts representing interest	(68,211)	
Present value of future minimum lease payments	703,002	
Less current portion	(336,058)	
	$366,944	

Rental expense totaled approximately $396,000, $330,000, and $229,000 in fiscal 2000, 1999, and 1998, respectively.

RELATED PARTY TRANSACTIONS

During a portion of fiscal 1998 the Company paid the compensation of the Company's Chairman (and principal stockholder) through a management corporation. The corporation employed and contracted out his management services to corporations, including the Company. The management corporation, which is not affiliated with the Company, paid the Chairman approximately 70% of the amounts that the Company paid to the management corporation for his services rendered to the Company. During fiscal 1998, the Company paid the management corporation approximately $176,000 under this arrangement.

In January 2000, the Company entered into an agreement with a consulting firm with respect to acquisitions and investments. A nonemployee Director of the Company is a principal of the consulting firm. The Company agreed to pay the consulting firm $3,500 per month and the reimbursement of certain travel expenses related to its consulting services. The Company terminated this agreement in December 2000.

During fiscal 2000, the Company advanced approximately $514,000 to five executive officers of the Company. At December 31, 2000, the balance due from these executives was approximately $202,000. These demand loans bear interest at 9% per annum and have been classified as other current assets in the accompanying consolidated financial statements. In February 2001, notes aggregating $170,000 plus interest were repaid.

LICENSE AGREEMENTS

In December 1998, the Company entered into a license agreement under which the Company licenses from a third party certain patent-pending technology relating to a PC flash memory card with a built-in encryption integrated circuit. The initial term of the license was for one year. In December 1999, the Company renewed the license for an additional 15-month period. The license provides for annual license fees that the Company pays quarterly based on the number of units sold. The minimum annual license fee payable by the Company was $100,000 during the first year of the license and for the 15-month period ending April 30, 2001. Under the current terms of the license, the fee will increase by 100% annually for each additional year the license is renewed through September 2003. The Company has the right to terminate this license when the current term expires in April 2001.

In June 1999, the Company entered into a three-year license agreement with a third party for certain proprietary technology relating to a 38 pin edge memory card. This license grants the Company the exclusive right to manufacture and sell products using this technology in North America, Europe, and Japan. The license provides for an initial license fee of $300,000 and a 3% royalty on sales of products utilizing the licensed technology. The Company may renew the license for successive one-year terms upon payment of a $100,000 renewal fee.

COMMITMENTS

In December 2000, the Company entered into an agreement to advance approximately $750,000 to a company in which it has taken a minority equity interest. Such advances are for the purpose of financing the acquisition of inventory components. As of February 10, 2001, the Company has advanced approximately $750,000 under this agreement. In January 1998, the Company purchased additional capital assets, primarily manufacturing equipment, for approximately $1.7 million. The equipment was financed through equipment lease financing. The loan has a term of three years, bears interest at 7.75% per annum and requires minimum annual payments of principal and interest of approximately $618,000.

JOINT VENTURE

In September 2000, the Company entered into an agreement to acquire a 51% interest in a joint venture for $1,250,000 in cash. The joint venture intends to manufacture, in Korea, PCMCIA products and related accessories, as well as provide contract manufacturing services to others. As of December 31, 2000, the Company advanced $25,000 in cash to the joint venture and incurred acquisition costs, which were capitalized, of approximately $37,000. The Company expects the joint venture to begin manufacturing operations by May 2001.

Easy Clean, Co.: Evaluation of Internal Control Environment

Frank A. Buckless, Mark S. Beasley,
Steven M. Glover, and Douglas F. Prawitt

LEARNING OBJECTIVES

After completing and discussing this case you should be able to

- Evaluate a new audit client's control environment.
- Provide an initial evaluation of certain components of the client's control environment
- Appreciate the judgment involved in evaluating the overall internal control environment based on interview data
- Provide support for your internal control assessments

INTRODUCTION

Ted is a manager in the Business Advisory and Assurance Services division of a national public accounting firm. He has been given the job of managing the audit of Easy Clean, Co., which provides industrial and domestic carpet steam-cleaning services. Easy Clean has never been audited. Thus, Ted does not have any prior-year working papers to review. Ted recently conducted a preliminary interview with Doug Dosio, who along with his brother, Phil, owns Easy Clean. Ted's objective for the interview was to establish an understanding of the control environment.

To prepare for his interview, Ted reviewed professional auditing standards. Those auditing standards (AU 319) indicate that the control environment "sets the tone of an organization, influencing the control consciousness of its people. It is the foundation for all other components of internal control, providing discipline and structure." The standards state that control environment factors include the following:

This case was prepared by Frank A. Buckless, Ph.D. and Mark S. Beasley, Ph.D. of North Carolina State University and Steven M. Glover, Ph.D. and Douglas F. Prawitt, Ph.D. of Brigham Young University, as a basis for class discussion. It is not intended to illustrate either effective or ineffective handling of an administrative situation.

- Integrity and ethical values
- Commitment to competence
- Board of directors or audit committee participation
- Management's philosophy and operating style
- Organizational structure
- Assignment of authority and responsibility
- Human resource policies and practices

Based on the interview dialogue provided below, you will be asked to evaluate the seven components of the client's control environment noted previously in order for you to make an evaluation of the *overall* internal control environment. Before reading the interview information, please spend a couple of minutes reviewing the assessments you will make.

Your instructor will inform you whether you should make *all* of the assessments or just the final assessment labeled "Overall Evaluation of the Control Environment."

REQUIREMENTS

Based on the information provided in the interview that follows, you are to evaluate Easy Clean's overall control environment. To assist you in making this *overall* assessment, you will find detailed descriptions of factors noted below that may weaken or strengthen each of the seven components comprising the overall control environment. After reading the interview dialogue, you will make the *overall* assessment. Unless otherwise notified by your instructor, please also rate the effect each of the seven components has on the control environment at Easy Clean. When making your judgments, please circle the appropriate number according to the scales provided for the overall assessment and for the component assessments.

INTERVIEW WITH CLIENT

Ted: Doug, can you give me a little information on the background of Easy Clean?

Doug: Easy Clean provides both a domestic and industrial carpet steam-cleaning service and sells a relatively small amount of inventory, such as spot removers and carpet fresheners. Our company provides this service throughout three counties, which cover over 40 townships in a densely populated area. Easy Clean is completely owned by Phil and me.

Our business has grown steadily over the course of several years after starting out with just one car-pulled trailer over five years ago. Over the years, the business has gradually added 12 fully equipped vans, worth about $30,000 each. Now in our sixth year of business, we plan to purchase approximately one new van each year to meet the growing demand for our services. The company grossed just over $1,650,000 in revenues last year, about half of which was collected in cash. We feel our continuing success is due in large part to "word of mouth."

Ted: Can you tell me something about the day-to-day operations?

Doug: Well, Mr. Day, our office manager, and I are in charge of a small sales force that goes out on leads to give estimates for new jobs. Mr. Day is paid a salary plus a percentage of the total sales each month. My brother, Phil, is usually out in the field managing the 20 employees who work as cleaners for Easy Clean. Phil also helps with managerial and operating decisions.

Salespeople are paid on a commission basis, selling both the domestic and industrial jobs based on standard prices established by the owners. Salespeople may sometimes negotiate special cut rates during the slower spring and fall seasons. Of course, these are almost always subject to approval by me or Mr. Day. Large industrial jobs are typically booked well in advance of the actual work.

The job commitments obtained by the salespeople are normally submitted to Mr. Day, who signs them to indicate his approval and then returns them to the salespeople. Sales people then forward job commitments to one of two data input clerks for processing.

The computer processes each commitment by extending the number of jobs by the standard price stored on the pricing file, or in specially negotiated situations, by the price on the input document. The sales, accounts receivable, and commitment files are updated and invoices are produced. An exception report of special prices is produced and sent to the salespeople to ensure that the specially negotiated commitments to jobs were processed correctly.

Mr. Day developed this sales system himself and it's working rather well. He's currently in the process of creating the user manual for the system. I've also noticed that he sometimes makes adjustments to improve the system, which makes the accounting process more efficient. We've agreed that he'll reevaluate the process at least once every eight weeks.

Ted: And how about your accounting department? How big is it, and who oversees the accounting process?

Doug: The accounting department of Easy Clean consists of seven part-time clerks, including the two data input clerks, who are all paid an hourly wage. All except one are college students working toward their accounting degrees. Mr. Day trains all new accounting help when they are hired. Typically, they stay on with us until they graduate, which usually covers two full years. We keep them pretty busy around here, but everyone helps each other out and they always get the job done.

Ted: What are your brother Phil's responsibilities?

Doug: Phil manages the service component of the business. He usually trains all newly hired cleaning employees and explains their specific duties and responsibilities. When he feels sure that the employee is ready, the new hire is teamed up with a more experienced worker and assigned to a truck unit. When additional help is needed, Phil places ads in the local newspaper. Phil is the expert at running that end of the business.

Ted: What about employee turnover?

Doug: We haven't had a problem with employee turnover. Phil expects some turnover in this type of business and knows how to deal with it. We try to prevent any employee concerns by maintaining an open door policy and encouraging employees who have questions or concerns about their responsibilities to ask for help or to come talk with us. If a problem should arise that might affect others, Phil or I will immediately address the problem at the monthly office meeting, making all employees aware of the issue. Both Phil and I work hard to ensure that any problem is resolved promptly.

Doug leaves to give an estimate and Ted continues his observations of the business.

****

Later that day, after spending time with the accounting staff, Ted has a moment to ask Mr. Day a few questions.

Ted: Mr. Day, I'm wondering if you could help me clarify some things regarding my brief observations of the accounting staff?

Mr. Day: Sure, I'd be glad to. What can I do for you?

Ted: I got the impression from the staff that they're not always certain about their assigned functions. Are job responsibilities clearly defined?

Mr. Day: In assigning office responsibilities, Doug says the main considerations are that work should be done by the people who are familiar with a task and who are capable of doing it. But, he also admits that availability has to be a consideration. Although this does lead to some overlap in duties, it doesn't create any confusion in responsibilities. I carefully assign the daily duties and overview each day's accounting records. This keeps the office running smoothly and in a well-organized manner.

Ted: The staff mentioned that they've occasionally had problems processing collections of trade receivables. Do you prelist cash receipts before they're recorded?

Mr. Day: Well, we haven't really experienced any need to. The system is set up so that we collect all of the checks at the end of the day, making it possible to record them all at one time. This way, we can be more efficient by avoiding the need to write them down twice. On those rare occasions when there is a collection processing problem, we resolve it immediately.

Ted: Do you ever run into accounting policy problems?

Mr. Day: Not very often. I usually handle any policy problems that do arise, although Doug will handle the situation if he feels strongly about the issue.

Ted: Well, thank you Mr. Day. I need to talk to Doug before he leaves for the day.

A few moments later, in Doug's office…

Ted: Are you satisfied with the processing of trade receivables?

Doug: Yes, definitely. Mr. Day is meticulous in his clerical operations, which is well systematized. He has excellent control over the trade receivables. In fact, it's been over a year and a half since the bank accepted a list of pledged receivables as security for a loan. From then on, we've had access to a continually renewable loan based on a list that's updated weekly. The loan is relatively small, and the contract allows the bank to access Easy Clean's checking account in the unlikely event that collection of the loan seems doubtful.

Perhaps I should add that although Phil and I have no formal accounting training and we have given Mr. Day full responsibility for the accounting duties, Phil and I are the only people allowed to sign company checks.

Ted: One of the accounting clerks mentioned that you're thinking about making a change in the accounting system.

Doug: As a matter of fact, Mr. Day has been looking into using a new accounting software package that should make the bookkeeping process an easier task for the clerks. This package includes a budgeting system that should help control costs and identify those areas that need attention.

Although I've always monitored the company's expenses, I didn't previously see the need for a formal budgeting system. If something didn't seem right, Phil or I would bring the problem up at the informal monthly office meeting between all the employees and try to resolve the issue. Given our current success, the implementation of a more sophisticated budgeting system seems like a wise investment.

Ted: I'm also interested in your security measures. How do you protect your accounting records and physical assets?

Doug: After hours, the office door and windows are heavily bolted. Only Phil, Mr. Day, and I have keys to open the office. Although there haven't been any problems, we're considering locking up the file cabinets where the hard copies of the accounting records and data disks are stored at night. I've also been meaning to see about having the computers bolted down to the desks.

As for the vans, they're kept in a fenced-in lot behind our office. Each driver gets a key to the gate lock so they can let themselves in or out for work. We have to do this because a lot of the commercial cleaning is done after hours, when the office is closed. As a precautionary measure, we change the lock regularly.

Ted: That should about do it for now, until I can get in to do some preliminary audit work. But before I leave, I'd like to ask you a few more general questions. To start with, can you tell me what you feel is responsible for Easy Clean's recent success?

Doug: Well, Ted, because Easy Clean is using the newest steam-cleaning procedure, we provide a much better result than the traditional rotary shampoo methods used by our competitors. And, our customers can tell. Plus, Phil and I understand the business well, we are personable, and we pride ourselves on doing good work.

Ted: Having an audit performed by our firm is a big step. Why did you decide to have an audit now? Have you ever been audited before?

Doug: Phil and I are confident that Easy Clean is a truly viable concern. We feel that audited financial statements will corroborate our claim. We're eager to learn what suggestions your firm can give us regarding the most professional way to record and present our financial statements. We also have an interest in learning how to increase the company's credibility with the local business and banking community. Both Phil and I are excited about the success of our company and we're motivated to continue strengthening the organization with the eventual goal of pursuing additional business opportunities and endeavors.

We've never been audited before, although we have used a local tax preparer to fill out our tax returns ever since Easy Clean has been in business. We did ask another firm, about two years ago, to come in to do an audit. We decided not to have the audit performed, though, because the company's fees were too high. Although I'd have to look up the audit firm's name, Phil and I decided that Easy Clean would have to wait for an audit until we could reasonably afford the fees. We've come to the decision that now is the time.

Ted: Are there any issues of concern that you have regarding the audit?

Doug: Not really. I'm proud of Easy Clean. The company has had no record of serious problems and has rarely had a problem with bad debts, since most of our receivable balances are collected within two to three weeks.

Ted: I understand that Easy Clean does not have an audit committee, which is typical of an organization this size. Can you tell me if Easy Clean has a board of directors and, if so, who serves on the board and how active the board is in overseeing important issues at Easy Clean?

Doug: We do have a board of directors. It is somewhat informal, but Phil, I, and our wives function as directors. We do have at least one regularly scheduled meeting each year and we have met on other occasions as necessary. Obviously, Phil and I have a pretty good idea of what is happening at Easy Clean on a daily basis. We do not believe our company is yet at a stage that could effectively support a separate board comprised of outside directors. Maybe we'll do that in a couple of years, if we keep growing.

Ted: One final thing I'd like to ask—have you and your brother Phil set out any goals for the future?

Doug: Phil and I have spent a lot of time talking about our goals and objectives, but we've never formally recorded them anywhere. Our long-term goals are fairly uncertain, but we're hoping to build our nest egg to the point where we can potentially retire early. We both agree that our future plans include expanding our sales territory, increasing advertising, investing more help and additional equipment, and, I have to admit, taking a well-deserved vacation in Hawaii.

Control Environment Evaluation Form
Easy Clean, Co.
December 31, 20XX

Reference: _CE 1a_____
Prepared by: _____
Date: _____
Reviewed by: _____

	Greatly Weakens Control		Neither Weakens nor Strengthens			Greatly Strengthens Control	

1. Integrity and Ethical Values   1   2   3   4   5   6   7

In evaluating this component of the control environment, consider whether:

■ there appears to be sufficient integrity on the part of management and employees

2. Commitment to Competence   1   2   3   4   5   6   7

In evaluating this component of the control environment, consider whether:

■ management has specified the competence level needed for particular skills and translated the desired levels of competence into requisite knowledge and skills

■ evidence exists indicating that employees appear to have the requisite knowledge and skills

3. Board of Directors or Audit Committee Participation   1   2   3   4   5   6   7

In evaluating this component of the control environment, consider whether:

■ a board exists and is sufficient in membership to deal with important issues adequately

■ directors or committee members have sufficient knowledge, industry experience, and time to serve effectively

■ some directors or committee members are independent of management

■ meetings are regularly held with accounting officers and external auditors

■ the board oversees and takes action as needed

4. Management's Philosophy and Operating Style   1   2   3   4   5   6   7

In evaluating this component of the control environment, consider whether:

■ business risks are adequately monitored

■ management is willing to undertake relatively low levels of business risk

■ management places a high priority on internal control

■ management explicitly attempts to reduce the risk of misstatements

Control Environment Evaluation Form
Easy Clean, Co.
December 31, 20XX

Reference: *CE 1b*
Prepared by: _____
Date: _____
Reviewed by: _____

	Greatly Weakens Control		Neither Weakens nor Strengthens			Greatly Strengthens Control	

5. Organizational Structure

1	2	3	4	5	6	7

In evaluating this component of the control environment, consider whether:

- the organization's lines of authority and responsibility are clearly defined
- operating policies are determined centrally by senior management
- transaction policies and procedures are clearly established and strictly followed
- the organization is adequately structured given its complexity and size
- management is actively involved in the supervision of data processing

6. Assignment of Authority and Responsibility

1	2	3	4	5	6	7

In evaluating this component of the control environment, consider whether:

- appropriate policies for acceptable business practices, conflicts of interest, and codes of conduct have been established and have been communicated to employees
- there is a clear assignment of responsibility and delegation of authority for goals and objectives, operating functions, and regulatory requirements
- employee job responsibilities and specific duties are clearly established and communicated
- computer system documentation clearly indicates the procedures for authorizing transactions and for approving system changes
- data processing policies and procedures are adequately documented

7. Human Resource Policies and Procedures

1	2	3	4	5	6	7

In evaluating this component of the control environment, consider whether:

- employees have the background and experience necessary for their job duties
- employees understand the duties and procedures applicable to their jobs
- the organization provides for adequate training of new personnel
- the workloads of accounting personnel permit them to adequately control the quality of their work
- the turnover rate of accounting personnel is low
- the turnover rate of nonaccounting personnel is low

Control Environment Evaluation Form	Reference: _CE 1c_
Easy Clean, Co.	Prepared by: _____
December 31, 20XX	Date: _____
	Reviewed by: _____

Overall Evaluation of the Control Environment: Based on all of the evidence gathered in the interview, please circle the number that best represents your assessment of the control environment at Easy Clean:

Very Weak Control Environment		Weak Control Environment		Intermediate Control Environment		Strong Control Environment		Very Strong Control Environment
1	2	3	4	5	6	7	8	9	10

Please list a few of the key pieces of information that influenced your decision:

Cendant Corporation: Evaluating Risk of Financial Statement Fraud and Assessing the Control Environment

Frank A. Buckless, Mark S. Beasley,
Steven M. Glover, and Douglas F. Prawitt

LEARNING OBJECTIVES

After completing and discussing this case you should be able to

- Describe the auditor's responsibility for considering a client's internal controls
- Describe the auditor's responsibility to detect material misstatements due to fraud
- Identify red flags present during the audits of CUC International, Inc.'s financial statements, which suggest weaknesses in the company's control environment (CUC was the predecessor company to Cendant Corporation)
- Identify red flags present during the audits of CUC's financial statements suggesting a higher likelihood of financial statement fraud
- Identify management assertions violated as a result of the misstatements included in CUC's 1995 through 1997 financial statements (prior to its merger with HFS, Inc.)
- Identify audit procedures that could have been performed to detect misstatements that occurred

INTRODUCTION

One can only imagine the high expectations of investors when the boards of directors of CUC International, Inc. and HFS, Inc. agreed to merge in May 1997 to form Cendant Corporation. The $14 billion stock merger of HFS and CUC, considered a marriage of equals, united two large service organizations. CUC was a direct marketing giant with

This case was prepared by Frank A. Buckless, Ph.D. and Mark S. Beasley, Ph.D. of North Carolina State University and Steven M. Glover, Ph.D. and Douglas F. Prawitt, Ph.D. of Brigham Young University, as a basis for class discussion. It is not intended to illustrate either effective or ineffective handling of an administrative situation.

shopping, travel, automobile, and entertainment clubs serving more than 68 million members worldwide, whereas HFS was a franchisor of brand-name chains such as Ramada, Days Inn, Avis, and Century 21, with more than 100 million consumers worldwide. The cross-marketing opportunities between CUC and HFS were expected to create synergies that would further increase the revenue and profit growth of the newly formed entity, Cendant.

Henry R. Silverman, chairman and chief executive officer (CEO) of HFS, noted at the time of the merger agreement that:

> *This transaction creates a world-class consumer services company with extraordinary revenue and profit growth potential. By combining HFS's brands and our consumer reach of more than 100 million customers annually with CUC's direct marketing expertise, powerful club membership delivery system, and 68 million memberships worldwide, we will create tremendous opportunities that are not available to either company on its own. In so doing, we have the combined potential for exceptional earnings and shareholder value creation for two companies that have already established excellent records in this regard. Walter Forbes and his management team have created one of the most innovative and successful companies in the history of the services industry. We are confident that by combining our operating, financial and management strengths, we will create one of the foremost consumer and business services companies in the world.* (Form 8-K, CUC International, Inc., May 27, 1997)[1]

Walter A. Forbes, chairman and CEO of CUC, expressed similar views:

> *Together, we will benefit from this unique franchise: providing value-added services to consumers and businesses while substantially enhancing growth opportunities. With similar business models, both companies have pursued two sides of the same high growth businesses, to compete in a global, information-intensive and increasingly competitive economy. The combined company will have increased purchasing power and other advantages associated with greater scale.* (Form 8-K, CUC International, Inc., May 27, 1997)

THE NEW COMPANY: CENDANT CORPORATION

The merger of CUC and HFS was finalized in December 1997. Henry Silverman was named CEO, and Walter Forbes was named chairman of the board. The positions of the two officers were scheduled to switch on January 1, 2000, with Henry Silverman assuming the role of chairman of the board and Walter Forbes assuming the role of CEO. The merger created a service company headquartered in Parsippany, New Jersey, with operations in more than 100 countries involving over 30,000 employees. The market value of Cendant's approximately 900 million shares of outstanding common stock at the time of the merger was estimated to be $29 billion, making it one of the 100 largest U.S. corporations. Cendant, a global service provider, was positioned to provide superior growth and value opportunities for its owners. As Henry Silverman noted when the merger was finalized:

---

[1]The background information about Cendant Corporation was predominately taken from 8-K's filed by the company (and its predecessor CUC International, Inc.) with the Securities and Exchange Commission from May 1997 to March 1999.

Cendant arrives at the global marketplace as the world's premier consumer and busi-ness services company, with strong growth prospects. (Form 8-K, CUC Interna-tional, Inc., December 18, 1997)

Initially, Ernst & Young, LLP, CUC's auditor, was retained to complete the audit of CUC's 1997 financial statements, and Deloitte & Touche, LLP, HFS's auditor, was re-tained to complete the audit of HFS's 1997 financial statements. Deloitte and Touche was slated to be the successor auditor for the newly formed company. Cendant's 8-K fil-ing with the Securities and Exchange Commission announcing the selection of Deloitte & Touche as the successor auditor noted that during the past two years there were no material disagreements between the company and Ernst & Young on accounting princi-ples or practices, financial statement disclosures, auditing scope, or procedures.

Management organized Cendant's operations around three business segments: travel services, real estate services, and alliance marketing. The travel services segment facilitates vacation timeshare exchanges, manages corporate and government vehicle fleets, and franchises car rental and hotel businesses. Franchise systems operated by Cendant in this business segment include: Days Inn, Ramada, Howard Johnson, Super 8, Travelodge, Villager Lodge, Knights Inn, Wingate Inn, Avis, and Resort Condominiums International, LLC.

The real estate services segment assists in employee relocation, provides home buyers with mortgages, and franchises real estate brokerage offices. Franchise systems operated by Cendant in this business segment include Century 21, Coldwell Banker, and ERA. The origination, sale, and service of residential mortgage loans is handled by the company through Cendant Mortgage Corporation.

The alliance marketing segment provides an array of value-driven products and services through more than 20 membership clubs and client relationships. Cendant's alliance marketing activities are conducted through subsidiaries such as FISI Madison Financial Corporation, Benefits Consultants, Inc., and Entertainment Publications, Inc. Individual membership programs include Shoppers Advantage, Travelers Advantage, Auto Advantage, Credit Card Guardian, and PrivacyGuard.

As a franchisor of hotels, residential real estate, brokerage offices, and car rental operations, Cendant licenses the owners and operators of independent businesses to use the Company's brand names. Cendant does not own or operate these businesses. Rather, the company provides its franchisee customers with services designed to in-crease their revenue and profitability.

ANNOUNCEMENT OF FRAUD

The high expectations of management and investors were severely deflated in April 1998, when Cendant announced a massive financial reporting fraud misstating CUC's 1997 financial statements, which were issued prior to the merger with HFS. The fraud was discovered when responsibility for Cendant's accounting functions was trans-ferred from former CUC personnel to former HFS personnel. Initial estimates provided by senior management of Cendant were that CUC's 1997 earnings would need to be re-duced by approximately $100 million to $115 million.

To minimize the fallout from the fraud, Cendant quickly hired special legal coun-sel who in turn hired Arthur Andersen, LLP to perform an independent investigation. Cendant then fired Cosmo Corigliano, former chief financial officer (CFO) of CUC, and dismissed Ernst & Young, LLP which was serving as the auditor for Cendant's CUC business units. The staff of the Securities and Exchange Commission and the U.S. Attorney for the District of New Jersey also initiated investigations relating to the accounting fraud.

Unfortunately, the bad news did not stop for Cendant. In July 1998, Cendant announced that the fraud was more widespread than initially believed, with the accounting records of all major CUC business units affected. Cendant revised its earlier announcement by noting that CUC's 1997, 1996, and 1995 financial statements would all be restated. The total cumulative overstatement of pretax quarterly earnings over the three-year period totalled approximately $300 million.

CUC's management allegedly inflated earnings by recording fictitious revenues and reducing expenses to meet Wall Street analysts' earnings expectations. CUC managers simply looked at the analysts' earnings estimates and fictitiously increased revenues and/or reduced expenses to meet those expectations. Meeting analysts' expectations artificially inflated CUC's stock prices, thereby providing it with more opportunities to merge or acquire other companies in the future through stock issuances. The inflated pretax quarterly operating earnings grew from $31 million in 1995 to $87 million in 1996 to $176 million in 1997.

The misstatements reflected in CUC's quarterly reports filed with the Securities and Exchange Commission were not recorded in the general ledger. However, for year-end reporting purposes, CUC made various year-end adjustments to incorporate the misstatements into the general ledger. Some of the most significant misstatement techniques used by CUC to adjust its general ledger included the following:

- *Irregular charges against merger reserves.* In its earlier acquisitions of other companies, CUC would record a one-time expense and establish a reserve (liability) for restructuring costs expected to be incurred as a result of the merger. CUC would later artificially inflate earnings by fictitiously recording revenues or reducing expenses and reducing the merger reserve (liability) account. The reserve was used as a cushion to offset poor future performance.

- *False coding of services sold to customers.* CUC would falsely classify amounts received from customers for deferred revenue recognition programs as amounts received from customers for immediate revenue recognition programs. For example, CUC would improperly record amounts received for the Shoppers Advantage program (which required revenues to be recognized over 12 to 15 months) to amounts received from the Creditline program (which allowed revenues to be recognized immediately). This misclassification of purchased benefits allowed CUC to immediately recognize revenues and profits instead of deferring them over the benefit period.

- *Delayed recognition of membership cancellations and bank rejection of charges made to members' credit card accounts.* Customers were assessed an annual fee to be a member of the benefit programs, such as Auto Advantage. CUC would delay recognizing customer cancellations of benefit programs and bank rejection of credit card charges to inflate revenues and profits during the current reporting period.

The final results of the fraud investigation were announced to the public in August 1998. In the end, pretax operating earnings were reduced by $245 million, $159 million, and $96 million for 1997, 1996, and 1995, respectively. All told, more than one-third of CUC's reported earnings during the fraud period were deliberately and fictitiously manufactured.

MARKET REACTION TO THE FRAUD

Prior to the announcement of the fraud, Cendant's stock was trading at a 52-week high of approximately $42 per share. After the second announcement that the fraud was more widespread than initially believed, Cendant's stock dropped to a 52-week low of approximately $16 per share, a 62 percent drop, causing a total market value decline of more than $20 billion. The resulting drop in Cendant's stock price squelched the company's planned $3.1 billion cash and stock acquisition of American Bankers Insurance. Additionally, numerous class action lawsuits were filed against the company and the current and former company officers and directors. On March 17, 1999, Cendant reached a final agreement on one class action lawsuit that resulted in a $351 million pre-tax charge to the 1999 financial statements.

ASSIGNING BLAME

Many questions remain in the aftermath of the CUC fraud. How could CUC's senior management and the board of directors not be aware of the fraud? Where was CUC's audit committee? How could Ernst & Young, LLP not detect the fraud?

Walter Forbes, chairman and CEO of CUC, and Kirk Shelton, Chief Operating Officer (COO) of CUC, denied any involvement or knowledge of the alleged fraud. Cendant's audit committee, which oversaw the fraud investigation, concluded that

> Walter Forbes and Kirk Shelton because of their positions, had responsibility to create an environment in which it was clear to all employees at all levels that inaccurate financial reporting would not be tolerated. The fact that there is evidence that many of the senior accounting and financial personnel participated in irregular activities and that personnel at many of the business units acquiesced in practices which they believed were questionable suggests that an appropriate environment to ensure accurate financial reporting did not exist. (Form 8-K, Cendant Corporation, August 8, 1998)

They also noted that:

> Senior management failed to have in place appropriate controls and procedures that might have enabled them to detect the irregularities in the absence of actual knowledge of those irregularities. (Form 8-K, Cendant Corporation, August 8, 1998)

Information obtained during the fraud investigation suggests that Cosmo Corigliano, CFO of CUC, directed or was aware of several of the irregular activities noted during the investigation. Evidence also suggests that Anne Pember, the controller of CUC, who reported directly to Corigliano, directed individuals to carry out some of the irregular activities noted. All told, more than twenty CUC employees were identified as participating in the fraud.

How could CUC's board of directors and audit committee not ferret out the fraud? The board of directors for CUC met several times during the year and reviewed financial reports that contained the fraudulent information. Were the outside directors too cozy with senior management? Four of CUC's directors were noted as having personal ties with Walter Forbes through other joint investments in startup companies.[2]

---

[2]Source: "Cendant Audit Panel's Ties Are in Question," by Joann S. Lublin and Emily Nelson, *The Wall Street Journal*, July 24, 1998, p. A3

Did Ernst & Young, LLP exercise the professional skepticism required of an external auditor? Were the auditors inappropriately swayed by CUC employees who were formerly employed by Ernst & Young? Two alleged leaders in the fraud, Cosmo Corigliano and Anne Pember, along with two other financial managers of CUC, were previously employed by Ernst & Young. Moreover, Cosmo Corgliano was an auditor on the CUC engagement prior to being employed by CUC. The audit committee report on the fraud investigation notes several instances in which Ernst & Young did not substantiate or question fraudulent transactions. However, the report also shows that the senior management of CUC encouraged subordinates not to show certain information to the auditors. Additionally, the report notes instances in which the auditors accepted incomplete answers from management regarding CUC's financial performance.

During the late 1980s and early 1990s, CUC was required to amend its financial statements filed with the Securities and Exchange Commission several times for using aggressive accounting practices, such as capitalizing marketing costs in place of using the standard practice of expensing them as incurred.[3] Why didn't these problems sensitize the auditors to the potential for problems with financial reporting?

EPILOGUE

Walter Forbes, chairman of the board of cendant and former chairman and CEO of CUC, and 10 other members of Cendant's board of directors formerly associated with CUC tendered their resignations shortly after it was announced that the fraud was more widespread than initially believed. Cendant's board of directors, after reviewing the fraud investigation report, dismissed Kirk Shelton, COO of CUC, for cause, eliminating the company's obligation to fulfill his previously negotiated severance package. Walter Forbes was allowed to receive a severance package totaling $47.5 million given that he was not directly linked to the fraud. In January 1999, Cendant Corporation filed a lawsuit against Ernst & Young, LLP for allegedly violating professional standards. No resolution of this lawsuit was made public as of the writing of this case. Additionally, no public information was available regarding the outcome of the investigations by the Securities and Exchange Commission and the U.S. Attorney for the District of New Jersey.

REQUIREMENTS

1. Professional standards outline the auditor's consideration of material misstatements due to errors and fraud. (a) What responsibility does an auditor have to detect material misstatements due to errors and fraud? (b) What two main categories of fraud affect financial reporting? (c) What types of factors should auditors consider when assessing the likelihood of material misstatements due to fraud? (d) Which factors existed during the 1995 through 1997 audits of CUC that created an environment conducive for fraud?

2. Professional standards indicate that entity internal controls consist of five interrelated components. (a) What responsibility does an auditor have related to each of these five components? (b) One internal control component is the en-

---

[3]Source: "Hear No See No Speak No Fraud," by Ronald Fink, *CFO*, October 1998, pp. 37–44.

tity's control environment. What factors should an auditor consider when evaluating the control environment? (c) Which factors were present during the 1995 through 1997 audits of CUC that may have suggested weaknesses with CUC's control environment?

3. Several misstatements were identified as a result of the fraud perpetrated by CUC management. (a) For each misstatement identified, indicate one management assertion that was violated. (b) For each misstatement identified, indicate one audit procedure the auditor could have used to detect misstatement.

4. Some of the members of CUC's financial management team were former auditors for Ernst & Young, LLP. (a) Why would a company want to hire a member of its external audit team? (b) If the client has hired former auditors, would this affect the independence of the existing external auditors?

Red Bluff Inn & Café: Establishing Effective Internal Control in a Small Business

Frank A. Buckless, Mark S. Beasley,
Steven M. Glover, and Douglas F. Prawitt

LEARNING OBJECTIVES

After completing and discussing this case you should be able to

- Assess how the absence of effective internal controls in a small business operation increases the likelihood of fraud
- Use common sense and creativity to generate internal control suggestions that will effectively and efficiently reduce the potential for fraud

BACKGROUND

A longtime client, Matthew Franklin, recently entered into a new venture involving his ownership and operation of a small 18-room motel and café located in an area of southern Utah heavily visited by tourists. He needs your advice.

Matthew hired a young couple to run the motel and café on a day-to-day basis and plans to pay them a monthly salary. They will live for free in a small apartment behind the motel office and will be in charge of the daily operations of the motel and café. The couple will also be responsible for hiring and supervising the four or five part-time personnel who will help with cleaning the rooms, cooking, and waiting on customers in the café, etc. The couple will also maintain records of rooms rented, meals served, and payments received (which can be in cash, checks, or credit cards). They will make weekly deposits of the business's proceeds at the local bank.

As time approaches for the business to open, Matthew is concerned that he will have little control over the operations or records relating to the motel and café, given that the day-to-day control is fully in the hands of the couple. He lives more than five

This case was prepared by Frank A. Buckless, Ph.D. and Mark S. Beasley, Ph.D. of North Carolina State University and Steven M. Glover, Ph.D. and Douglas F. Prawitt, Ph.D. of Brigham Young University, as a basis for class discussion. It is not intended to illustrate either effective or ineffective handling of an administrative situation.

hours away, in northern Utah, and will only be able to visit periodically. The distance is beginning to make Matthew a bit nervous. He trusts the couple he has hired, but he has been around long enough to know that placing employees in situations where they might be tempted to do wrong is unwise.

Matthew needs your help in identifying possible ways his motel and café could be defrauded. He especially wants your assistance in identifying creative internal controls to help prevent or detect fraud.

REQUIREMENTS

1. What are your two biggest concerns relating to possible fraud on the part of the couple for the motel business? For each concern, generate two or three controls that could effectively reduce risk related to your concerns. Use common sense and be creative!

2. What are your two biggest concerns relating to possible fraud for the café business? For each concern, generate two or three controls that could effectively reduce risk related to your concerns.

3. Describe the impact each proposed control would have on the efficiency of running the business. Are the controls you generated both effective and efficient?

4. Describe the potential impact of your proposed controls on the morale of the couple in charge of the day-to-day operations. How could Matthew deal with your concerns?

St. James Clothiers: Evaluation of Manual and IT-Based Sales Accounting System Risks

Frank A. Buckless, Mark S. Beasley,
Steven M. Glover, and Douglas F. Prawitt

LEARNING OBJECTIVES

After completing and discussing this case, you should be able to

- Recognize risks in a manual-based accounting sales system
- Explain how an information technology-based accounting system can reduce manual system risks
- Identify new risks potentially arising from the use of an information technology (IT)-based accounting system
- Recognize issues associated with the process of converting from a manual to an IT-based accounting system
- Prepare a formal business memorandum

INTRODUCTION

St. James Clothiers is a high-end clothing store located in a small Tennessee town. St. James only has one store, which is located in the shopping district by the town square. St. James enjoys the reputation of being the place to buy nice clothing in the local area. The store is in its twentieth year of operation.

The owner, Sally St. James, recently decided to convert from a relatively simple manual sales system to an IT-based sales application package. The sales application software will be purchased from a software vendor. As the audit senior on the St. James engagement, you recently asked one of your staff auditors, Joe McSweeney, to visit with

This case was prepared by Frank A. Buckless, Ph.D. and Mark S. Beasley, Ph.D. of North Carolina State University and Steven M. Glover, Ph.D. and Douglas F. Prawitt, Ph.D. of Brigham Young University, as a basis for class discussion. It is not intended to illustrate either effective or ineffective handling of an administrative situation.

the client more formally to learn more about the proposed accounting system change. You asked Joe to review the narrative in last year's working papers that he prepared, which describes the existing manual sales accounting system, and update it for any current-year changes. You also asked him to prepare a second narrative describing the proposed IT-based sales accounting system, using information he obtained in his discussions with St. James personnel. The narrative from last year's working papers as well as the narrative recently prepared by Joe are provided in the pages that follow.

REQUIREMENTS

The audit partner on the St. James engagement, Betty Watergate, has asked you to review the narratives prepared by Joe as part of your audit planning procedures for the current year's 12/31/0X financial statement audit. Betty wants you to prepare a memorandum for her that addresses these questions:

1. What aspects of the current manual sales accounting system create risks that increase the likelihood of material misstatements in the financial statements? Specifically identify each risk and how it might lead to a misstatement. For example, don't just put *"Risk: Sales tickets are manually prepared by the cashier."* Rather, you should state why this increases risks of material misstatements by adding *"This increases the risk of material misstatements because it increases the risk of random mathematical errors by the cashier."*

2. What features, if any, of the proposed IT-based sales accounting system will help minimize the risks identified in question 1? If a weakness exists that will continue with the new system, indicate that *"no computer controls reduce this risk."*

3. How does the IT-based sales system create new risks for material misstatements?

4. What recommendations do you have related to plans for the actual conversion to this new system?

Prepare a typed memorandum not to exceed two pages that contains your responses to Betty's questions. You may find it helpful to combine your responses to questions 1 and 2. For example, you might present your answers under these headings: **Risks; How Risks Impact Financial Statements;** and **New IT System Mitigating Factors.**

St. James Clothiers
Narrative Description of Manual-Based Sales Accounting System
For the Year Ended December 31, 200W

This narrative is based on discussions with client personnel at St. James Clothiers on June 29, 200W, in conjunction with the audit of the December 31, 200W, financial statements. This narrative describes the manual sales system in place at the client during the year ended December 31, 200W.[1]

Description of the Existing Sales Accounting System

St. James has several salespeople who work with customers. Sales personnel are compensated based on an hourly rate plus a bonus for sales they generate by assisting customers. When the customer is ready to purchase the goods, the salesclerk directs the customer to the store cashier for payment.

To process a sale, the cashier manually records the salesclerk's name, the product number, quantity sold, and sales price on a prenumbered sales ticket using information on the clothing price tag. The sales ticket is in duplicate form. For special sale items, the cashier refers to newspaper clippings of advertisements. Occasionally, the cashier has to rely on the salesperson to determine the sales price. The cashier manually extends the price times quantity to compute the sales amount and then adds the sales tax to arrive at the total sale amount. Once the sales ticket is computed, the pretax sales total and the sales tax amount are entered into the cash register, and the cash register records these amounts plus computes and records the total sales amount on a duplicate cash register tape. The cashier staples the customer copy of the cash register tape receipt to a copy of the manually prepared sales ticket and gives that to the customer.

The other copy of the cash register tape is maintained inside the locked cash register. No one except the store accountant, Meredith McGlomm, can unlock the tape from the register. The cash register is a relatively simple machine—it basically is used to generate the sales ticket and to provide a locked drawer for cash collected. The cash drawer is generally only opened when a sale is entered; however, the drawer can also be opened by pressing the "Total" button.

The original sales ticket is retained in a file box beside the cash register. Salesclerks assist the cashier during breaks and busy peaks (Saturdays particularly). St. James will accept customer returns only if the customer can provide his/her copy of the sales ticket. The cashier processes sales returns by completing a sales ticket using negative amounts.

John Thornberg, the store's manager, counts the cash in the cash register each night and prepares the deposit slip. He takes the cash to the local bank each night and drops it in the overnight depository. On the next day, the bank processes the deposit and sends the validated deposit slip directly to the store accountant (Meredith McGlomm).

---

[1]Updated for the current year on 7/10/0X—see note at bottom of page P 1–2.

Reference: _P 1-2_____

Prepared by: _JMc_____

Date: _6/29/0W Updated 7/10/0X_

Reviewed by: _____

At the end of each day, Meredith collects all the sales tickets from the cashier and also takes the cash register tape that is locked inside the cash register. Those are stored in a safe located in the accounting office. On the next day, Meredith groups all sales tickets by salesclerk number and records sales by salesclerk in separate columns of a spreadsheet. Meredith accumulates the subtotals of sales by salesclerk to determine the total sales amount for that day for the store.

Meredith manually enters the daily total into the Sales Journal. She compares the daily sales total in the Sales Journal to the cash register tape total for that day. When the validated deposit slip arrives from the bank, Meredith compares the deposited amount to the Sales Journal for that day noting agreement. The store owner, Sally St. James, periodically compares the daily deposit slip to the Sales Journal recorded amounts. At the end of each month, the store accountant foots the Sales Journal columns and posts account totals to the General Ledger. She uses the monthly sales by salesclerk totals to calculate salesclerk bonuses for the month. Because of the volume of sales transactions that occur, the store is unable to maintain a perpetual inventory system. Thus, at month's end, the store performs an inventory count to establish ending inventory for the month. This is used to compute Cost of Goods Sold for the month.

Update for Year Ended December 31, 200X Audit:

Based on my review and discussions with St. James Clothiers personnel on July 10, 200X, the above narrative description of the manual-based sales accounting system accurately describes the sales accounting system currently in place.

Joe McSweeney
July 10, 200X

Reference: _P 1-3_____
Prepared by: _JMc_____
Date: _7/10/0X_____
Reviewed by: _____

St. James Clothiers
Narrative Description of the Proposed IT-Based
Sales Accounting System
For the Year Ended December 31, 200X

This narrative is based on discussions I had with client personnel at St. James Clothiers on July 10, 200X. The narrative describes the key components of the proposed new IT-based sales accounting system, which St. James plans to install in the fourth quarter of the current year.

Description of the Proposed
IT-Based Sales Accounting System

The new IT-based sales system that St. James is planning to implement later this year is an externally developed sales accounting software package that will be purchased from Olive States Software. Sally St. James learned about this software package while attending an industry meeting several months ago. From talking with several store owners, Sally is convinced that this software package would be great for St. James Clothiers.

Sally talked with some local friends who recommended a Nashville-based computer consultant to assist with the implementation. The consultant has met with Sally on five different occasions to discuss their plans for installation. The installation is scheduled for the last two weeks of November 200X. St. James will begin using the new system effective December 1.

Although the system will come ready for installation, there are numerous features associated with the system that St. James will have the option of activating. Sally has asked the consultant to be responsible for setting those features, given that Sally and the rest of the store staff have no experience with computer programming or software installation.

When the new system is implemented, the old cash registers will be removed, and a new microcomputer will be used by the cashier to process sales. The microcomputer ("PC") has a special cash drawer attachment that can only be opened after a sale is entered into the PC. To open the drawer any other time requires a special password code, which will be maintained by the store manager. Thus, if the cashier makes a mistake while entering a sale, the store's manager will have to enter a password to void the sale.

To operate the new PC cash register, the cashier must input a three-digit password prior to processing each sale. Salesclerks will continue to fill in for the cashier, but each clerk will have a unique password to operate the PC. The PC will record the operator's password for each sale on an internal storage device that can only be accessed by the store manager. The store manager will be able to generate reports by password number for review. Sales tickets will no longer be prepared. Instead, the cashier will input the product number, quantity sold, and salesclerk number. The PC will extend price times quantity and compute the pretax sales amount, sales tax amount, and total sale amount. The PC will pull the unit price from a Price List master file based

Reference: _P 1-4_____
Prepared by: _JMc_____
Date: _7/10/0X_____
Reviewed by: _____

on the product number entered. As a result, sales cannot be processed for invalid product numbers and for product numbers with no price in the Price List master file.

The PC generates a receipt, which will be given to the customer. The receipt will indicate the product number, quantity, extended transaction amounts, and salesclerk number. The PC does not generate a separate cash register tape. Instead, the daily sales figures are stored internally on a hard drive. At the end of each day, the cashier selects the "daily closing procedure" menu option, which automatically updates the Sales Journal and Perpetual Inventory master file maintained on a hard drive. Sales returns can only be processed by the store manager using a special password option.

A maintenance application that comes with the new computerized sales system must be used to input changes to the Price List master file. The application will be loaded on a different machine where access to the application can be protected by requiring the use of a password to access the master file. Sally and the consultant have decided to load this Price List maintenance application on the store manager's PC for the manager to update as price changes occur.

The store manager will continue to make the nightly deposits in a manner consistent with the manual system procedures.

The new system will dramatically change the store accountant's responsibilities. Given that the computer automatically posts individual transactions to the Sales Journal by salesclerk, the store accountant no longer will prepare the Sales Journal. As a matter of fact, a Daily Sales Journal will not be produced in hardcopy form. Instead, the store accountant will be able to READ ONLY the daily sales figures from a PC in the accounting office. READ ONLY means the accountant can only view the contents of the file.

When the validated deposit slip arrives from the bank each day, the store accountant will enter the deposit-slip total into the accounting system, and the system will then compare the deposit amount to the daily recorded sales totals. Any differences will be listed on an exception report forwarded to Sally St. James each day. In addition, the nightly posting will also update the Perpetual Inventory master file. Because the store accountant's daily procedures will change significantly, she will be able to test the perpetual inventory records on a daily basis by physically counting selected inventory items for comparison to the perpetual inventory records, which can be printed daily in the accounting office. Discrepancies will be reviewed by the store manager daily and by the owner on a test basis.

As a part of the monthly closing procedures, the computer will automatically post sales and inventory transactions to the General Ledger accounts. The store accountant will print the General Ledger Trial Balance to prepare monthly financial statement reports. No other hardcopy reports or journals will be generated.

Joe McSweeney
July 10, 200X

Collins Harp Enterprises: Assessing IT Risks and Recommending General Controls

Frank A. Buckless, Mark S. Beasley,
Steven M. Glover, and Douglas F. Prawitt

LEARNING OBJECTIVES

After completing and discussing this case you should be able to

- Recognize risks associated with the IT organizational structure and systems development process at a potential audit client
- Identify general controls that, if implemented, could reduce risks associated with IT system development
- Communicate negative information to a potential new client in a way that might lead to new audit and consulting services for that company

BACKGROUND

You are the new information technology (IT) audit specialist at the accounting firm of Townsend and Townsend, LLP. One of the audit partners, Harold Mobley, asked you to evaluate the effectiveness of general and application IT-related controls for a potentially new audit client, Collins Harp Enterprises. During a round of golf last week, an executive of Collins Harp Enterprises asked Harold to have someone with good IT training to take a look at the company's IT systems development process. Harold recently summarized the following information about Collins Harp's IT systems development process based on his recent conversation with Linda Seth, IT vice president at Collins Harp.

IT SUMMARY

Collins Harp Enterprises develops most of its computer applications in-house. Over the past several years, Linda Seth has been able to hire several good programmers with

This case was prepared by Frank A. Buckless, Ph.D. and Mark S. Beasley, Ph.D. of North Carolina State University and Steven M. Glover, Ph.D. and Douglas F. Prawitt, Ph.D. of Brigham Young University, as a basis for class discussion. It is not intended to illustrate either effective or ineffective handling of an administrative situation.

relatively strong programming experience. She has assembled a team of five programmers who handle most of the application and systems programming needs. Because of their strong backgrounds, Ms. Seth involves all five programmers in new application developments or modifications to existing applications and also involves all of them in operating system and utility software programming tasks. The staff is relatively versatile, and any one of them is able to handle the programming demands of most changes.

Linda notes that because programmers are typically the more "free-spirited, pony-tail type," she prefers to give the programmers relatively free latitude in the development of new applications or modifications to existing applications. She comments that the programmers like to view their work as a form of art. As a result, she notes that the programmers "attack" the programming logic development using their own, unique programming style and approach. She believes that such "freedom" for the programming staff enhances the quality of the application development.

New applications are generally initiated by Linda after she identifies suggestions for changes to existing applications based on conversations with similar IT personnel at other companies. Because she regularly attends IT development conferences, she believes that she is in the best position to identify ways to improve current application procedures. Occasionally, non-IT personnel (like the accounting department personnel who work with the accounting systems) identify suggested changes. Linda notes that she generally hears about application changes or new application ideas from the non-IT personnel in informal settings such as over lunch in the company cafeteria or when bumping into people in the office hallways. When that occurs, she makes a mental note to take back to her programming staff.

When applications are developed or changes are made, the assigned programmer generally telephones the non-IT personnel primarily responsible for the application to discuss the programmer's suggested modification and to get their unofficial "blessing" to proceed. Occasionally, the programmer meets with the respective personnel, if requested. However, the programmers generally feel that such meetings are a waste of time because the users have very little understanding of the programming logic used. Programmers prefer to minimize their contact with user personnel.

If the programmer is making a modification to an existing application, he or she makes a copy of the current program tape or disk so that they do not have to reprogram the entire application. Before beginning, the programmer generally tries to meet with the programmer who was previously involved with any programming associated with this application to get a "big picture feel" for the application. Given the small size of the programming staff, the programmer can generally identify who was last involved with this application by talking with the other programmers. The programmer locates documents related to the programming logic maintained in the programming department's files. Generally, this documentation includes a hardcopy of the program logic along with notes made by the prior programmer about the format of the logic used. The newly assigned programmer is able to recreate a trail of the most recent modifications to the application from these notes.

Programmers test all application developments and modifications. To increase the independence of the testing, Linda assigns a different programmer to perform the testing of the application before implementation. The test programmer creates a fictitious data set by copying one of the actual data sets used in the relevant application. The test programmer performs a test of the new application or modification and documents the results. Linda says that there are tight controls over program testing because of her detailed reviews of all program test results and personal approval of each program before implementation into live production. And, she adds that copies of all test results are maintained in the files for subsequent review.

Once Linda believes that the program is accurately processing the test data, she approves the program for implementation into live production. Linda notes that it is a big event for the programmers when their application is ready for implementation. She comments that the programmers take pride in the completion of the project and that all the programmers celebrate once the project programmer announces that he or she has compiled the final version into object code and forwarded the object code version to the Librarian.

REQUIREMENTS

Harold would like you to prepare a draft letter to Linda Seth that addresses the following:

1. Describe any weaknesses you note in the Collins Harp IT system development and program change process.
2. For each weakness identified in question 1, provide a brief description of your primary concern about the presence of that weakness.
3. For each weakness identified in question 1, provide a recommendation of a general control that could be implemented to minimize your concern.

Remember your response will be to Linda Seth at Collins Harp. Therefore, you want to prepare your response in a letter (not memo) format. Be sure to be professional in your response. You want to be critical of obvious weaknesses, but you do not want to be offensive, as Collins Harp could become a new client. Harold does not want the letter to exceed two single-spaced pages.

Dell Computer Corporation: Determination of Planning Materiality and Tolerable Misstatement

Frank A. Buckless, Mark S. Beasley,
Steven M. Glover, and Douglas F. Prawitt

LEARNING OBJECTIVES

After completing and discussing this case you should be able to

- Determine planning materiality for an audit client
- Allocate planning materiality to financial statement elements
- Provide support for your materiality decisions

INTRODUCTION

Dell Computer Corporation[1] (Dell) designs, develops, manufactures, markets, services, and supports a wide range of computer systems, including desktops, notebooks, workstations, and network servers. The company also markets software, computer peripherals, and post-sale service and support programs. The company's products are sold in more than 170 countries and it has manufacturing facilities in Round Rock, Texas; Limerick, Ireland; and Penang, Malaysia. Net revenue for fiscal 1998 was $12.3 billion and net income was $944 million. Dell generally experiences stronger revenues in the second and third fiscal-year quarters.

The company's business strategy is to deliver the best customer experience through direct, comprehensive customer relationships, cooperative research and development with technology partners, custom-built computer systems, and service and support programs tailored to customer needs. The direct customer approach eliminates

---

[1]The background information about Dell Computer Corporation was taken from Dell Computer Corporation's February 1, 1998, Form 10-K and August 2, 1998, Form 10-Q filed with the Securities and Exchange Commission.

This case was prepared by Frank A. Buckless, Ph.D. and Mark S. Beasley, Ph.D. of North Carolina State University and Steven M. Glover, Ph.D. and Douglas F. Prawitt, Ph.D. of Brigham Young University, as a basis for class discussion. It is not intended to illustrate either effective or ineffective handling of an administrative situation.

the need to support an extensive network of wholesale and retail dealers. This direct customer focus allows the company to reduce the cost of its products by avoiding typical dealer markups and avoiding higher inventory costs associated with the wholesale/retail channel. In addition, direct customer contact allows the Company to maintain, monitor, and update a database of information about customers and their current and future product and service needs, which can be used to shape future product and service programs. The company's partnerships with leading-edge technology companies create efficient procurement, manufacturing, and distribution processes that allow Dell to bring relevant technology to its customers faster and more competitively priced than many of its competitors.

Dell common stock is traded on the NASDAQ national market, and Dell is required to have an annual audit pursuant with the 1934 Securities and Exchange Act. As of the close of business on September 8, 1998, Dell had 1,273,510,968 shares of common stock outstanding with a trading price of $59\frac{15}{16}$.

BACKGROUND INFORMATION ABOUT THE AUDIT

Your firm, Smith and Jones, P.A., is in the initial planning phase for the fiscal 1999 audit of Dell Computer Corporation. As the audit manager, you have been assigned responsibility for determining planning materiality and tolerable misstatement. Your firm's materiality and tolerable misstatement guidelines have been provided to assist you with this assignment.

Donna Fontain, the audit partner, has performed a preliminary analysis of the company and its performance and believes the likelihood of management fraud is very low. Donna's initial analysis of the company's performance is documented in the memo referenced as G 3–1 and G 3–2 (top right corner of the document). Additionally, Donna has documented current events noted while performing the preliminary analysis in a separate memo, G 4. You have recorded the fiscal 1998 balance sheet numbers along with projections for fiscal 1999 on audit schedules G 6–1 and G 6–2. Selected information from the company's fiscal 1998 notes to the financial statements have been provided on the following pages. Assume no misstatements were discovered during the fiscal 1998 audit.

REQUIREMENTS

Review the audit memos (G 3–1, G 3–2 and G 4), selected information from the fiscal 1998 notes to the financial statements, and audit schedules (G 5, G 6–1, and G 6–2). Based on your review, complete audit schedules G 5, G 6–1, and G 6–2.

Smith and Jones, PA.
Policy Statement: Materiality

This policy statement provides general guidelines for firm personnel when determining planning materiality and tolerable misstatement for purposes of determining the nature, timing, and extent of audit procedures. The intent of this policy statement is not to suggest that these materiality guidelines must be followed on all audit engagements. The appropriateness of these materiality guidelines must be determined on an engagement by engagement basis, using professional judgment.

Planning Materiality Guidelines

Planning materiality represents the maximum, combined, financial statement misstatement or omission that could occur before influencing the decisions of reasonable individuals relying on the financial statements. The magnitude and nature of financial statement misstatements or omissions will not have the same influence on all financial statement users. For example, a 5 percent misstatement with current assets may be more relevant for a creditor than a stockholder, whereas a 5 percent misstatement with net income before income taxes may be more relevant for a stockholder than a creditor. Therefore, the primary consideration when determining materiality is the expected users of the financial statements.

Relevant financial statement elements and presumptions on the effect of combined misstatements or omissions that would be considered immaterial and material are provided below:

- Net Income Before Income Taxes—combined misstatements or omissions less than 5 percent of Net Income Before Income Taxes are presumed to be immaterial, and combined misstatements or omissions greater than 10 percent are presumed to be material. (Note: Net Income Before Income Taxes may not be an appropriate base if the client's Net Income Before Income Taxes is substantially below other companies of equal size or is highly variable.)

- Net Revenue—combined misstatements or omissions less than 1 percent of Net Revenue are presumed to be immaterial, and combined misstatements or omissions greater than 3 percent are presumed to be material.

- Current Assets—combined misstatements or omissions less than 5 percent of Current Assets are presumed to be immaterial, and combined misstatements or omissions greater than 10 percent are presumed to be material.

- Current Liabilities—combined misstatements or omissions less than 5 percent of Current Liabilities are presumed to be immaterial, and combined misstatements or omissions greater than 10 percent are presumed to be material.

- Total Assets—combined misstatements or omissions less than 1 percent of Total Assets are presumed to be immaterial, and combined misstatements or omissions greater than 3 percent are presumed to be material. (Note: Total Assets may not be an appropriate base for service organizations or other organizations that have few operating assets.)

The specific amounts established for each financial statement element must be determined by considering the primary users as well as qualitative factors. For example, if the client is close to violating the minimum current ratio requirement for a loan agreement, a smaller planning materiality amount should be used for current assets and liabilities. Conversely, if the client is substantially above the minimum current ratio requirement for a loan agreement, it would be reasonable to use a higher planning materiality amount for current assets and current liabilities.

Planning materiality should be based on the smallest amount established from relevant materiality bases to provide reasonable assurance that the financial statements, taken as a whole, are not materially misstated for any user.

(Continued on next page)

Continued

Tolerable Misstatement Guidelines

In addition to establishing materiality for the overall financial statements, materiality for individual financial statement accounts should be established. The amount established for individual accounts is referred to as "tolerable misstatement." Tolerable misstatement represents the amount an individual financial statement account can differ from its true amount without affecting the fair presentation of the financial statements taken as a whole. Establishment of tolerable misstatement for individual accounts enables the auditor to design and execute an audit strategy for each audit cycle.

Tolerable misstatement should be established for all balance sheet accounts (except "retained earnings" because it is the residual account). Tolerable misstatement need not be allocated to income statement accounts because many misstatements affect both income statement and balance sheet accounts and misstatements affecting only the income statement are normally less relevant to users.

The objective in setting tolerable misstatement for individual balance sheet accounts is to provide reasonable assurance that the financial statements taken as a whole are fairly presented in all material respects at the lowest cost. Factors to consider when setting tolerable misstatement include:

- <u>Relevance of Account to Users</u>—tolerable misstatement should not exceed that amount that would influence the decision of reasonable users.

- <u>Cost of Audit Evidence</u>—tolerable misstatement should be higher for balance sheet accounts that cost more to audit.

- <u>Competence of Evidence</u>—tolerable misstatement should be higher for balance sheet accounts with less competent evidence available.

- <u>Expected Misstatement</u>—tolerable misstatement should at a minimum equal the expected misstatement for an account if it is unlikely that the client will adjust the financial statements for misstatements found during the audit.

- <u>Size of Account</u>—tolerable misstatement should be higher for larger balance sheet accounts.

To provide reasonable assurance that the financial statements taken as a whole do not contain material misstatements, the tolerable misstatement established for individual accounts should not exceed planning materiality and the sum of tolerable misstatements should not exceed three times planning materiality. The sum of tolerable misstatements should be lower as the expectation for management fraud increases. In many audits it is reasonable to expect that some individual accounts will be misstated less than tolerable misstatement and that misstatements across accounts will offset each other. This expectation is not reasonable when the likelihood of management fraud is high. If management is intentionally trying to misstate the financial statements, it is likely that misstatements will be systematically biased in one direction across accounts.

Approved: April 24, 1995.

Dell Computer Corporation
Information from the Fiscal 1998 Notes to Consolidated Financial Statements

Fiscal Year   The company's fiscal year is the 52- or 53-week period ending on the Sunday nearest January 31.

Marketable Securities   The company's marketable securities are classified as available-for-sale and are reported at fair value. Unrealized gains and losses are reported, net of taxes, as a component of stockholders' equity. Unrealized losses are charged against income when a decline in fair value is determined to be other than temporary. The specific identification method is used to determine the cost of securities sold. Gains and losses on marketable securities are included in financing and other when realized. The company accounts for highly liquid investments with maturities of three months or less at date of acquisition as marketable securities and reflects the related cash flows as investing cash flows. As a result, a significant portion of its gross marketable securities purchases and maturities disclosed as investing cash flows is related to highly liquid investments. The fair value of the company's holdings of marketable securities by security type is as follows:

	February 1, 1998	February 2, 1997
	(In Millions)	
Preferred stock	$ 172	$ 172
Mutual funds, principally invested in debt securities	800	182
Debt securities:		
State and municipal securities	190	317
U.S. corporate and bank debt	307	415
U.S. government and agencies	40	98
International corporate and bank debt	15	53
Total debt securities	552	883
Total marketable securities	$1,524	$1,237

Inventories   Inventories are stated at the lower of cost or market. Cost is determined on a first-in, first-out basis. The components of the company's inventory were as follows:

	February 1, 1998	February 2, 1997
	(In Millions)	
Production materials	$ 189	$ 223
Work-in-process and finished goods	44	28
	$ 233	$ 251

Property, Plant, and Equipment   Property, plant, and equipment are carried at depreciated cost. Depreciation is provided using the straight-line method over the estimated economic lives of the assets, which range from 10 to 30 years for buildings and two to five years for all other assets. Leasehold improvements are amortized over the shorter of five years or the lease term. The components of the company's property, plant, and equipment were as follows:

	February 1, 1998	February 2, 1997
	(In Millions)	
Land and buildings	$ 137	$ 133
Computer equipment	135	104

(continued)

	February 1, 1998	February 2, 1997
	(In Millions)	
Office furniture and fixtures	45	32
Machinery and other equipment	126	59
Leasehold improvements	66	46
Total property, plant, and equipment	509	374
Accumulated depreciation and amortization	(167)	(139)
	$ 342	$ 235

Foreign Currency Translation   The majority of the company's international sales are made by international subsidiaries that have the U.S. dollar as their functional currency. International subsidiaries that have the U.S. dollar as the functional currency are remeasured into U.S. dollars using current rates of exchange for monetary assets and liabilities and historical rates of exchange for nonmonetary assets. Gains and losses from remeasurement are included in financing and other. The company's subsidiaries that do not have the U.S. dollar as their functional currency translate assets and liabilities at current rates of exchange in effect at the balance sheet date. The resulting gains and losses from translation are included as a component of stockholders' equity. Items of income and expense for the company's international subsidiaries are translated using the monthly average exchange rates in effect for the period in which the items occur.

Foreign Currency Hedging Instruments   The company enters into foreign exchange contracts to hedge its foreign currency risks. These contracts must be designated at inception as hedges and measured for effectiveness both at inception and on an ongoing basis. Realized and unrealized gains or losses and premiums on foreign currency purchased option contracts that are designated and effective as hedges of probable, anticipated, but not firmly committed, foreign currency transactions are deferred and recognized in income as a component of revenue, cost of sales and/or operating expenses in the same period as the hedged transaction. Forward contracts designated as hedges of probable, anticipated, or firmly committed transactions are accounted for on a mark-to-market basis, with realized and unrealized gains or losses recognized currently.

Equity Instruments Indexed to the Company's Common Stock   Proceeds received upon the sale of equity instruments and amounts paid upon the purchase of equity instruments are recorded as a component of stockholders' equity. Subsequent changes in the fair value of the equity instrument contracts are not recognized. If the contracts are ultimately settled in cash, the amount of cash paid or received is recorded as a component of stockholders' equity.

Revenue Recognition   Sales revenue is recognized at the date of shipment to customers. Provision is made for an estimate of product returns and doubtful accounts and is based on historical experience. Revenue from separately priced service and extended-warranty programs are deferred and recognized over the extended-warranty period. The components of the company's net accounts receivable are as follows:

	February 1, 1998	February 2, 1997
	(In Millions)	
Gross accounts receivable	$1,514	$ 934
Allowance for doubtful accounts	(28)	(31)
	$1,486	$ 903

Warranty and Other Post-Sales Support Programs The company provides currently for the estimated costs that may be incurred under its initial warranty and other post-sales support programs. The components of the company's accrued and other liabilities were as follows:

	February 1, 1998	February 2, 1997
	(In Millions)	
Accrued compensation	$ 236	$ 113
Deferred revenue on warranty contracts	193	126
Book overdrafts	146	27
Accrued warranty costs	139	111
Taxes other than income taxes	122	74
Other	218	167
	$1,054	$ 618

Advertising Costs Advertising costs are charged to expense as incurred. Advertising expenses for fiscal years 1998, 1997, and 1996 were $137 million, $87 million, and $83 million, respectively.

Stock-Based Compensation The company adopted Statement of Financial Accounting Standards No. 123, "Accounting for Stock-Based Compensation," in the fiscal year ended February 2, 1997. On adoption, the company continued to apply Accounting Principles Board Opinion No. 25, "Accounting for Stock Issued to Employees," in accounting for its stock option and stock purchase plans. As a result, no expense has been recognized for options granted with an exercise price equal to market value at the date of grant or in connection with the employee stock purchase plan. For stock options that have been issued at discounted prices, the company accrues for compensation expense over the vesting period for the difference between the exercise price and fair market value on the measurement date.

Income Taxes The provision for income taxes is based on income before income taxes as reported in the Consolidated Statement of Income. Deferred tax assets and liabilities are determined based on the difference between the financial statement and tax basis of assets and liabilities using enacted tax rates in effect for the year in which the differences are expected to reverse. The components of the company's net deferred tax asset (included in other current assets) were as follows:

	Fiscal Year Ended		
	February 1, 1998	February 2, 1997	January 28, 1996
	(In Millions)		
Provisions for product returns and doubtful accounts	$ 20	$ 31	$ 25
Inventory and warranty provisions	24	21	18
Deferred service contract revenue	124	107	53
Other	(62)	(26)	(29)
Net deferred tax asset	$106	$133	$ 67

Reference: _G 3-1_____
Prepared by: _DF_____
Date: _8/14/98_____
Reviewed by: _____

Dell Computer Corporation
Memo: Analysis of Performance for First Six Months
Year Ended: January 31, 1999

Net Revenue increased 53% in the first six months of fiscal 1999 over the comparable period of fiscal 1998 (from $5.40 billion to $8.25 billion). The increase in Net Revenue was primarily attributable to increased units sold. Unit sales increased 70% in the first six months of fiscal 1999 compared to the same period of fiscal 1998. Unit sales increased across all product lines for the first six months of fiscal 1999 compared to the same period of fiscal 1998. Desktop products continue to remain the primary component of unit sales, comprising 80% of total units sold during the first six months of fiscal 1999. However, the unit sales growth rate in enterprise systems (which include both servers and workstations) and notebooks exceeded the unit sales growth rate of desktop products. The effect of the increased unit sales on Net Revenue for the first six months of fiscal 1999 compared to the same period of fiscal 1998 was partially offset by a decline in average revenue per unit sold of 10%. The decrease in average revenue per unit sold was primarily attributable to price reductions as a result of component cost declines.

Net Revenue increased in all geographic regions in the first six months of fiscal 1999 as compared to the same period of fiscal 1998. The percentage of total Net Revenue derived from each region for the first six months of fiscal 1999 was 67.7% from the Americas, 25.6% from Europe, and 6.7% from Asia Pacific/Japan. The comparable percentages for the first six months of the previous fiscal year were 69.1% from the Americas, 23.4% from Europe, and 7.5% from Asia Pacific/Japan.

The Company's Gross Margin as a percentage of Net Revenue increased to 22.5% in the first six months of fiscal 1999 compared to 21.9% in the corresponding period of the prior fiscal year. The increase resulted primarily from component cost declines, which were mostly passed through to customers, resulting in the aforementioned declines in average revenue per unit sold.

The company continues to successfully manage its operating activities. Days of Sales In Accounts Receivable was 37 on August 2, 1998, compared to 36 on February 1, 1998. Days of Supply in Inventory was 8 on August 2, 1998, compared to 7 on February 1, 1998, and Days in Accounts Payable was 52 on August 2, 1998, compared to 51 on February 1, 1998.

Selling, General and Administrative Expenses as a percentage of Net Revenue increased to 10% for the first six months of fiscal 1999 from 9.6% in the comparable period of the prior fiscal year. The increase was due primarily to the company's increased staffing worldwide and increased infrastructure expenses, including those for information systems, to support the company's continued growth.

Reference: _G 3-2_____
Prepared by: __DF_____
Date: __8/14/98_____
Reviewed by: _____

Dell Computer Corporation
Memo: Analysis of Performance for First Six Months
Year Ended: January 31, 1999

Research Development and Engineering Expenses as a percentage of Net Revenue decreased to 1.5% for the first six months of fiscal 1999 from 1.6% in the comparable period of the prior fiscal year. In absolute dollar amounts, these costs increased due to increased staffing levels and product development costs.

Net Income as a percentage of Net Revenue increased to 7.9% for the first six months of fiscal 1999 from 7.6% in the comparable period of the prior year.

Cash Flow from Operating Activities was $1.1 billion for the first six months of fiscal 1999 compared to $0.6 billion for the same period of the prior fiscal year. The company's Cash Flow from Operating activities was generated primarily from the company's net income and increases in operating working capital.

Overall, the company's first six months' performance has been very strong and compares favorably with major competitors. Compaq's Net Revenue for the first six months of 1998 grew 6.8% over the comparable 1997 period (to $11.52 billion from $10.79 billion). Compaq's Net Income/(Loss) as a percentage of Net Revenue decreased to (31.2%) for the first six months of 1998 compared to 6.2% for the first six months of 1997. Gateway 2000's Net Revenue for the first six months of 1998 grew 19% over the comparable 1997 period (to $3.35 billion from $2.81 billion). Gateway 2000's Net Income as a percentage of Net Revenue decreased to 4.1% for the first six months of 1998 compared to 4.4% for the first six months of 1997.

Reference: _G 4_

Prepared by: _DF_

Date: _8/14/98_

Reviewed by: _____

Dell Computer Corporation
Memo: Current Events
Year Ended: January 31, 1999

The company utilized $155 million in cash during the first six months of fiscal 1999 to improve and equip facilities. Cash flows for capital expenditures for fiscal 1999 are expected to be approximately $360 million.

Subsequent to the second quarter of fiscal 1999, the company entered into an additional master lease facility providing funds up to $593 million. This agreement along with the agreement entered into last fiscal year provide Dell the ability to lease certain real property, buildings and equipment to be constructed or acquired. Currently, $85 million of these facilities have been utilized.

In April 1998, the company issued $200 million 6.55% fixed-rate senior notes due April 15, 2008 (the "Senior Notes") and $300 million 7.10% fixed-rate senior debentures due April 15, 2028 (the "Senior Debentures"). Interest on the Senior Notes and Senior Debentures is paid semiannually. The Senior Notes and Senior Debentures are redeemable, in whole or in part, at the election of the company, for principal, any accrued interest and a redemption premium based on the present value of interest to be paid over the term of the debt agreements. The Senior Notes and Senior Debentures generally contain no restrictive covenants, other than a limitation on liens on the company's assets and a limitation on sale-leaseback transactions.

On July 17, 1998, the company's stockholders approved an amendment to the company's Certificate of Incorporation to increase the number of shares of common stock, par value $.01 per share, that the company is authorized to issue from one billion to three billion.

The company intends to issue approximately 634 million authorized shares of common stock to complete a two-for-one stock split.

During the current fiscal year, the company repurchased 11 million shares of common stock at an average cost of $36 per share. The company is currently authorized to repurchase up to 50 million additional shares of its common stock and anticipates that such repurchases will constitute a significant use of future cash resources. The above per share information does not reflect the company's expected two-for-one stock split.

Dell Computer Corporation
Planning Materiality Assessment
Year Ended: January 31, 1999

Reference: _G 5_
Prepared by: _DF_
Date: _8/14/98_
Reviewed by: _____

Primary Users of Financial Statements (list):

| |
| |

Likelihood of Management Fraud (check one):

_____ Low Likelihood of Management Fraud
_____ Reasonably Low Likelihood of Management Fraud
_____ Moderate Likelihood of Management Fraud

Materiality Bases (in Millions):

Base	Fiscal 1998 Actual Financial Statement Amounts	Fiscal 1999 Projected Financial Statement Amounts	Planning Materiality Levels			
			Lower Limit		Upper Limit	
			Percent	Dollar Amount	Percent	Dollar Amount
Income Before Taxes	$1,368	$2,109	5		10	
Net Revenues	$12,327	$19,000	1		3	
Current Liabilities	$2,697	$4,115	5		10	
Current Assets	$3,912	$6,155	5		10	
Total Assets	$4,268	$6,771	1		3	

Planning Materiality (in Millions):

Explanation:

Cumulative Materiality Amount to be Allocated to Accounts (in Millions):

Planning Materiality:	
Multiplication Factor (3 if low likelihood of management fraud, 2 if reasonably low likelihood of management fraud, and 1 if high likelihood of management fraud):	X

Dell Computer Corporation
Tolerable Misstatement for Balance Sheet Accounts
Year Ended: January 31, 1999 (All Amounts Are in Millions)

Reference: _G 6-1_
Prepared by: _____
Date: _____
Reviewed by: _____

Account	Actual 2/1/98 Balances	Projected 1/31/99 Balances	Tolerable Mis- statement	Explanation
Cash	$ 320	$ 500	$10	*A low tolerable misstatement is assigned because low-cost competent evidence is available to test account items.*
Marketable securities	1,524	2,300		
Accounts receivable, net	1,486	2,290		
Inventories	233	365		
Other, current	349	700		
Property, plant, and equipment, net	342	602		
Other, noncurrent assets	14	14		
Accounts payable	1,643	2,515		
Accrued and other current liabilities	1,054	1,600		
Page Total				

Dell Computer Corporation
Tolerable Misstatement for Balance Sheet Accounts
Year Ended: January 31, 1999 (All Amounts Are in Millions)

Account	Actual 2/1/98 Balances	Projected 1/31/99 Balances	Tolerable Mis-statement	Explanation
Long-term debt	$ 17	$ 512		
Deferred revenue on warranty contracts	225	260		
Other noncurrent liabilities	36	100		
Commitments and contingent liabilities	—	—		
Preferred stock capital accounts	—	—		
Common stock capital accounts	747	1,290		
Retained earnings	607	555		
Other stockholders' equity	(61)	(61)		
Page Total				
Total				

Laramie Wire Manufacturing: Using Analytical Procedures in Audit Planning

Frank A. Buckless, Mark S. Beasley,
Steven M. Glover, and Douglas F. Prawitt

LEARNING OBJECTIVES

After completing and discussing this case you should be able to

- Review and analyze information relating to a company's inventory and related accounts
- Identify potential risks and areas requiring a greater amount of substantive audit attention
- Understand how preliminary analytical procedures can help in planning the audit of inventory

INTRODUCTION

Analytical procedures can be powerful tools in conducting an audit. They help the auditor understand a client's business, and they are useful in identifying potential risks and problem areas requiring greater substantive audit attention. If formulated carefully enough that they allow the auditor to arrive at a precise expectation of what an account balance *ought* to be, "analytics" can provide a source of inexpensive and powerful substantive evidence that replaces time-consuming detailed testing. Finally, analytical procedures are useful in helping the auditor assess whether a client faces a going-concern issue and whether a client's financial statements "make sense" after required audit adjustments are made.

The three general uses of analytical procedures listed above correspond to the three stages of an audit in which they are typically used—planning, evidence gathering, and final review. Statement on Auditing Standards (SAS) No. 56, *Analytical Procedures*, provides guidance to auditors on how and when to use analytical procedures. SAS No. 56 *requires* auditors to use analytics in the planning and final review stages, and encourages—but does not require—the use of analytics in the substantive-evidence-gathering stage of the audit.

This case addresses the use of analytical procedures in the planning stage of the audit. During planning, analytics help the auditor gain an overall understanding of the client and its business environment. They also help the auditor plan the evidence that will be gathered in various audit areas by helping the auditor identify potential risks and problem areas requiring more extensive substantive testing.

BACKGROUND ABOUT LARAMIE WIRE MANUFACTURING

You are a senior auditor assigned to the Laramie Wire Manufacturing audit. This is the first year your firm has conducted the audit for this particular client. In fact, although Laramie has previously engaged accountants to perform limited-review services for the purpose of obtaining bank loans, this is the first year Laramie has contracted for a full-scale audit of its financial statements. The company is planning an initial public offering (IPO) of its stock in the next two or three years and has hired your firm to conduct its first financial statement audit in preparation for the upcoming IPO.

Laramie is a medium-sized company that buys copper rod and plastic materials used to make insulated copper wiring. Laramie operates out of a single building complex totaling 500,000 square feet, which includes office space (3%), production area (57%), shipping and receiving (15%), and finished goods and raw materials inventory warehousing (25%). Laramie supplies insulated copper wiring in the northeastern part of the United States. The company has a good reputation for quality products and has had a good working relationship with its outside accountants over the past 10 years. You have been assigned responsibility for auditing Laramie's inventories. You are in the planning stages of the audit, and you are preparing to conduct some analytical procedures to help you identify risk areas that may require further attention.

Your staff assistant assembled information relating to inventories and other items, including a brief description of Laramie's production and inventory areas. Because your assistant is new, he is usually not very good about weeding out irrelevant information, so you may not need to use every piece of information he has provided. The information is listed below.

	1999	1998
Sales	$8,450,000	$8,150,000
Cost of Sales	$6,242,500	$6,080,000
Finished Goods Inventory (Approx. 300 million ft.—1999)	$1,654,500	$1,175,500
Copper Rod Inventory (Approx. 5.9 million lbs.—1999)	$2,625,000	$1,650,000
Plastics Inventory (Approx. 1.1 million lbs.—1999)	$ 224,500	$ 182,000
Accounts Payable (for Inv. purchases)	$ 450,000	$ 425,000
Days Purchases in A/P	43.6 days	44.2 days
Days Sales in Receivables	56.3 days	48.4 days
Market Price of Insulated Wire (per foot)	$ .008	$ .009
Market Price of Copper Rod (per lb.)	$ .480	$ .480
Market Price of Plastics (per lb.)	$ .120	$ .190

Laramie makes several different gauges and types of insulated copper wire for use in applications ranging from residential telephone and electrical wiring to industrial-grade, high-voltage power cables. The production area is divided into three areas, with each area specializing in a particular product group, including residential products, industrial products, and special-order products. Production is done in batches according to orders placed with the firm. For each batch, machinery is adjusted and calibrated according to the type and size of product to be manufactured, and the size of the batch depends on the amount of product needed. Average machine setup time from start to finish is approximately six hours, which is slightly below the industry average.

The different types of products Laramie manufactures all use similar raw materials, so raw material inventory is stored in a single location, divided only into copper and plastics materials. Finished insulated copper wire is stored on large, stackable spools of various sizes, with approximately 500,000 feet of wire per spool. Copper rod inventory is stored on pallets, which are not stackable. Each pallet measures 6 feet by 6 feet, stands 5 feet tall, and holds 1,500 pounds of copper rod. Plastics inventory is stored in 4-foot-tall stackable barrels, with approximately 350 lbs. of plastic per barrel. The raw materials inventory storage area is located near the shipping and receiving area for convenience. Inbound and outbound shipments of inventory are trucked to the nearest rail yard, from which they are distributed around the northeastern region of the United States. A single 18-wheeler can carry up to 15 pallets of copper rod, 40 barrels of plastics, or 24 spools of finished wire.

Laramie's production process is semiautomated, but it still requires a relatively large amount of labor. Thus, Laramie's conversion costs are fairly evenly divided between direct labor and factory overhead. Overhead consists primarily of the costs of the production facilities and depreciation and maintenance on the machinery. Laramie uses a hybrid product costing system (i.e., a system that combines characteristics of both job-order and process costing systems) to accommodate both the continuous and homogeneous nature of the manufacturing process and the fact that production runs are performed in separately identifiable batches. In accordance with the relatively homogenous nature of Laramie's products, overhead is allocated from a single cost pool based on a combination of machine and direct labor hours.

As wire product is completed, it is rolled onto large spools of various sizes, usually in lengths of about 500,000 linear feet. These spools of finished inventory are stored next to the raw materials inventory near the facility's eight loading and unloading docks. In many cases the inventory is produced in response to specific customer orders received, in which case the spools are tagged for shipment to customers according to date requested. Inventory that has been produced without a customer order to provide a "cushion" for rush orders is stored toward the far end of the finished goods storage area, away from the shipping area.

The inventory and production areas are well organized and seem to flow smoothly. Machines appear to be well maintained. A cursory visual examination of inventories reveals no problems. Two spools in the finished goods area were tagged as being of the type of residential wiring recently banned by federal safety guidelines. These spools are clearly marked, and the inventories supervisor indicated they are to be destroyed within the next week. Procedures and records for tracking materials upon arrival, through the production process, and into finished goods and shipping, appear to be well designed.

REQUIREMENTS

1. With the five management assertions in mind (existence or occurrence, completeness, valuation or allocation, rights and obligations, and presentation and disclosure), perform analytical procedures to help you identify areas that indicate the need for further attention, if any.

2. For each of the five management assertions as they relate to Laramie's inventory balance, briefly explain identified risks or issues requiring further attention, if any.

Burlington Bees:
Using Analytical Procedures
as Substantive Tests

Frank A. Buckless, Mark S. Beasley,
Steven M. Glover, and Douglas F. Prawitt

LEARNING OBJECTIVES

After completing and discussing this case you should be able to

- Use analytical procedures to develop expectations for revenue accounts
- Recognize factors that lead to precise expectations of account balances
- Appreciate the degree of professional judgment involved in evaluating differences between expected and reported account balances
- Understand the audit planning implications of using analytical procedures as substantive tests of account balances

BACKGROUND

Burlington Bees, an independent, minor league baseball team, competes in the Northwest Coast League. The team finished in second place in 200X with an 87–57 record. The Bees' 200X cumulative season attendance of 434,348 spectators set a new record high for the team, up from 390,000 in 200W.

Bank-loan covenants require the Bees to submit audited financial statements annually to the bank. The accounting firm of Hickman and Snowden, CPAs, has served as the Bees' auditors for the past five years.

One of the major audit areas involves testing ticket revenues. Those revenues reached nearly $1.9 million in 200W. In prior years, the audit plan called for extensive detail testing of revenue accounts to gain assurance that reported ticket revenues were fairly stated.

This case was prepared by Frank A. Buckless, Ph.D. and Mark S. Beasley, Ph.D. of North Carolina State University and Steven M. Glover, Ph.D. and Douglas F. Prawitt, Ph.D. of Brigham Young University, as a basis for class discussion. It is not intended to illustrate either effective or ineffective handling of an administrative situation.

Michelle Kramme, a new audit manager, just received the assignment to be the manager on the 200X audit. Michelle worked previously on the Bees' prior-year audits as a staff auditor. When she learned she would be managing the current-year engagement, she immediately thought back to all the hours of detailed testing of ticket sales she performed. On some of her other clients, Michelle has been successful at redesigning audit plans to make better use of analytical procedures as substantive tests. She is beginning to wonder if there is a more efficient way to gather substantive evidence related to ticket revenues on the Bees' engagement.

In her first meeting with Bees' management for the 200X audit, Michelle learned that the Bees now use an outside company, Tickets R Us, to operate ticket gates for home games. The terms of the contract require Tickets R Us to collect ticket stubs so that they can later report total tickets collected per game. Although Tickets R Us does not break down the total ticket sales into the various price categories, Michelle thinks there may be a way to develop an analytical procedure using the independently generated total ticket numbers and data from prior audits. To investigate this possibility, Michelle asked a staff person to gather some information related to reported sales. Here is the information the staff person gathered from the records of the client, Tickets R Us, and prior-year working papers:

200X Park Attendance

Total park attendance	434,348

200X Number of Games

Weekday games	43
Weekend games	29

Information from prior-year audit working papers indicates that average per-game attendance for weekend games was 25% higher than average per-game attendance for weekday games.

200X Per-Game Ticket Prices

Club seats		$10
Box seats		$ 6
General seats:	Adult	$ 4
	Child (Senior Citizens)	$ 2

Comparison of 200W ticket prices to 200X ticket prices reveals an average increase of 10% between the two years.

Sales Mix		**Weekday**	**Weekend**
Club seats		30%	25%
Box seats		35%	30%
General seats:	Adult	20%	25%
	Child (Senior Citizens)	15%	20%

Information from prior-year audit working papers shows that sales mix has remained fairly constant over the past several years.

200X Promotions: Number of Games

Weekday	7
Weekend	10

Information from prior-year audit working papers shows that attendance generally increases by 10 percent when there is a promotion (e.g., free baseball cap, poster, or special entertainment).

REQUIREMENTS

1. Using the information provided, please develop an expectation for ticket revenues for the 200X fiscal year.

2. How close would the Bees' reported ticket revenue have to be to your expectation for you to consider reported ticket revenue reasonable or fairly stated? If reported ticket revenues are outside your "reasonableness range," what could explain the difference?

3. What are the advantages of using analytical procedures as substantive tests? If the engagement team decides to use analytical procedures for the Bees' audit, how will the audit plan differ from prior years? Do you believe that analytical procedures should be used as substantive tests for the Bees 200X audit?

Henrico Retail, Inc.: Understanding the IT Accounting System and Identifying Audit Evidence for Retail Sales

Frank A. Buckless, Mark S. Beasley,
Steven M. Glover, and Douglas F. Prawitt

LEARNING OBJECTIVES

After completing and discussing this case you should be able to

- Outline the audit trail for processing retail sales transactions
- Develop audit plans for gathering evidence to test the existence and valuation of retail sales
- Recognize when audit evidence must be gathered electronically if a traditional paper trail is absent

BACKGROUND

Henrico Retail, Inc., is a first-year audit client. The audit partner obtained this background information about the sales system after recently meeting with client personnel at the corporate office.

Sales System Background Information

Henrico's sales system is computer-based with computerized cash registers on the floors of all of its stores. At the point of sale, Henrico's sales personnel enter product number, quantity per product, and indication of whether it is a cash sale or credit sale. Additionally for credit sales, the sales personnel must enter customer credit card number and credit approval number obtained directly from the credit card agency approving the credit sale. Henrico only

This case was prepared by Frank A. Buckless, Ph.D. and Mark S. Beasley, Ph.D. of North Carolina State University and Steven M. Glover, Ph.D. and Douglas F. Prawitt, Ph.D. of Brigham Young University, as a basis for class discussion. It is not intended to illustrate either effective or ineffective handling of an administrative situation.

accepts VISA or MasterCard credit cards and a copy of the credit charge slip is maintained in the cash drawer. The computerized cash register performs the following:

- Identifies correct price based on product number
- Notifies clerk if product number is invalid
- Calculates total price of purchase (price × quantity)
- Extends totals, calculates sales taxes, and determines final transaction amount
- Generates a customer receipt and a duplicate record of the transaction on a cash register tape that is locked inside the register. Cash register tapes indicate all inputted information. Only accounting department personnel have access to the tape.

Store clerks are allowed to operate any machine on the floor. If a cash register is not currently being used, all the clerk has to do is turn the machine on, and once the system is booted, the clerk begins by entering the product number. Generally, operation of the cash register is self-explanatory although some problems have occurred previously. Henrico has no formal training for cash register operation because management believes "on the job experience" is more effective.

At the end of each day, sales personnel count the cash in the drawer and list the total cash count on the Daily Deposit Sheet (a preprinted blank form). In addition, the sales personnel summarize total credit sales on the Daily Deposit Sheet by listing total amounts from the credit sales slips in the register. The sales personnel take the cash drawer, which includes credit slips, to the store cashier. The cashier verifies the Daily Deposit Sheet and initials the total cash and credit sales columns listed on the Daily Deposit Sheet. The cashier leaves $200 in each cash drawer to begin the following day. Cash drawers are stored overnight in the store's vault. The store cashier takes the cash plus credit charge slips to the bank at the end of each day. The bank immediately credits the store's cash account for all cash and credit card receipts presented. An independent person in accounting verifies that the sum of the cash and credit card slip totals on all Daily Deposit Sheets for the prior day reconcile to the validated deposit slip. After performing the reconciliation, the accounting clerk attaches the Daily Deposit Sheets to the validated deposit slip and files them together by date.

Accounting personnel close out the machines each night. As a part of this procedure, the machine prints subtotals of cash and credit sales for the day at the end of the cash register tape. Accounting personnel remove the cash register tapes from the machines each night, and the tapes are stored in the accounting department.

Overnight, the computer system processes all transactions for each cash register and summarizes this information on a Daily Sales Report. The Daily Sales Report is generated for each store nightly. It summarizes total store sales, as well as subtotals of cash and credit sales, by store cash register. These reports are filed by date at each store. In addition, the computer updates perpetual inventory records daily, which are stored on magnetic disk. No reports of this interface are generated daily by the computer.

At month's end, the computer generates a detailed Inventory Listing, which provides quantity information by product number. Also, the computer generates a Monthly Sales Report for each store. This report shows daily sales totals for the store for each day of the month. The computer also prepares and prints a consolidated General Ledger, which summarizes the postings of monthly sales totals from each store to the consolidated sales account.

REQUIREMENTS

You are the audit senior assigned to the audit of Henrico Retail, Inc. The audit partner recently asked you to assist in planning the audit of the sales system based on your review of the client-prepared sales system narrative. The partner has asked you to address the following issues:

1. Describe the audit trail from the point of sale to the general ledger posting of the consolidated sales and cash accounts. Be sure to emphasize whether the audit trail is in paper or electronic form.
2. Develop a proposed strategy for auditing the **existence** of sales. Is there a sufficient paper audit trail to be able to audit that assertion without relying on IT audit specialists?
3. What source would you use to select a sample of sales transactions to test the **existence** of sales at one store? Why this source? What evidence would you examine?
4. Develop a proposed strategy for auditing the **valuation** of the sales account. Is there a sufficient paper trail to be able to audit that assertion without relying on IT audit specialists?
5. What portion, if any, of the sales system will likely require the assistance of an IT systems auditor, who evaluates evidence existing only in electronic form?
6. What control weaknesses can you identify in the existing sales system?

Southeast Shoe Distributor, Inc.: Identification of Tests of Controls for the Revenue Cycle (Sales and Cash Receipts)

Frank A. Buckless, Mark S. Beasley,
Steven M. Glover, and Douglas F. Prawitt

LEARNING OBJECTIVES

After completing and discussing this assignment you should be able to

- Recognize common documents and records used to record transactions in the revenue cycle
- Recognize common control activities used to process transactions in the revenue cycle
- Identify client control activities that reduce the likelihood of material misstatements
- Link client control activities to management assertions
- Identify tests of controls for each control activity identified

INTRODUCTION

Southeast Shoe Distributor (SSD) is a closely-owned business that was founded 10 years ago by Stewart Green and Paul Williams. SSD is a distributor that purchases and sells men's, women's, and children's shoes to retail shoe stores located in small to midsize communities. The company's basic strategy is to obtain a broad selection of designer-label and name-brand merchandise at low prices and resell the merchandise to small, one-location, retail stores that have difficulty obtaining reasonable quantities of designer and name-brand merchandise. The company is able to keep the cost of merchandise low by (1) selectively purchasing large blocks of production overruns, overorders, mid- and late-season deliveries, and previous season's stock from manufacturers and other retailers at significant discounts, (2) sourcing in-season name-brand and branded designer merchandise directly from factories in Brazil, Italy, and Spain, and (3) negotiating favorable prices with manufacturers by ordering merchandise during off-peak production periods and taking delivery at one central warehouse.

During the year, the company purchased merchandise from more than 50 domestic and international vendors, independent resellers, manufacturers, and other retailers that frequently have excess inventory. Designer and name-brand footwear sold by the company during the year include the following: Amalfi, Clarks, Dexter, Fila, Florsheim, Naturalizer, and Rockport. At the current time, SSD has one warehouse located in Atlanta, Georgia. Last year, SSD had 123 retail shoe store customers and had net sales of $7,311,214. Sales are strongest in the second and fourth calendar-year quarters, with the first calendar-year quarter substantially weaker than the rest.

BACKGROUND INFORMATION ABOUT THE AUDIT

SSD is required to have an audit of its annual financial statements to fulfill requirements of loan agreements with financial institutions. The general ledger accounts SSD has related to sales and cash collection activities are

- Sales
- Sales Discounts
- Sales Returns and Allowances
- Uncollectible Account Expense
- Accounts Receivable
- Allowance for Uncollectible Accounts

In accordance with professional standards, Susan Mansfield, audit manager, reviewed SSD's control environment, risk assessment policies, and monitoring system and has assessed them as strong. Bill Zander, staff auditor, reviewed SSD's information system and control activities related to sales and cash receipts and prepared the enclosed flowcharts (referenced in the top right-hand corner as *R 30–1, R 30–2, R 30–3,* and *R 30–4*). The number and size of sales returns and allowances and write-offs of specific customer accounts is relatively small. Thus Susan has decided there is no need to document the company's policies nor perform tests of controls for these two business activities. As the audit senior, you have been assigned responsibility for (1) identifying internal control activities that assure that sales and cash receipt transactions are not materially misstated and (2) identifying tests of controls that would test the design and operating effectiveness of internal control activities identified.

REQUIREMENTS

Complete steps 5 through 7 in the Revenue Cycle Planning Audit Program—Identification of Tests of Controls (working paper *R 1–1*) and document your work in working papers *R 1–1, R 31, R 32, R 33, R 40–1,* and *R 40–2*. Bill Zander completed steps 1 through 4 and has documented the results of his work in working papers *R1–1, R 30–1, R 30–2, R 30–3,* and *R 30–4* (Note: you should assume that only control activities identified in the flowcharts exist). Audit steps 5, 6, and 7 can be completed separately. Your instructor will indicate which steps you are to complete.

Reference: _R 1–1_____
Prepared by: _BZ_____
Date: ___6/12/0X_____
Reviewed by: _____

Southeast Shoe Distributor, Inc.
Revenue Cycle Planning Audit Program—Identification of Tests of Controls
Year Ended: December 31, 200X

Audit Procedures	Initial	Date	W/P Ref.
1. Obtain and study a copy of the client's policies and procedures manuals related to sales and cash receipts.	BZ	6/12/0X	N/A
2. Discuss with and observe client personnel performing control activities related to sales and cash receipts.	BZ	6/12/0X	N/A
3. Perform a document walk-through of the client's policies and procedures related to sales and cash receipts.	BZ	6/12/0X	N/A
4. Obtain or prepare a flowchart for sales and cash receipts showing control activities, document flows, and records.	BZ	6/12/0X	R30–1 to R30–4
5. Use the control activities matrix to identify client control activities that reduce the likelihood of material misstatements for management assertions related to sales and cash receipts.			R31 R32
6. Use the planning audit test matrices to identify potential tests of controls.			R40–1 R40–2
7. Based on the previous procedures, identify internal control deficiencies that may need to be reported to the client on the internal control deficiencies schedule.			R33

Reference: _R 30–1_
Prepared by: _BZ_
Date: _6/12/0X_
Reviewed by: _____

Southeast Shoe Distributor, Inc.
Revenue Cycle—Sales Flowchart
For the Year Ended December 31, 200X

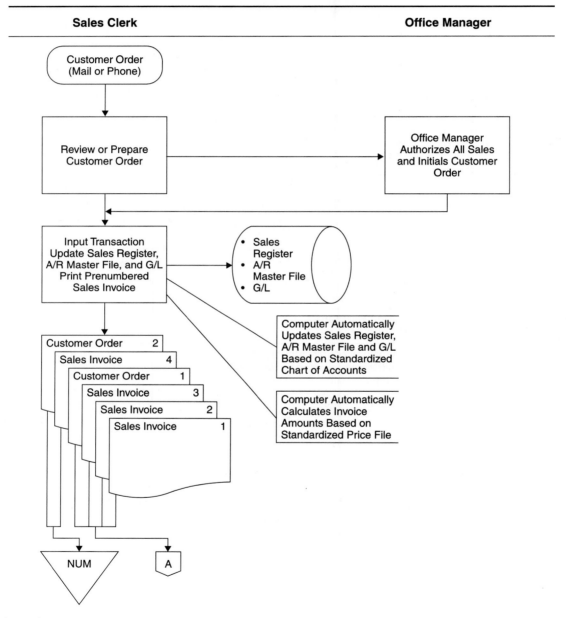

Legend:
  NUM - filed numerically by Sales Invoice number
  A - off-page connecter

Reference: _R 30–2_
Prepared by: _BZ_
Date: _6/12/0X_
Reviewed by: _____

Southeast Shoe Distributor, Inc.
Revenue Cycle—Sales Flowchart
For the Year Ended December 31, 200X

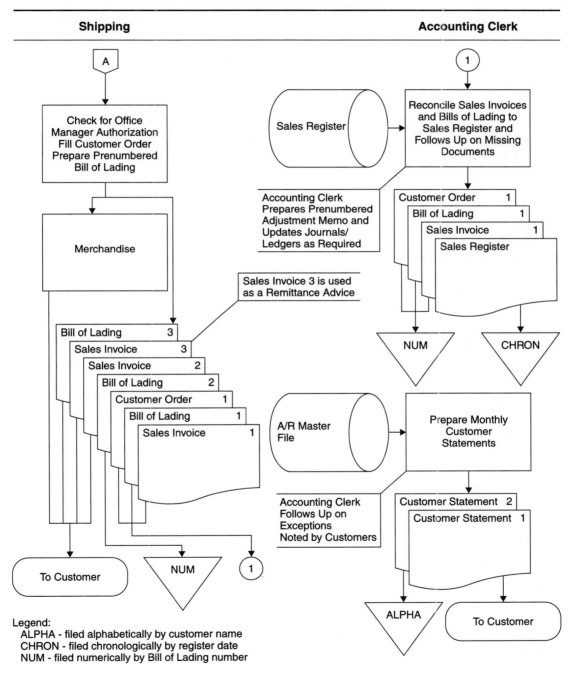

Legend:
ALPHA - filed alphabetically by customer name
CHRON - filed chronologically by register date
NUM - filed numerically by Bill of Lading number

Reference: _R 30–3_
Prepared by: _BZ_
Date: _6/12/0X_
Reviewed by: _____

Southeast Shoe Distributor, Inc.
Revenue Cycle—Cash Receipts Flowchart
For the Year Ended December 31, 200X

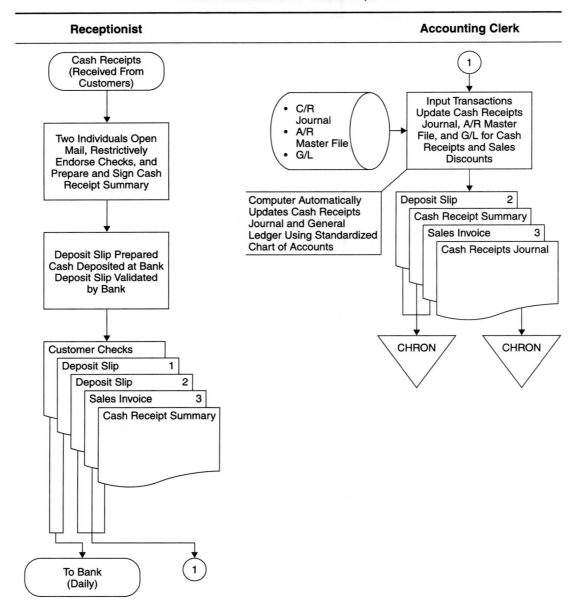

Legend:
CHRON - filed chronologically by summary/journal date

Reference: _R 30–4_
Prepared by: _BZ_
Date: _6/12/0X_
Reviewed by: _____

**Southeast Shoe Distributor, Inc.
Revenue Cycle—Cash Receipts Flowchart
For the Year Ended December 31, 200X**

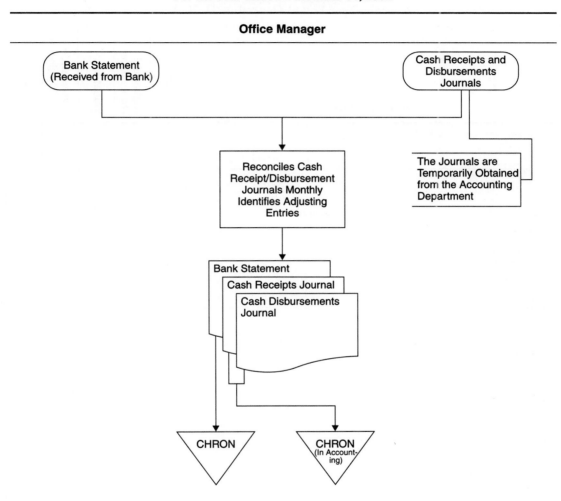

Office Manager

Legend:
  CHRON - filed chronologically by statement/journal date

Reference: _R 31_

Prepared by: _____

Date: _____

Reviewed by: _____

Southeast Shoe Distributor, Inc.
Revenue Cycle—Sales Control Activities Matrix
For the Year Ended December 31, 200X

Control Activities	Existence	Rights and Obligations	Valuation	Presentation and Disclosure	Completeness
1) *All sales are approved by the office manager.*	X		X		
Identify the management assertion(s) each control activity affects with an "X."					

Reference: _____R 32_____
Prepared by: _____
Date: _____
Reviewed by: _____

Southeast Shoe Distributor, Inc.
Revenue Cycle—Cash Receipts Control Activities Matrix
For the Year Ended December 31, 200X

Control Activities	Existence	Rights and Obligations	Valuation	Presentation and Disclosure	Completeness
Identify the management assertion(s) each control activity affects with an "X."					

Reference: ____R 33____
Prepared by:_____
Date: _____
Reviewed by: _____

Southeast Shoe Distributor, Inc.
Revenue Cycle—Internal Control Deficiencies
For the Year Ended December 31, 200X

Internal Control Deficiencies	Client Personnel Discussed With	RC	MW
1) *The client does not internally verify the proper general ledger account classification for sales and cash-receipt transactions.*		*No*	*No*

Legend:
RC—Reportable Condition (Yes or No)
MW—Material Weakness (Yes or No)

Southeast Shoe Distributor, Inc.
Revenue Cycle—Tests of Controls Planning Matrix
For the Year Ended December 31, 200X

Reference: ___R 40-1___
Prepared by: _____
Date: _____
Reviewed by: _____

Tests of Controls	Sales					Cash Receipts					Accounts Receivable				
	Existence	Rights /Obligations	Valuation	Presentation /Disclosure	Completeness	Existence	Rights/Obligations	Valuation	Presentation /Disclosure	Completeness	Existence	Rights/Obligations	Valuation	Presentation/Disclosure	Completeness
TC1) Inquire and observe the office manager authorizing sales.	W										W		W		

Indicate whether the test provides Strong (S), Moderate (M), or Weak (W) evidence for the specific management assertion.

Southeast Shoe Distributor, Inc.
Revenue Cycle—Tests of Controls Planning Matrix
For the Year Ended December 31, 200X

Reference: _R 40-2_
Prepared by: _____
Date: _____
Reviewed by: _____

Tests of Controls	Sales					Cash Receipts					Accounts Receivable				
	Existence	Rights/Obligations	Valuation	Presentation /Disclosure	Completeness	Existence	Rights/Obligations	Valuation	Presentation /Disclosure	Completeness	Existence	Rights/Obligations	Valuation	Presentation /Disclosure	Completeness

Indicate whether the test provides Strong (S), Moderate (M), or Weak (W) evidence for the specific management assertion.

Southeast Shoe Distributor, Inc.: Identification of Substantive Tests for the Revenue Cycle (Sales and Cash Receipts)

Frank A. Buckless, Mark S. Beasley,
Steven M. Glover, and Douglas F. Prawitt

LEARNING OBJECTIVES

After completing and discussing this assignment you should be able to

- Recognize common documents and records used in the revenue cycle
- Identify analytical tests to detect material misstatements
- Identify substantive tests of transactions to detect material misstatements
- Identify substantive tests of balances to detect material misstatements
- Link audit tests to management assertions

INTRODUCTION

Southeast Shoe Distributor (SSD) is a closely-owned business that was founded 10 years ago by Stewart Green and Paul Williams. SSD is a distributor that purchases and sells men's, women's, and children's shoes to retail shoe stores located in small- to mid-size communities. The company's basic strategy is to obtain a broad selection of designer-label and name-brand merchandise at low prices and resell the merchandise to small, one-location, retail stores that have difficulty obtaining reasonable quantities of designer and name-brand merchandise. The company is able to keep the cost of merchandise low by (1) selectively purchasing large blocks of production overruns, overorders, mid- and late-season deliveries, and previous season's stock from manufacturers and other retailers at significant discounts, (2) sourcing in-season name-brand and branded designer merchandise directly from factories in Brazil, Italy, and Spain, and (3) negotiating favorable prices with manufacturers by ordering merchandise during off-peak production periods and taking delivery at one central warehouse.

This case was prepared by Frank A. Buckless, Ph.D. and Mark S. Beasley, Ph.D. of North Carolina State University and Steven M. Glover, Ph.D. and Douglas F. Prawitt, Ph.D. of Brigham Young University, as a basis for class discussion. It is not intended to illustrate either effective or ineffective handling of an administrative situation.
Copyright © 2000 by Prentice-Hall, Inc. ISBN 0-13-016946-3.

During the year, the company purchased merchandise from more than 50 domestic and international vendors, independent resellers, manufacturers, and other retailers that frequently have excess inventory. Designer and name-brand footwear sold by the company during the year include the following: Amalfi, Clarks, Dexter, Fila, Florsheim, Naturalizer, and Rockport. At the current time, SSD has one warehouse located in Atlanta, Georgia. Last year, SSD had 123 retail shoe store customers and had net sales of $7,311,214. Sales are strongest in the second and fourth calendar-year quarters, with the first calendar-year quarter substantially weaker than the rest.

BACKGROUND INFORMATION ABOUT THE AUDIT

SSD is required to have an audit of its annual financial statements to fulfill requirements of loan agreements with financial institutions. The general ledger accounts SSD has related to sales and cash collection activities are

- Sales
- Sales Discounts
- Sales Returns and Allowances
- Uncollectible Account Expense
- Accounts Receivable
- Allowance for Uncollectible Accounts

Bill Zander, staff auditor, reviewed SSD's information system and control activities related to sales and cash receipts and prepared the enclosed flowcharts (referenced in the top right-hand corner as R 30–1, R 30–2, R 30–3, and R 30–4). The number and size of sales returns and uncollectible accounts is relatively small. Thus Susan Mansfield, audit partner, decided not to have Bill document the company's policies and procedures related to sales returns and allowances and uncollectible accounts.

As the audit senior, you have been assigned responsibility for identifying substantive tests of transactions to detect material misstatements related revenue cycle accounts. You have conducted some preliminary discussions with client personnel and noted the following:

- Sales returns and allowances transactions are recorded in the sales register.
- Sales discounts are recorded in the cash receipts journal.
- The estimation and write-off of uncollectible accounts are recorded in the general journal and require preparation of a prenumbered adjustment memo.
- Misstatements to sales, cash receipts, and accounts receivable are recorded in the general journal and require preparation of a prenumbered adjustment memo.

REQUIREMENTS

Complete audit steps 1–3 in the Revenue Cycle Planning Audit Program—Identification of Substantive Tests (working paper R 1–2) and document your work in working papers R 1–2, R 41–1, R 41–2, R 42–1, R 42–2, R 43–1, and R 43–2. Audit steps 3a, 3b, and 3c can be completed separately. Your instructor will indicate which steps you are to complete.

Reference: _____R 1–2_____
Prepared by: _____
Date: _____
Reviewed by: _____

Southeast Shoe Distributor, Inc.
Revenue Cycle Planning Audit Program—Identification of Substantive Tests
Year Ended: December 31, 200X

Audit Procedures	Initial	Date	W/P Ref.
1. Obtain an understanding of the documents and records used for sales and cash receipts transactions by reviewing the flowcharts documenting our understanding.			R 30–1 to R 30–4
2. Obtain an understanding of the documents and records used for recording adjustments to sales, cash receipts, and accounts receivable by discussing with client personnel.			N/A
3. Use the planning audit test matrices to identify potential a. substantive tests of transactions, b. tests of balances, c. and analytical tests that can be performed related to revenue cycle accounts.			R 41–1 R 41–2 R 42–1 R 42–2 R 43–1 R 43–2

Reference: _R 30–1_
Prepared by: _BZ_
Date: _6/12/0X_
Reviewed by: _____

Southeast Shoe Distributor, Inc.
Revenue Cycle—Sales Flowchart
For the Year Ended December 31, 200X

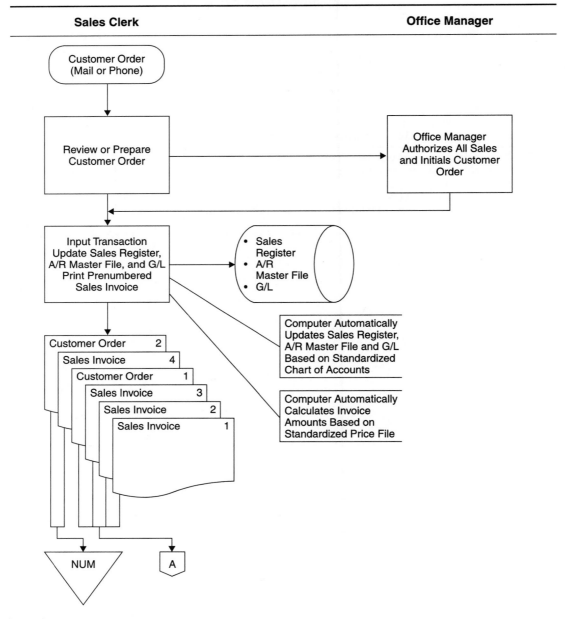

Legend:
NUM - filed numerically by Sales Invoice number
A - off-page connecter

Reference: _R 30–2_
Prepared by: _BZ_
Date: _6/12/0X_
Reviewed by: _____

**Southeast Shoe Distributor, Inc.
Revenue Cycle—Sales Flowchart
For the Year Ended December 31, 200X**

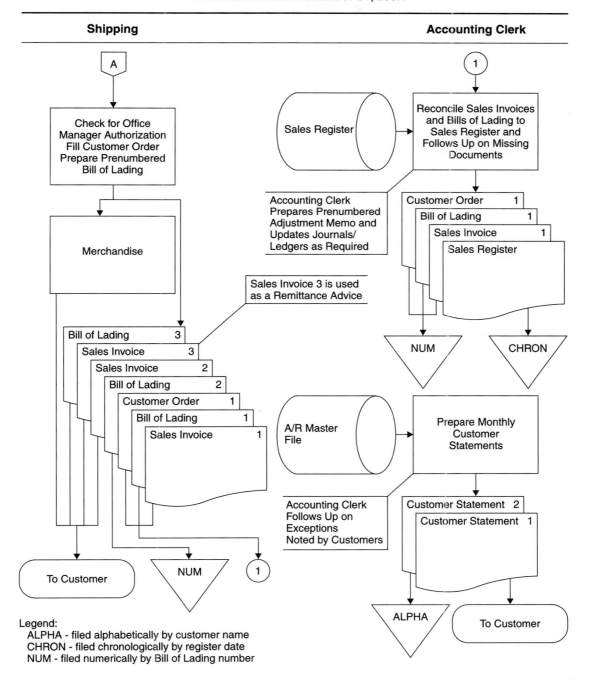

Legend:
 ALPHA - filed alphabetically by customer name
 CHRON - filed chronologically by register date
 NUM - filed numerically by Bill of Lading number

Reference: _R 30–3_
Prepared by: _BZ_
Date: _6/12/0X_
Reviewed by: _____

Southeast Shoe Distributor, Inc.
Revenue Cycle—Cash Receipts Flowchart
For the Year Ended December 31, 200X

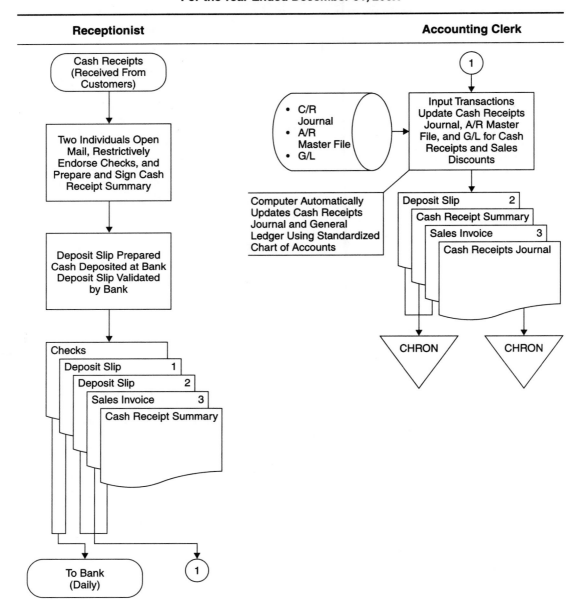

Legend:
CHRON - filed chronologically by summary/journal date

Reference: _R 30–4_
Prepared by: _BZ_
Date: _6/12/0X_
Reviewed by: _____

Southeast Shoe Distributor, Inc.
Revenue Cycle—Cash Receipts Flowchart
For the Year Ended December 31, 200X

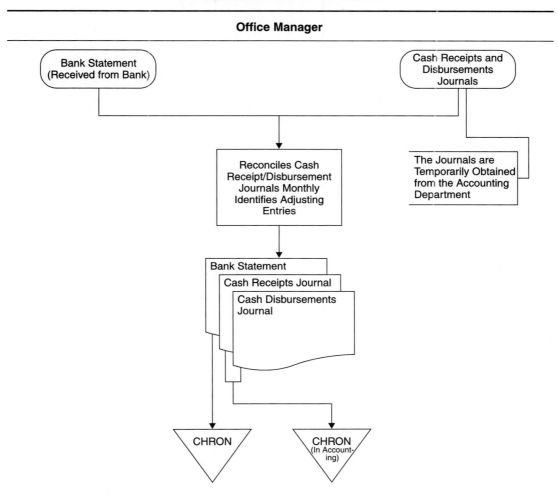

Office Manager

Legend:
 CHRON - filed chronologically by statement/journal date

Southeast Shoe Distributor, Inc.
Revenue Cycle—Subtantive Tests of Transactions Planning Matrix
For the Year Ended December 31, 200X

Reference: _R 41-1_
Prepared by: _____
Date: _____
Reviewed by: _____

Subtantive Tests of Transactions	Sales					Cash Receipts					Accounts Receivable				
	Existence	Rights/Obligations	Valuation	Presentation/Disclosure	Completeness	Existence	Rights/Obligations	Valuation	Presentation/Disclosure	Completeness	Existence	Rights/Obligations	Valuation	Presentation/Disclosure	Completeness
TC1) Vouch sales transactions recorded in the sales register to supporting documents	M		M	M							M		M	M	

Indicate whether the test provides Strong (S), Moderate (M), or Weak (W) evidence for the specific management assertion.

Reference: _R 41-2_
Prepared by: _____
Date: _____
Reviewed by: _____

Subtantive Tests of Transactions	Sales					Cash Receipts					Accounts Receivable				
	Existence	Rights/Obligations	Valuation	Presentation/Disclosure	Completeness	Existence	Rights/Obligations	Valuation	Presentation/Disclosure	Completeness	Existence	Rights/Obligations	Valuation	Presentation/Disclosure	Completeness

Indicate whether the test provides Strong (S), Moderate (M), or Weak (W) evidence for the specific management assertion.

Southeast Shoe Distributor, Inc.
Revenue Cycle—Analytical Tests Planning Matrix
For the Year Ended December 31, 200X

Analytical Tests	Sales					Cash Receipts					Accounts Receivable				
	Existence	Rights/Obligations	Valuation	Presentation/Disclosure	Completeness	Existence	Rights/Obligations	Valuation	Presentation/Disclosure	Completeness	Existence	Rights/Obligations	Valuation	Presentation/Disclosure	Completeness
AT1) Scan the sales journal for large unusual, or related-party transactions.	M		M	M							M		M	M	

Indicate whether the test provides Strong (S), Moderate (M), or Weak (W) evidence for the specific management assertion.

Southeast Shoe Distributor, Inc.
Revenue Cycle—Analytical Tests Planning Matrix
For the Year Ended December 31, 200X

Reference: _R 42-2_
Prepared by: _____
Date: _____
Reviewed by: _____

Analytical Tests	Sales					Cash Receipts					Accounts Receivable				
	Existence	Rights/Obligations	Valuation	Presentation/Disclosure	Completeness	Existence	Rights/Obligations	Valuation	Presentation/Disclosure	Completeness	Existence	Rights/Obligations	Valuation	Presentation/Disclosure	Completeness

Indicate whether the test provides Strong (S), Moderate (M), or Weak (W) evidence for the specific management assertion.

Southeast Shoe Distributor, Inc.
Revenue Cycle—Tests of Balances Planning Matrix
For the Year Ended December 31, 200X

Reference: ___R 43-1___
Prepared by: _____
Date: _____
Reviewed by: _____

Tests of Balances	Sales					Cash Receipts					Accounts Receivable				
	Existence	Rights/Obligations	Valuation	Presentation/Disclosure	Completeness	Existence	Rights/Obligations	Valuation	Presentation/Disclosure	Completeness	Existence	Rights/Obligations	Valuation	Presentation/Disclosure	Completeness
TB1) Confirm accounts receivable using positive confirmations	S		M					M		S	S	W	M		

Indicate whether the test provides Strong (S), Moderate (M), or Weak (W) evidence for the specific management assertion.

Southeast Shoe Distributor, Inc.
Revenue Cycle—Tests of Balances Planning Matrix
For the Year Ended December 31, 200X

Reference: _R 43-2_
Prepared by: _____
Date: _____
Reviewed by: _____

Tests of Balances	Sales					Cash Receipts					Accounts Receivable				
	Existence	Rights/Obligations	Valuation	Presentation/Disclosure	Completeness	Existence	Rights/Obligations	Valuation	Presentation/Disclosure	Completeness	Existence	Rights/Obligations	Valuation	Presentation/Disclosure	Completeness

Indicate whether the test provides Strong (S), Moderate (M), or Weak (W) evidence for the specific management assertion.

Southeast Shoe Distributor, Inc.: Selection of Audit Tests and Risk Assessment for the Revenue Cycle (Sales and Cash Receipts)

Frank A. Buckless, Mark S. Beasley,
Steven M. Glover, and Douglas F. Prawitt

LEARNING OBJECTIVES

After completing and discussing this assignment you should be able to

- Design an overall audit strategy for the revenue cycle (i.e., select tests of controls, substantive tests of transactions, analytical tests, and tests of balances to be performed)
- Assess planned control risk for the revenue cycle based on the tests of controls selected
- Assess planned detection risk for the revenue cycle based on the substantive tests selected

INTRODUCTION

Southeast Shoe Distributor (SSD) is a closely-owned business that was founded 10 years ago by Stewart Green and Paul Williams. SSD is a distributor that purchases and sells men's, women's, and children's shoes to retail shoe stores located in small- to mid-size communities. The company's basic strategy is to obtain a broad selection of designer-label and name-brand merchandise at low prices and resell the merchandise to small, one-location, retail stores that have difficulty obtaining reasonable quantities of designer and name-brand merchandise. The company is able to keep the cost of merchandise low by (1) selectively purchasing large blocks of production overruns, overorders, mid- and late-season deliveries, and previous season's stock from manufacturers and other retailers at significant discounts, (2) sourcing in-season name-brand

This case was prepared by Frank A. Buckless, Ph.D. and Mark S. Beasley, Ph.D. of North Carolina State University and Steven M. Glover, Ph.D. and Douglas F. Prawitt, Ph.D. of Brigham Young University, as a basis for class discussion. It is not intended to illustrate either effective or ineffective handling of an administrative situation.

and branded designer merchandise directly from factories in Brazil, Italy, and Spain, and (3) negotiating favorable prices with manufacturers by ordering merchandise during off-peak production periods and taking delivery at one central warehouse.

During the year, the company purchased merchandise from more than 50 domestic and international vendors, independent resellers, manufacturers, and other retailers that frequently had excess inventory. Designer and name-brand footwear sold by the company during the year include the following: Amalfi, Clarks, Dexter, Fila, Florsheim, Naturalizer, and Rockport. At the current time, SSD has one warehouse located in Atlanta, Georgia. Last year, SSD had 123 retail shoe store customers and had net sales of $7,311,214. Sales are strongest in the second and fourth calendar-year quarters, with the first calendar-year quarter substantially weaker than the rest.

BACKGROUND INFORMATION ABOUT THE AUDIT

SSD is required to have an audit of its annual financial statements to fulfill requirements of loan agreements with financial institutions. The general ledger accounts SSD has related to sales and cash collection activities are

- Sales
- Sales Discounts
- Sales Returns and Allowances
- Uncollectible Account Expense
- Accounts Receivable
- Allowance for Uncollectible Accounts

In accordance with professional standards, Susan Mansfield, audit manager, reviewed SSD's control environment, risk assessment policies, and monitoring system and has assessed them as strong. Additionally, Susan determined that tolerable misstatement should be $40,000 for the revenue cycle and that acceptable audit risk should be low. Bill Zander, staff auditor, assessed inherent risk related to sales, cash receipts, and accounts receivable and prepared the enclosed audit risk matrix (referenced in the top right-hand corner as *R 50* and *R 50–1*). As the audit senior, you have been assigned responsibility for selecting audit procedures to perform for the revenue cycle that will achieve the desired acceptable audit risk at the lowest possible cost.

REQUIREMENTS

This case assignment cannot be completed until the previous two audit-planning case assignments related to SSD are completed. Complete audit steps 3 and 4 in the Revenue Cycle Planning Audit Program—Risk Assessment and Selection of Audit Tests (working paper *R 1–3*) and document your work in working papers *R 1–3, R 40–1, R 40–2, R 41–1, R 41–2, R 42–1, R 42–2, R 43–1, R 43–1, R 50, R 50–2,* and *R 50–3*. Bill Zander completed audit steps 1 and 2 and has documented the results of his work in the working papers *R 1–3, R 50,* and *R 50–1*.

Reference: _R 1–3_____

Prepared by: _BZ_____

Date: ___6/12/0X_____

Reviewed by: _____

Southeast Shoe Distributor, Inc.
Revenue Cycle Planning Audit Program—Risk Assessment and Selection of Audit Tests
Year Ended: December 31, 200X

Audit Procedures	Initial	Date	W/P Ref
1. Complete the acceptable audit risk section of the revenue cycle planning audit risk matrix by obtaining the acceptable audit risk from the general planning working papers.	BZ	6/12/0X	R 50
2. Form an initial assessment of inherent risk related to revenue cycle accounts and complete the initial inherent-risk assessment section of the planning audit risk matrix.	BZ	6/12/0X	R 50 R 50–1
3. Select audit tests to perform by circling the procedure number on the audit tests planning matrices.			R 40–1 R 40–2 R 41–1 R 41–2 R 42–1 R 42–2 R 43–1 R 43–2
4. Based on the procedures selected in audit step 3, complete the planned control risk and detection risk sections of the revenue cycle planning audit risk matrix.			R 50 R 50–2 R 50–3

Southeast Shoe Distributor, Inc.
Revenue Cycle—Planning Audit Risk Matrix
For the Year Ended December 31, 200X

Tolerable Misstatement: $40,000, G6	Reference	Existence*	Rights and Obligations	Valuation	Presentation and Disclosure	Completeness**
Acceptable Audit Risk	G5	L	L	L	L	L
Initial Inherent Risk—Sales		M		M	L	H
Initial Inherent Risk—Cash Receipts		H		H	L	H
Initial Inherent Risk—Accounts Receivable		M	L	M	L	L
Planned Control Risk—Sales						
Planned Control Risk—Cash Receipts						
Planned Detection Risk—Sales						
Planned Detection Risk—Cash Receipts						
Planned Detection Risk—Accounts Receivable						

Initial Inherent Risk should be assessed as:

High (H) unless the combination of inherent risk factors present justify a lower assessment.
Medium (M) if the combination of inherent risk factors present justify this assessment.
Low (L) if the combination of inherent risk factors present justify this assessment.
Factors justifying a lower inherent risk assessment are:
High management integrity, Low motivation to materially misstate for external parties, Repeat engagement, No material prior-year misstatements, No related-party transactions, Routine transactions, Limited judgment required to correctly record transactions, Low susceptibility to defalcation, Stable business environment.

Planned Control Risk should be assessed as:

Low (L) if control activity(ies) reduces the likelihood of a material misstatement to a negligible level and persuasive tests of controls are planned to be performed.
Medium (M) if control activity(ies) reduces the likelihood of a material misstatement to a negligible level and moderately persuasive tests of controls are planned or control activity(ies) reduces the likelihood of a material misstatement to a moderate level and persuasive tests of controls are planned.
High (H) if control activity(ies) does not reduce the likelihood of a material misstatement to a reasonable level or no tests of controls are planned.

Planned Detection Risk should be assessed at:

Low (L) if persuasive substantive tests are planned to be performed.
Medium (M) if moderately persuasive substantive tests are planned to be performed.
High (H) if minimal substantive tests are planned to be performed.

Note: *completeness for cash receipts,
**existence for cash receipts

Reference: _R 50–1_____
Prepared by: _BZ_____
Date: __6/12/0X_____
Reviewed by: _____

Southeast Shoe Distributor
Revenue Cycle—Comments Initial Inherent Risk Assessment
For the Year Ended December 31, 200X

Comments:

The inherent risk assessment for the existence, valuation, and completeness assertions for cash receipt transactions and completeness assertion for sales transactions is set at a high level because of the susceptibility of cash to theft.

The inherent risk assessment for the existence of sales transactions is set at a medium level even though no misstatements were discovered in previous years because of the external incentives for management and employees to inflate sales.

The inherent risk assessment for the valuation assertion is set at a medium level even though no misstatements were discovered in previous years because of the large number of products and price points offered.

The inherent risk assessment for the presentation and disclosure assertion for sales transactions is set at a low level because no misstatements were discovered in prior years and few nontrade sales occur during any year.

The inherent risk assessment for the presentation and disclosure assertion for cash receipts is set at a low level because no misstatements occurred in previous years and few nontrade receivable cash receipts are received during any year.

The inherent risk assessment for the completeness, rights and obligations, presentation, and disclosure assertions for accounts receivable is set at a low level because of the lack of external incentives and misstatements in prior years.

The inherent risk assessment for the valuation assertion for accounts receivable is set at a medium level even though no misstatements were observed in prior years because of the subjectivity of estimating uncollectible accounts and the large number of products and price points offered.

The inherent risk assessment for the existence of accounts receivable is set at a medium level even though no misstatements were discovered in prior years because of the management and employee external incentives to inflate accounts receivable.

Reference: <u>R 50–2</u>
Prepared by: <u>BZ</u>
Date: <u>6/12/0X</u>
Reviewed by: _____

Southeast Shoe Distributor
Revenue Cycle—Comments Planned Control Risk Assessment
For the Year Ended December 31, 200X

Comments:

Reference: _R 50–3_____

Prepared by: _BZ_____

Date: __6/12/0X_____

Reviewed by: _____

Southeast Shoe Distributor
Revenue Cycle—Comments Planned Control Risk Assessment
For the Year Ended December 31, 200X

Comments:

Southeast Shoe Distributor, Inc.: Performance of Tests of Transactions for the Expenditure Cycle (Acquisitions and Cash Disbursements)

Frank A. Buckless, Mark S. Beasley,
Steven M. Glover, and Douglas F. Prawitt

LEARNING OBJECTIVES

After completing and discussing this case you should be able to

- Recognize common documents and records used to record purchase and cash disbursement transactions
- Recognize common control activities used to process purchase and cash disbursement transactions
- Recognize potential tests of controls and substantive tests of transactions for auditing purchase and cash disbursement transactions
- Perform tests of controls and substantive tests of transactions for purchase and cash disbursement transactions
- Evaluate the results of tests of controls and substantive tests of transactions for purchase and cash disbursement transactions using a nonstatistical approach
- Recognize the linkage between control activities, tests of controls, and management assertions
- Recognize the linkage between substantive tests of transactions and management assertions

INTRODUCTION

Southeast Shoe Distributor (SSD) is a closely-owned business founded 10 years ago by Stewart Green and Paul Williams. SSD is a distributor that purchases and resells men's,

This case was prepared by Frank A. Buckless, Ph.D. and Mark S. Beasley, Ph.D. of North Carolina State University and Steven M. Glover, Ph.D. and Douglas F. Prawitt, Ph.D. of Brigham Young University, as a basis for class discussion. It is not intended to illustrate either effective or ineffective handling of an administrative situation.

women's, and children's shoes to retail shoe stores located in small- to midsize communities. The company's basic strategy is to obtain a broad selection of designer-label and name-brand footwear at low prices to resell to small, one-location, retail stores. SSD targets stores that have a difficult time obtaining reasonable quantities of designer and name-brand footwear. The company is able to keep the cost of footwear low by (1) selectively purchasing large blocks of production overruns, overorders, mid- and late-season deliveries, and previous season's stock from manufacturers and other retailers at significant discounts, (2) sourcing in-season name-brand and branded designer footwear directly from factories in Brazil, Italy, and Spain, and (3) negotiating favorable prices with manufacturers by ordering footwear during off-peak production periods and taking delivery at one central warehouse.

During the year, the company purchased merchandise from more than 50 domestic and international vendors, independent resellers, manufacturers, and other retailers that have frequent excess inventory. Designer and name-brand footwear sold by the company include the following: Amalfi, Clarks, Dexter, Fila, Florsheim, Naturalizer, and Rockport. At the current time, SSD has one warehouse located in Atlanta, Georgia. Last year, SSD had net sales of $7,311,214. Sales are strongest in the second and fourth-calendar-year quarters, with the first calendar-year quarter substantially weaker than the rest.

BACKGROUND INFORMATION ABOUT THE AUDIT

SSD is required to have an audit of its annual financial statements to fulfill requirements of loan agreements with financial institutions. Jorge Hernandez, audit senior, reviewed SSD policies and procedures related to acquisitions and cash disbursements and prepared the enclosed flowcharts (working papers referenced in the top right-hand corner as *E 20–1*, *E 20–2*, and *E 21*) and planned control risk matrix (working paper *E 22*). As a result of this process, Jorge developed the enclosed audit program (working papers *E 1–1*, *E 1–2*). The audit program was approved by Susan Mansfield, audit manager, and Katherine Smith, audit partner. The two staff auditors assigned to this engagement are Joy Avery and you. Together, you and Joy are responsible for performing the tests of transactions outlined in the expenditure cycle audit program (working papers *E 1–1* and *E 1–2*). The general ledger accounts related to purchasing and cash disbursement activities at SSD include the following:

- Inventory Purchases
- Purchase Discounts
- Purchase Returns and Allowances
- Freight In
- Administrative Expenses
- Warehousing Expenses
- Selling Expenses
- Prepaid Assets
- Accounts Payable

Joy Avery has already selected the audit samples for purchases and cash disbursements and completed audit procedures 2, 3, 5, 6, and 7. Joy's work is documented on working papers *E 1–1, E 1–2, E 30, E 32, E 33, E 34, E 40, E 41, E 42, E 43,* and *E 44.*

REQUIREMENTS

You have been assigned responsibility for completing audit steps 1a-h and 4a listed on audit program *E 1–1.* You will want to review the flowcharts on working papers *E 20–1* and *E 20–2* to become familiar with the documents and records used with purchases. Assume that you have already completed audit steps 1f, g, and h for all 40 sample items and no deviations or misstatements were found. Also assume you have tested 35 of the sample items selected for audit steps 1a-e and 35 of the sample items selected for audit step 4a. No deviations or misstatements were observed for these sample items. The documents and records related to the remaining five sample items for audit steps 1a-e and 4a are provided behind the audit working papers. Note that receiving reports are only generated for purchases of inventory and fixed assets and that purchase orders are not generated for recurring services, such as utilities and cleaning. The audit firm has a policy of using the same audit sample for planned tests of controls and substantive tests of transactions (dual-purpose test) whenever possible to maximize audit efficiency. Thus, the results of the test-of-controls aspect of audit steps 1a-e and 4a should be documented on working paper *E 31,* whereas the substantive test aspect should be documented on working paper *E 35.* Adjusting entries should be proposed on schedule *E 11* for any observed misstatements. You should assume that there was no systematic pattern or intent to commit a fraud based on a review and discussion with client personnel concerning observed deviations and misstatements. Finally, you may want to review the working papers already completed by Joy Avery to have an idea of how each is to be completed.

Reference: _E 1–1_____
Prepared by: _JA_____
Date: ___2/19/0Y_____
Reviewed by: _____

Southeast Shoe Distributor
Expenditure Cycle Audit Program for
Analytical Procedures and Tests of Transactions
Year Ended: December 31, 200X

Audit Procedures	Initial	Date	Ref.
1. Select a sample of 40 transactions recorded in the purchase journal throughout the year and perform the following:	JA	2/14/0Y	E 30
a. Determine if vendor invoices, purchase orders, and receiving reports were properly included in the voucher packages or the invoices were properly initialed by the executive secretary (Karen Tucci as "KT").			E 31
b. Examine vendor invoices, purchase orders, and receiving reports for authenticity and reasonableness.			E 31 E 35
c. Determine if the purchase orders were signed by the supervisor (Bruce Penny).			E 31
d. Determine if the voucher cover was initialed by the supervisor (Janet Sotiriadis as "JS").			E 31
e. Determine if the purchase journal amounts were correct based on the voucher package documents.			E 31 E 35
f. Determine if the vouchers had correct general ledger account codes.			E 31 E 35
g. Determine if the vouchers were posted to the correct general ledger accounts.			E 31 E 35
h. Determine if the vouchers were posted to the correct vendor's accounts payable subsidiary file.			E 31 E 35
2. Scan the purchase journal for large, unusual transactions and perform follow-up procedures for each one identified.	JA	2/15/0Y	E 32
3. Examine the weekly exception reports for receiving reports and determine if proper follow-up procedures were performed.	JA	2/15/0Y	E 33
_60, JA_			
4. Select a sample of ~~40~~ receiving reports issued during the current year and perform the following for each:	JA	2/14/0Y	E 34
a. Obtain the related purchase order and vendor invoice and determine if receiving report was properly accounted for in the purchase journal.			E 35

Reference: _E 1–2_____

Prepared by: _JA_____

Date: ___2/19/0Y_____

Reviewed by: _____

Southeast Shoe Distributor
Expenditure Cycle Audit Program
Year Ended: December 31, 200X

Audit Procedures	Initial	Date	Ref.
5. Scan the cash disbursement journal for related-party or large, unusual transactions and perform follow-up procedures for each one identified	JA	2/15/0Y	E 42
6. Select a sample of 40 transactions recorded in the cash disbursement journal throughout the year and perform the following:	JA	2/14/0Y	E 40
a. Determine if the voucher packages were properly stamped "paid."	JA	2/19/0Y	E 41
b. Examine cancelled checks for proper endorsement and reasonableness.	JA	2/19/0Y	E 41 E 44
c. Determine if cash disbursement journal amounts agree with the cancelled checks.	JA	2/19/0Y	E 41 E 44
d. Determine if disbursements were posted to the correct general ledger accounts.	JA	2/19/0Y	E 41 E 44
e. Determine if disbursements were posted to the correct vendor accounts payable subsidiary file.	JA	2/19/0Y	E 41 E 44
7. Obtain the bank reconciliations completed during the year and perform the following:	JA	2/16/0Y	E 43
a. Determine who prepared the bank reconciliations.	JA	2/16/0Y	E 43
b. Review the bank reconciliations for reasonableness.	JA	2/16/0Y	E 43
c. Reperform the bank reconciliation for one month.	JA	2/16/0Y	E 43

Reference: _E 11_

Prepared by: _____

Date: _____

Reviewed by: _____

Southeast Shoe Distributor
Expenditure Cycle—Proposed Adjusting Entry Schedule
For the Year Ended December 31, 200X

Account	Debit	Credit
Explanation:		
Explanation:		
Explanation:		
Explanation:		

Reference: _E 20–1_
Prepared by: _JH_
Date: _9/16/0X_
Reviewed by: _____

Southeast Shoe Distributor
Expenditure Cycle—Purchases Flowchart
For the Year Ended December 31, 200X

Buying/Purchasing

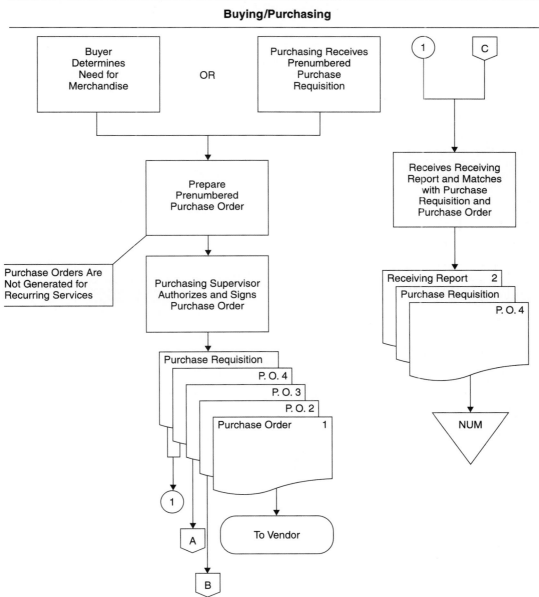

Legend:
  NUM - filed numerically by Purchase Order number
  A - off-page connector
  B - off-page connector
  C - off-page connector

Reference: _E 20–2_
Prepared by: _JH_
Date: _9/16/0X_
Reviewed by: _____

Southeast Shoe Distributor
Expenditure Cycle—Purchases Flowchart
For the Year Ended December 31, 200X

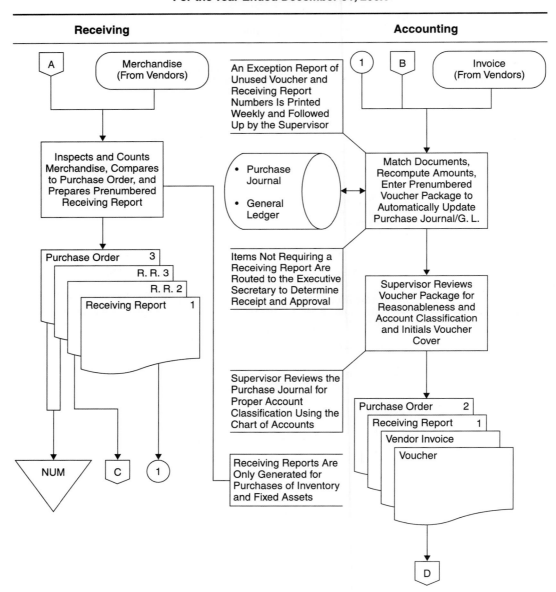

Legend:
   NUM - filed numerically by Receiving Report number
   A - off-page connector
   B - off-page connector
   C - off-page connector

Reference: _E 21_

Prepared by: _JH_

Date: _9/16/0X_

Reviewed by: _____

Southeast Shoe Distributor
Expenditure Cycle—Cash Disbursement Flowchart
For the Year Ended December 31, 200X

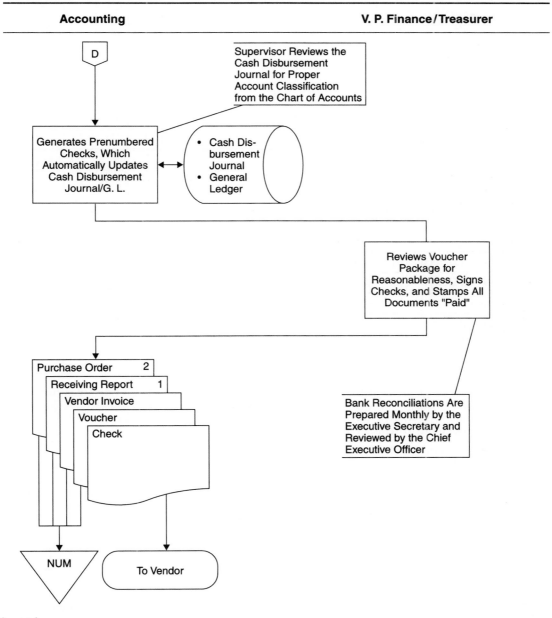

Accounting	V. P. Finance/Treasurer

D

Supervisor Reviews the Cash Disbursement Journal for Proper Account Classification from the Chart of Accounts

Generates Prenumbered Checks, Which Automatically Updates Cash Disbursement Journal/G. L.

- Cash Disbursement Journal
- General Ledger

Reviews Voucher Package for Reasonableness, Signs Checks, and Stamps All Documents "Paid"

Purchase Order   2
Receiving Report   1
Vendor Invoice
Voucher
Check

Bank Reconciliations Are Prepared Monthly by the Executive Secretary and Reviewed by the Chief Executive Officer

NUM

To Vendor

Legend:
NUM - filed numerically by Voucher number
O - off-page connector

183

Southeast Shoe Distributor
Expenditure Cycle—Planned Audit Risk Matrix
For the Year Ended December 31, 200X

Tolerable Misstatement:	Existence*	Rights and Obligations	Valuation	Presentation and Disclosure	Completeness**
Acceptable Audit Risk	L	L	L	L	L
Inherent Risk—Purchases	M		M	M	H
Inherent Risk—Cash Disbursements	M		L	L	H
Inherent Risk—Accounts Payable	L	L	M	L	H
Planned Control Risk—Purchases	M		M	M	M
Planned Control Risk—Cash Disbursements	M		L	H	L
Planned Detection Risk—Purchases	M		M	M	M
Planned Detection Risk—Cash Disbursements	M		H	M	H
Planned Detection Risk—Accounts Payable	M	H	M	M	M

Planned Inherent Risk should be assessed as:

    High (H) if the combination of inherent risk factors present do not justify a lower assessment.
    Medium (M) if the combination of inherent risk factors present justify this assessment.
    Low (L) if the combination of inherent risk factors present justify this assessment.

Factors justifying a lower inherent risk assessment are:

    High management integrity, Low motivation to misstate numbers for external parties, Repeat engagement, No prior-year misstatements, No related-party transactions, Routine transactions, Limited judgment required to correctly record transactions, Low susceptibility to defalcation, Stable business environment.

Planned Control Risk should be assessed as:

    Low (L) if control activity(ies) reduces the likelihood of a material misstatement to a negligible level and persuasive tests of controls are planned to be performed.
    Medium (M) if control activity(ies) reduces the likelihood of a material misstatement to a negligible level and moderately persuasive tests of control are planned or control activity(ies) reduces the likelihood of a material misstatement to a moderate level and persuasive tests of controls are planned.
    High (H) if control activity(ies) does not reduce the likelihood of a material misstatement to a reasonable level or no tests of controls are planned.

Planned Detection Risk should be assessed at:

    Low (L) if persuasive substantive tests are planned to be performed.
    Medium (M) if moderately persuasive substantive tests are planned to be performed.
    High (H) if minimal substantive tests are planned to be performed.

Note: *completeness for cash disbursements,
      **existence for cash disbursements

Southeast Shoe Distributor
Nonstatistical Tests of Transactions Sample Plan—Expenditure Cycle Purchases
For the Year Ended December 31, 200X

Sampling Frame	Beg. Doc. # or Page #	End. Doc. # or Page #	Sample Size
Lines recorded in the purchase journal during the year	Page 1 (Line 1)	Page 100 (Line 1,293)	40

Sample Selection Method:
  The sample was selected by using the "=randbetween(1,1293)" Microsoft Excel spreadsheet function. Line numbers drawn twice were discarded and a new line number was selected using the Excel "randbetween" function.

Sample: *Line number starting with line 1 on page 1 to line 1,293 on page 100*

Sample Item	Sample Ref.	Sample Item	Sample Ref.	Sample Item	Sample Ref.
1	39	16	363	31	953
2	43	17	368	32	969
3	68	18	484	33	1,025
4	79	19	514	34	1,054
5	87	20	582	35	1,070
6	91	21	586	36	1,159
7	99	22	604	37	1,161
8	219	23	606	38	1,254
9	235	24	652	39	1,272
10	237	25	682	40	1,281
11	238	26	811		
12	301	27	903		
13	326	28	907		
14	341	29	918		
15	356	30	942		

Reference: _E 31_

Prepared by: _____

Date: _____

Reviewed by: _____

Southeast Shoe Distributor
Nonstatistical Tests of Controls Evaluation—Expenditure Cycle Purchases
For the Year Ended December 31, 200X

Sampling Frame: *Lines recorded in the purchase journal during the year*

Attribute	RCL	Sample Size	SDR	TDR	ASR
Voucher contains Vendor Invoice, Purchase Order, and Receiving Report (if necessary).	M	40		5%	
Vendor Invoice, Purchase Order, and Receiving Report look authentic and reasonable.	M	40		5%	
Purchase Order is signed by Bruce Penny or Vendor Invoice is initialed by Karen Tucci.	M	40		5%	
Voucher Cover is initialed by Janet Sotiriadis.	M	40		5%	
Purchase Journal amount is correct based on Voucher Package documents.	M	40		5%	
Voucher Cover has correct general ledger account code.	M	40	0	5%	5%
Voucher is posted to the correct general ledger account.	M	40	0	5%	5%
Voucher is posted to correct vendor accounts payable subsidiary file.	M	40	0	5%	5%

Conclusions:

Legend:
ASR—Allowance for Sampling Risk (TDR-SDR)
RCL—Risk of Assessing Control Risk Too Low (L—Low or M—Moderate)
SDR—Sample Deviation Rate
TDR—Tolerable Deviation Rate

Reference: _E 32_
Prepared by: _JA_
Date: _2/15/0Y_
Reviewed by: _____

Southeast Shoe Distributor
Unusual Transactions—Expenditure Cycle Purchases
For the Year Ended December 31, 200X

Date	Account Description or Payee	Check or Voucher #	Account IDs	Amount
	No unusual transactions noted.			
	See conclusion below.			

Follow-up procedures performed:
No unusual purchase transactions were identified from scanning the purchase journal (audit step 2). Thus, no follow-up procedures are needed.

Reference: _E 33_____
Prepared by: _JA_____
Date: __2/15/0Y_____
Reviewed by: _____

Southeast Shoe Distributor
Nonsampling Tests of Transactions—Expenditure Cycle Purchases
For the Year Ended December 31, 200X

Procedure:

The weekly exception reports of unused vouchers and receiving reports were scanned and the follow-up procedures were discussed with Janet Sotiriadis, Accounting Manager (audit step 3).

Exceptions/Misstatements:

Janet indicated that she resolved all unmatched vouchers but did not resolve all unmatched receiving reports. She said she did not have enough time to follow up on unmatched receiving reports. Janet indicated that unmatched receiving reports always resulted from vendors not invoicing SSD on a timely basis and that these unmatched receiving reports were eventually captured in the system when the invoice was received from the vendor. No specific misstatements were noted as a result of this audit procedure.

Conclusion:

The results of this procedure do not support a lower control risk assessment related to the completeness assertion for purchases (i.e., there may be unrecorded purchases). Control risk for the completeness of purchases will be increased to the maximum level and additional substantive audit procedures will be performed. The sample size for audit step 4 will be increased from its planned size of 40 to 60 receiving reports. Additionally, more emphasis will be placed on purchase transactions occurring in the last calendar-year quarter to ensure that there are no material unrecorded purchases and payables at year-end.

Reference: _E 34_
Prepared by: _JA_
Date: _2/14/0Y_
Reviewed by: _____

Southeast Shoe Distributor
Nonstatistical Tests of Transactions Sample Plan—Expenditure Cycle Purchases
For the Year Ended December 31, 200X

Sampling Frame	Beg. Doc. # or Page #	End. Doc. # or Page #	Sample Size
Receiving reports issued during the year	2,387	2,810	60

Sample Selection Method:
The first 40 sample items were selected from the first three calendar-year quarters by using the "=randbetween(2387,2673)" Microsoft Excel spreadsheet function. The last 20 sample items were selected from the last calendar-year quarter by using the "=randbetween(2674,2810)" Microsoft Excel spreadsheet function. Receiving report numbers drawn twice were discarded and a new random number was selected using the Excel "randbetween" function.

Sample: _Receiving Report Number_

Sample Item	Sample Ref.	Sample Item	Sample Ref.	Sample Item	Sample Ref.	Sample Item	Sample Ref.
1	2,389	16	2,529	31	2,598	46	2,695
2	2,394	17	2,533	32	2,599	47	2,696
3	2,395	18	2,539	33	2,610	48	2,702
4	2,409	19	2,540	34	2,624	49	2,703
5	2,412	20	2,548	35	2,633	50	2,706
6	2,415	21	2,549	36	2,635	51	2,709
7	2,419	22	2,563	37	2,636	52	2,723
8	2,421	23	2,568	38	2,647	53	2,726
9	2,424	24	2,570	39	2,666	54	2,741
10	2,450	25	2,579	40	2,668	55	2,759
11	2,463	26	2,584	41	2,674	56	2,764
12	2,490	27	2,587	42	2,677	57	2,778
13	2,494	28	2,588	43	2,679	58	2,784
14	2,522	29	2,593	44	2,685	59	2,787
15	2,523	30	2,597	45	2,694	60	2,801

Southeast Shoe Distributor
Nonstatistical Substantive Tests Evaluation—Expenditure Cycle Purchases
For the Year Ended December 31, 200X

Misstatements:	Recorded Amount	Audited Amount	Misstatement Amount
Total Sample Misstatement			
Projected Misstatement:			
Total Sample Misstatement			
Dollar Value of Sample		÷	$1,061,410.43
Percentage Sample Dollar Misstatement		=	
Dollar Value of Population per Journal		×	$6,206,243.81
Projected Population Dollar Misstatement		=	
Allowance for Sampling Risk			
Tolerable Misstatement			$ 40,000.00
Projected Population Dollar Misstatement		−	
Recorded Adjustments		+	
Allowance for Sampling Risk		=	
Conclusions:			

Southeast Shoe Distributor
Nonstatistical Tests of Transactions Sample Plan—
Expenditure Cycle Cash Disbursements
For the Year Ended December 31, 200X

Sampling Frame	Beg. Doc. # or Page #	End. Doc. # or Page #	Sample Size
Lines recorded in the cash disbursement journal during the year	Page 1 (Line 1)	Page 47 (Line 1,032)	40

Sample Selection Method:
The sample was selected by using the "=randbetween(1,1043)" Microsoft Excel spreadsheet function. Line numbers drawn twice were discarded and a new line number was selected using the Excel "randbetween" function.

Sample: *Line number starting with line 1 on page 1 to line 1,293 on page 47*

Sample Item	Sample Ref.	Sample Item	Sample Ref.	Sample Item	Sample Ref.
1	37	16	446	31	819
2	117	17	449	32	845
3	139	18	499	33	867
4	159	19	516	34	884
5	168	20	536	35	902
6	197	21	539	36	914
7	232	22	579	37	987
8	271	23	612	38	992
9	273	24	636	39	997
10	285	25	648	40	1,000
11	321	26	670		
12	345	27	694		
13	374	28	720		
14	396	29	736		
15	403	30	739		

Reference: _E 41_____
Prepared by: _JA_____
Date: _2/19/0Y_____
Reviewed by: _____

Southeast Shoe Distributor
Nonstatistical Tests of Controls Evaluation—Expenditure Cycle Cash Disbursements
For the Year Ended December 31, 200X

Population: *Lines recorded in the cash disbursement journal during the year*

Attribute	RCL	Sample Size	SDR	TDR	ASR
Voucher package documents stamped "paid."	*M*	*40*	*0%*	*5%*	*5%*
Canceled check and endorsement look authentic and reasonable.	*M*	*40*	*0%*	*5%*	*5%*
Cash disbursement journal amount agrees with cancelled check.	*M*	*40*	*0%*	*5%*	*5%*
Disbursement posted to correct general ledger accounts.	*M*	*40*	*0%*	*5%*	*5%*
Disbursement posted to correct vendor accounts payable subsidiary file.	*M*	*40*	*0%*	*5%*	*5%*

Conclusions:
No deviations were noted as a result of performing tests of controls 6a-e for cash disbursements. Thus, a reduced control risk assessment is supported for the existence of purchases and the existence, valuation, and presentation and disclosure of cash disbursements.

Legend:
ASR—Allowance for Sampling Risk (TDR-SDR)
RCL—Risk of Assessing Control Risk Too Low (L—Low or M—Moderate)
SDR—Sample Deviation Rate
TDR—Tolerable Deviation Rate

Reference: _E 42_____

Prepared by: _JA_____

Date: ___2/15/0Y_____

Reviewed by: _____

Southeast Shoe Distributor
Unusual Transactions—Expenditure Cycle Cash Disbursements
For the Year Ended December 31, 200X

Date	Account Description or Payee	Check or Voucher #	Account IDs	Amount
	No unusual or related-party transactions			
	were noted. See conclusion below.			

Follow-up procedures performed:
No unusual or related-party cash disbursement transactions were identified from scanning the cash disbursement journal (audit step 5). Thus, no follow-up procedures are needed.

Reference: _E 43_____
Prepared by: _JA_____
Date: __2/16/0Y_____
Reviewed by: _____

Southeast Shoe Distributor
Nonsampling Tests of Transactions—Expenditure Cycle Cash Disbursements
For the Year Ended December 31, 200X

Procedure:

The monthly bank reconciliations were scanned and the bank reconciliation process was discussed with Karen Tucci, Executive Secretary (audit steps 7a and b). Additionally, the April 200X bank reconciliation was reperformed (audit step 7c).

Exceptions/Misstatements:

Karen indicated that she receives the bank statements directly from the mail room and performs the monthly bank reconciliations. She also noted that the bank reconciliations are reviewed by Stewart Green, Chief Executive Officer, after she has completed the reconciliations. This process is consistent with the stated company policy.

Review of the monthly bank reconciliations and reperformance of the April 200X bank reconciliation revealed no exceptions or misstatements.

Conclusion:

The results of these tests support a reduced control risk assessment for the existence, completeness, and valuation of cash disbursements.

Southeast Shoe Distributor
Nonstatistical Substantive Tests Evaluation—Expenditure Cycle Cash Disbursements
For the Year Ended December 31, 200X

Misstatements:	Recorded Amount	Audited Amount	Misstatement Amount
No misstatements were identified as a result of			
performing audit steps 6b-e			
Total Sample Misstatement			0

Projected Misstatement:			
Total Sample Misstatement			0
Dollar Value of Sample		÷	$316,319.78
Percentage Sample Dollar Misstatement		=	0%
Dollar Value of Population per Journal		×	$8,151,977.17
Projected Population Dollar Misstatement		=	0

Allowance for Sampling Risk			
Tolerable Misstatement			$ 40,000.00
Projected Population Dollar Misstatement		--	0
Recorded Adjustments		+	0
Allowance for Sampling Risk		=	$ 40,000.00

Conclusions:
  No misstatments were noted as a result of performing substantive tests for 6b-e for cash
  disbursements. Thus, a reduction of the substantive tests of balances for the valuation,
  existence, and completeness assertions of accounts payable is supported.

Southeast Shoe Distributor, Inc.
Chart of Accounts

Account Description	Account Number	Account Description	Account Number
Petty Cash	10000	Sales	40000
Regular Checking Account	10100	Sales Returns and Allowances	41000
Payroll Checking Account	10200	Sales Discounts	42000
Accounts Receivable	11000	Other Income	43000
Allowance for Doubtful Accounts	11100	Cost of Goods Sold	50000
Notes Receivable	11200	Inventory Adjustments	51000
Other Receivables	11300	Purchase Returns and Allowances	52000
Inventory	12000	Purchase Discounts	53000
Prepaid Expenses	13000	Advertising Expense	60000
Other Current Assets	14000	Amortization Expense	60500
Furniture and Fixtures	15000	Auto Expense	61000
Vehicles	15100	Bad Dept Expense	61500
Leasehold Improvements	15200	Cleaning Expense	62000
Buildings	15300	Charitable Contributions	62500
Accumulated Depreciation—Furniture		Depreciation Expense	63000
and Fixtures	16000	Dues and Subscriptions	63500
Accumulated Depreciation—Vehicles	16100	Employee Benefit Programs Expense	64000
Accumulated Depreciation—		Freight Expense	64500
Leasehold Improvements	16200	Gifts Expense	65000
Accumulated Depreciation—Buildings	16300	Income Tax Expense	65500
Land	17000	Insurance Expense	66000
Organizational Costs	18000	Interest Expense	66500
Other Assets	19000	Legal and Professional Expense	67000
Accounts Payable	20000	Licenses Expense	67500
Accrued Expenses	21000	Maintenance Expense	68000
Salaries and Wages Payable	21100	Meals and Entertainment Expense	68500
Federal Payroll Taxes Payable	21200	Office Expense	69000
State Payroll Taxes Payable	21300	Other Taxes	69500
FICA Taxes Payable	21400	Payroll Tax Expense	70000
FUTA Taxes Payable	21500	Postage Expense	70500
SUTA Taxes Payable	21600	Rent or Lease Expense	71000
Property Taxes Payable	21700	Repairs Expense	71500
Income Taxes Payable	21800	Salaries Expense	72000
Other Taxes Payable	21900	Salaries Bonus Expense	72500
Notes Payable—Current Portion	22000	Salaries Commission Expense	73000
Notes Payable—Short-Term	22100	Supplies Expense	73500
Other Current Liabilities	23000	Telephone Expense	74000
Notes Payable—Long-Term	24000	Travel Expense	74500
Common Stock	30000	Utilities Expense	75000
Paid-in Capital	31000	Wages Expense	75500
Retained Earnings	32000	Other Expense	80000
Dividends	32100	Gain/Loss on Sale of Assets	90000

Southeast Shoe Distributor, Inc.
Purchase Journal for Audit Procedure 1*
For the Period from January 1, 200X to December 31, 200X

Date	G/L Account ID Account Description	Invoice #	Voucher #	Debit Amount	Credit Amount
02/16/0X (68)	74000 Telephone Expense	404–555–5555	7893	837.27	
	20000 Accounts Payable				837.27
04/23/0X (238)	75000 Utilities Expense	21790–1778	8063	376.85	
	20000 Accounts Payable				376.85
05/07/0X (301)	69000 Office Expense	11235	8126	113.24	
	20000 Accounts Payable				113.24
11/08/0X (1054)	12000 Inventory	26710	8879	6,677.76	
	20000 Accounts Payable				6,677.76
12/23/0X (1281)	12000 Inventory	789938	9106	24,575.60	
	20000 Accounts Payable				24,575.60

*Abstracted from the Purchase Journal using the exact format of the Purchase Journal. Note that the number in parenthesis under the transaction date is not normally included in the Purchase Journal. This number is provided because it represents the line number of the transaction in the Purchase Journal.

SSD
Documents for Audit Procedure 1

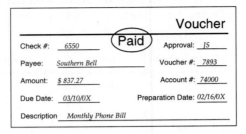

Voucher		
Check #: _6550_	(Paid)	Approval: _JS_
Payee: _Southern Bell_		Voucher #: _7893_
Amount: _$ 837.27_		Account #: _74000_
Due Date: _03/10/0X_		Preparation Date: _02/16/0X_
Description _Monthly Phone Bill_		

Southern Bell
A BellSouth Company

Account Number: 404-555-5555   535   371

Bill Date: February 10, 200X   Atlanta

Page   1

Current Charges Due Before	Total Amount Due
March 10, 200X	837.27

KT

Amount of Last Bill	Less Payments	Adjustments	Current Charges
1,051.58	1,051.58		837.27

(Paid)

Detailed Statement of Regulated Charges

**** Please Note: An additional charge at the rate of 1.0%
**** per month will apply to any unpaid balance
**** after March 13.

Monthly Service Charges
    Montly Service 01/01 thru 01/31 200X
    Basic Services   **Quantity**

Amount	Total

(continued)

Helpful Numbers

	Orders and Billing	Payment Questions
Southern Bell	780-2800	780-2187
Outside of Georgia	1(800)404-2800	1(800)404-5233

Numbers for other companies are listed with their charges

SSD
Documents for Audit Procedure 1 (continued)

Voucher

Check #:	6558	Approval:	JS
Payee:	Georgia Power	Voucher #:	8063
Amount:	$ 376.85 **Paid**	Account #:	75000
Due Date:	05/15/0X	Preparation Date:	04/23/0X
Description	Monthly Electric Bill		

Retain bottom portion for your records, detach and return stub with payment.

Service For:	Southeast Shoe Distributor, Inc. 1102 Memorial Avenue Atlanta, Georgia 30303	Your Account Number 21790-1778	Rate Class Commercial	Billing Date 04/20/0X

Meter Number	Service Period	Days	Type of Reading	Multiplier	Units	Meter Readings Current	Meter Readings Past	Usage
43869800	03/09/0X - 04/10/0X	32	Actual	1	KWH	68418.00	64178.00	4240.00

	Usage
Previous Balance	237.98
Payment **Paid**	237.98
Balance Forward *KT*	0.00
Curent Charges	
Consumption	365.87
Sales Tax (3%)	10.98

	Due Date	Total Due
	05/15/0X	376.85

Georgia Power Company
62 Lake Mirror RD, Forest Park, GA 30297, (404) 608-9843

SSD
Documents for Audit Procedure 1 (continued)

Voucher

Check #:	6731		Approval:	JS
Payee:	Express Supplies		Voucher #:	8126
Amount:	$ 113.24	**Paid**	Account #:	69000
Due Date:	06/04/0X		Preparation Date:	05/07/0X

Description Purchase of office supplies

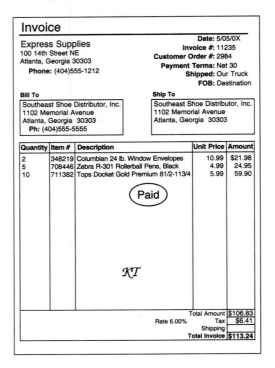

Invoice

Express Supplies
100 14th Street NE
Atlanta, Georgia 30303
Phone: (404)555-1212

Date: 5/05/0X
Invoice #: 11235
Customer Order #: 2984
Payment Terms: Net 30
Shipped: Our Truck
FOB: Destination

Bill To
Southeast Shoe Distributor, Inc.
1102 Memorial Avenue
Atlanta, Georgia 30303
Ph: (404)555-5555

Ship To
Southeast Shoe Distributor, Inc.
1102 Memorial Avenue
Atlanta, Georgia 30303

Quantity	Item #	Description	Unit Price	Amount
2	348219	Columbian 24 lb. Window Envelopes	10.99	$21.98
5	708446	Zebra R-301 Rollerball Pens, Black	4.99	24.95
10	711382	Tops Docket Gold Premium 81/2-113/4	5.99	59.90

Paid

KT

Total Amount	$106.83
Rate 6.00% Tax	$6.41
Shipping	
Total Invoice	**$113.24**

Purchase Order

Bill To

Express Supplies
100 14th Street NE
Atlanta, Georgia 30303
(404) 555-1212

PO#: 2984
Date: 05/04/0X   Date Required: 05/05/0X
Terms: Net 30
Ship by: Your Truck
Buyer: Mary Tally

Vendor
Brown Group, Inc.
8300 Maryland Drive
St. Louis, MO 63105
Ph: (314)854-4000

Ship To
Southeast Shoe Distributor, Inc.
1102 Memorial Avenue
Atlanta, Georgia 30303

Item #	Description	Size	Quantity	Unit Price	Amount
348219	Columbian 24 lb. Window Envelopes		2	$10.99	$21.98
708446	Zebra R-301 Rollerball Pens, Black		5	4.99	24.95
711382	Tops Docket Gold Premium 8½-11¾ Pads		10	5.99	59.90

Paid

Total Amount	$106.83
Tax	$6.41
Total Purchase Order	$113.24

Message

Authorization
Name: Bruce Penny
Date: 05/04/0X
Title: Purchasing Supervisor
Signature: *Bruce Penny*

Voucher

Check #:	7372	Approval:	JS
Payee:	Jones Apparel Group, Inc.	Voucher #:	8879
Amount:	$ 6,677.76	Account #:	12000
Due Date:	12/19/0X	Preparation Date:	11/08/0X

Paid

Description Purchase of Women's Shoes

Invoice

Jones Apparel Group, Inc.
250 Rittenhouse Circle
Bristol, PA 19007

Fax: (215)785-1795
Ph: (215)785-4000

Date: 11/4/0X
Invoice #: 26710
PO#: 3272
Terms: Net 45
Shipped: FreightWay Services
FOB: Shipping Point

Bill To
Southeast Shoe Distributor, Inc.
1102 Memorial Avenue
Atlanta, Georgia 30303
Ph: 404-555-5555

Ship To
Southeast Shoe Distributor, Inc.
1102 Memorial Avenue
Atlanta, Georgia 30303

Item #	Description	Size	Quantity	Unit Price	Amount
w4568	Alto by Evan Picone Shell	5.5 m	12	$33.44	$401.28
w4568	Alto by Evan Picone Shell	6.0 m	12	33.44	401.28
w4568	Alto by Evan Picone Shell	6.5 m	24	33.44	802.56
w4568	Alto by Evan Picone Shell	7.0 m	24	33.44	802.56
w4568	Alto by Evan Picone Shell	7.5 m	24	33.44	802.56
w4568	Alto by Evan Picone Shell	8.0 m	24	33.44	802.56
w4568	Alto by Evan Picone Shell	8.5 m	24	33.44	802.56
w4568	Alto by Evan Picone Shell	9.0 m	24	33.44	802.56
w4568	Alto by Evan Picone Shell	9.5 m	12	33.44	401.28
w4568	Alto by Evan Picone Shell	10.0 m	12	33.44	401.28

Total Amount		$6,420.48
Rate N/A	Tax	
	Shipping	$257.28
Paid	**Total Invoice**	**$6,677.76**

Message

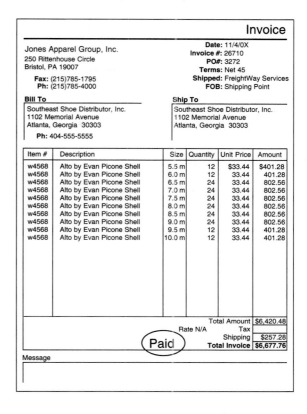

Receiving Report

Southeast Shoe Distributor, Inc.   Date Received: 11/05/0X
1102 Memorial Avenue   Receiving Report #: **2726**
Atlanta, Georgia 30303

Received from	**Purchase Order #:**
Jones Apparel Group, Inc.	3272

Freight carrier	**Received by**
FreightWay Services	Sue Ravens

Quantity	Item #	Size	Description
12	w4568	5.5 M	Alto
12	w4568	6.0 M	"
24	w4568	6.5 M	"
24	w4568	7.0 M	"
24	w4568	7.5 M	"
24	w4568	8.0 M	"
24	w4568	8.5 M	"
24	w4568	9.0 M	"
12	w4568	9.5 M	"
12	w4568	10 M	"

Paid

Condition:
    Excellent

Purchase Order

Bill To
Southeast Shoe Distributor, Inc.
1102 Memorial Avenue
Atlanta, Georgia 30303
Ph: (404)555-5555

PO#: 3272
Date: 10/29/0X   Date Required: 11/15/0X
Terms: Net 30
Ship by: FreightWay Services
Buyer: Mary West

Vendor
Jones Apparel Group, Inc.
250 Ritenhouse Circle
Bristol, PA 19007
Ph: (215)785-4000

Ship To
Southeast Shoe Distributor, Inc.
1102 Memorial Avenue
Atlanta, Georgia 30303

Item #	Description	Size	Quantity	Unit Price	Amount
w4568	Alto by Evan Picone Shell	5.5 M	12	$33.44	$401.28
w4568	Alto by Evan Picone Shell	6.0 M	12	33.44	401.28
w4568	Alto by Evan Picone Shell	6.5 M	24	33.44	802.56
w4568	Alto by Evan Picone Shell	7.0 M	24	33.44	802.56
w4568	Alto by Evan Picone Shell	7.5 M	24	33.44	802.56
w4568	Alto by Evan Picone Shell	8.0 M	24	33.44	802.56
w4568	Alto by Evan Picone Shell	8.5 M	24	33.44	802.56
w4568	Alto by Evan Picone Shell	9.0 M	24	33.44	802.56
w4568	Alto by Evan Picone Shell	9.5 M	12	33.44	401.28
w4568	Alto by Evan Picone Shell	10.0 M	12	33.44	401.28

Paid

Total Amount		$6,420.48
Tax		
Total Purchase Order		$6,420.48

Message   Authorization

Name: Bruce Penny
Date: 10/29/0X
Title: Purchasing Supervisor

Signature: Bruce Penny

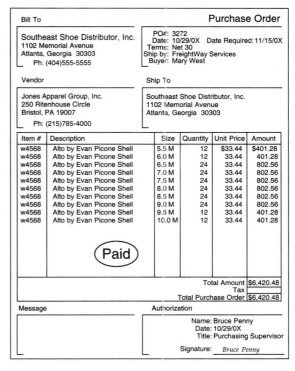

Voucher

Check #:	7572	Approval:	JS
Payee:	Wolverine World Wide, Inc.	Voucher #:	9106
Amount:	$24,575.60	Account #:	12000
Due Date:	02/21/0Y	Preparation Date:	12/23/0X

Paid

Description: *Purchase of Men's Shoes*

Invoice

Wolverine World Wide, Inc.
9341 Courtland Drive
Rockford, MI 49351

Fax: (616)866-5500
Ph: (616)866-0257

Date: 12/23/0X
Invoice #: 789938
PO#: 3342
Terms: Net 90
Shipped: Transit Freight Company
FOB: Shipping Point

Bill To
Southeast Shoe Distributor, Inc.
1102 Memorial Avenue
Atlanta, Georgia 30303
Ph: 404-555-5555

Ship To
Southeast Shoe Distributor, Inc.
1102 Memorial Avenue
Atlanta, Georgia 30303

Item #	Description	Size	Quantity	Unit Price	Amount
19421	Hush Puppies Trail Brown	7.0 M	20	$39.20	$784.00
19421	Hush Puppies Trail Brown	7.5 M	20	39.20	784.00
19421	Hush Puppies Trail Brown	8.0 M	20	39.20	784.00
19421	Hush Puppies Trail Brown	8.5 M	20	39.20	784.00
19421	Hush Puppies Trail Brown	9.0 M	20	39.20	784.00
19421	Hush Puppies Trail Brown	9.5 M	40	39.20	1,568.00
19421	Hush Puppies Trail Brown	10.0 M	40	39.20	1,568.00
19421	Hush Puppies Trail Brown	10.5 M	40	39.20	1,568.00
19421	Hush Puppies Trail Brown	11.0 M	40	39.20	1,568.00
19421	Hush Puppies Trail Brown	11.5 M	40	39.20	1,568.00
19421	Hush Puppies Trail Brown	12.0 M	40	39.20	1,568.00
19421	Hush Puppies Trail Brown	13.0 M	20	39.20	784.00
19421	Hush Puppies Trail Brown	14.0 M	20	39.20	784.00
18335	Hush Puppies Monroe Dark Brown	9.0 M	20	34.30	686.00
18355	Hush Puppies Monroe Dark Brown	9.5 M	40	34.30	1,372.00
18355	Hush Puppies Monroe Dark Brown	10.0 M	40	34.30	1,372.00
18355	Hush Puppies Monroe Dark Brown	10.5 M	40	34.30	1,372.00
18355	Hush Puppies Monroe Dark Brown	11.0 M	40	34.30	1,372.00
18355	Hush Puppies Monroe Dark Brown	11.5 M	40	34.30	1,372.00
18355	Hush Puppies Monroe Dark Brown	12.0 M	20	34.30	686.00
18355	Hush Puppies Monroe Dark Brown	13.0 M	20	34.30	686.00

Total Amount		$23,814.00
Paid Rate N/A	Tax	
	Shipping	$761.60
	Total Invoice	$24,575.60

Message

Receiving Report

Southeast Shoe Distributor, Inc.
1102 Memorial Avenue
Atlanta, Georgia 30303

Date Received: 12/23/0x
Receiving Report #: 2798

Received from
Wolverine World Wide, Inc.

Purchase Order #:
3342

Freight carrier
Transit Freight Company

Received by
Sue Ravens

Quantity	Item #	Size	Description
20	18355	9.0 M	Hush Puppies Monroe Dark Brown
40	18355	9.5 M	"
40	18355	10.0 M	"
40	18355	10.5 M	"
40	18355	11.0 M	"
40	18355	11.5 M	"
20	18355	12.0 M	"
20	18355	13.0 M	"
20	19421	7.0 M	Hush Puppies Trail Brown
20	19421	7.5 M	"
20	19421	8.0 M	"
20	19421	8.5 M	"
20	19421	9.0 M	"
40	19421	9.5 M	"
40	19421	10.0 M	"
40	19421	10.5 M	"
40	19421	11.0 M	"
40	19421	11.5 M	"
40	19421	12.0 M	"
20	19421	13.0 M	"
20	19421	14.0 M	"

Paid

Condition:
Excellent

Purchase Order

Bill To
Southeast Shoe Distributor, Inc.
1102 Memorial Avenue
Atlanta, Georgia 30303
Ph: (404)555-5555

PO#: 3342
Date: 12/15/0X   **Date Required:** 01/15/0Y
Terms: Net 60
Ship by: Transit Freight Company
Buyer: Doug Scott

Vendor
Wolverine World Wide, Inc.
9341 Courtland Drive
Rockford, MI 49351
Ph: (616)866-0257

Ship To
Southeast Shoe Distributor, Inc.
1102 Memorial Avenue
Atlanta, Georgia 30303

Item #	Description	Size	Quantity	Unit Price	Amount
19421	Hush Puppies Trail Brown	7.0 M	20	$39.20	$784.00
19421	Hush Puppies Trail Brown	7.5 M	20	39.20	784.00
19421	Hush Puppies Trail Brown	8.0 M	20	39.20	784.00
19421	Hush Puppies Trail Brown	8.5 M	20	39.20	784.00
19421	Hush Puppies Trail Brown	9.0 M	20	39.20	784.00
19421	Hush Puppies Trail Brown	9.5 M	40	39.20	1,568.00
19421	Hush Puppies Trail Brown	10.0 M	40	39.20	1,568.00
19421	Hush Puppies Trail Brown	10.5 M	40	39.20	1,568.00
19421	Hush Puppies Trail Brown	11.0 M	40	39.20	1,568.00
19421	Hush Puppies Trail Brown	11.5 M	40	39.20	1,568.00
19421	Hush Puppies Trail Brown	12.0 M	40	39.20	1,568.00
19421	Hush Puppies Trail Brown	13.0 M	20	39.20	784.00
19421	Hush Puppies Trail Brown	14.0 M	20	39.20	784.00
18335	Hush Puppies Monroe Dark Brown	9.0 M	20	34.30	686.00
18355	Hush Puppies Monroe Dark Brown	9.5 M	40	34.30	1,372.00
18355	Hush Puppies Monroe Dark Brown	10.0 M	40	34.30	1,372.00
18355	Hush Puppies Monroe Dark Brown	10.5 M	40	34.30	1,372.00
18355	Hush Puppies Monroe Dark Brown	11.0 M	40	34.30	1,372.00
18355	Hush Puppies Monroe Dark Brown	11.5 M	40	34.30	1,372.00
18355	Hush Puppies Monroe Dark Brown	12.0 M	20	34.30	686.00
18355	Hush Puppies Monroe Dark Brown	13.0 M	20	34.30	686.00

Total Amount		$23,814.00
Paid Tax		
	Total Purchase Order	$23,814.00

Message

Authorization
Name: Bruce Penny
Date: 04/18/0X
Title: Purchasing Supervisor
Signature: *Bruce Penny*

Southeast Shoe Distributor, Inc.
Purchase Journal for Audit Procedure 4*
For the Period from January 1, 200X to December 31, 200X

Date	G/L Account ID Account Description	Invoice #	Voucher #	Debit Amount	Credit Amount
01/21/0X	12000 Inventory	541105	7855	31,086.00	
	20000 Accounts Payable				31,086.00
01/25/0X	61000 Auto Expense	LS–6341	7861	2,034.00	
	20000 Accounts Payable				2,034.00
02/19/0X	12000 Inventory	5166–B–12	7898	5,408.00	
	20000 Accounts Payable				5,408.00
03/14/0X	12000 Inventory	8992	7930	10,471.68	
	20000 Accounts Payable				10,471.68
04/24/0X	12000 Inventory	15622	8065	25,900.20	
	20000 Accounts Payable				25,900.20
05/13/0X	60000 Advertising Expense	2456–d22	8128	421.36	
	20000 Accounts Payable				421.36
06/03/0X	15000 Furniture and Fixtures	47948	8217	3,590.00	
	20000 Accounts Payable				3,590.00
08/11/0X	12000 Inventory	32501	8522	1,097.52	
	20000 Accounts Payable				1,097.52

*Abstracted from the Purchase Journal using the exact format of the Purchase Journal

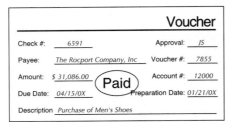

Voucher

Check #: _6591_ Approval: _JS_

Payee: _The Rocport Company, Inc_ Voucher #: _7855_

Amount: _$ 31,086.00_ **Paid** Account #: _12000_

Due Date: _04/15/0X_ Preparation Date: _01/21/0X_

Description _Purchase of Men's Shoes_

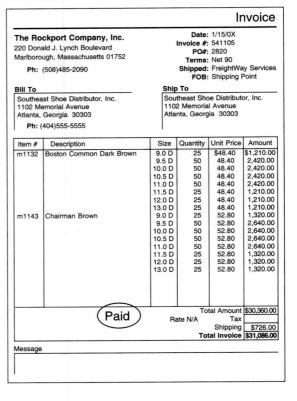

Invoice

The Rockport Company, Inc.
220 Donald J. Lynch Boulevard
Marlborough, Massachusetts 01752
Ph: (508)485-2090

Date: 1/15/0X
Invoice #: 541105
PO#: 2820
Terms: Net 90
Shipped: FreightWay Services
FOB: Shipping Point

Bill To
Southeast Shoe Distributor, Inc.
1102 Memorial Avenue
Atlanta, Georgia 30303
Ph: (404)555-5555

Ship To
Southeast Shoe Distributor, Inc.
1102 Memorial Avenue
Atlanta, Georgia 30303

Item #	Description	Size	Quantity	Unit Price	Amount
m1132	Boston Common Dark Brown	9.0 D	25	$48.40	$1,210.00
		9.5 D	50	48.40	2,420.00
		10.0 D	50	48.40	2,420.00
		10.5 D	50	48.40	2,420.00
		11.0 D	50	48.40	2,420.00
		11.5 D	25	48.40	1,210.00
		12.0 D	25	48.40	1,210.00
		13.0 D	25	48.40	1,210.00
m1143	Chairman Brown	9.0 D	25	52.80	1,320.00
		9.5 D	50	52.80	2,640.00
		10.0 D	50	52.80	2,640.00
		10.5 D	50	52.80	2,640.00
		11.0 D	50	52.80	2,640.00
		11.5 D	25	52.80	1,320.00
		12.0 D	25	52.80	1,320.00
		13.0 D	25	52.80	1,320.00

Paid

Total Amount	$30,360.00
Rate N/A Tax	
Shipping	$726.00
Total Invoice	$31,086.00

Message

Receiving Report

Southeast Shoe Distributor, Inc. Date Received: _01/18/0X_
1102 Memorial Avenue Receiving Report #: **2395**
Atlanta, Georgia 30303

Received from **Purchase Order #:**
The Rockport Company, Inc. _2820_

Freight carrier **Received by**
FreightWay Services _Sue Ravens_

Quantity	Item #	Size	Description
25	m1132	9.0 D	Boston Common Dark Brown
50	m1132	9.5 D	„
50	m1132	10.0 D	„
50	m1132	10.5 D	„
50	m1132	11.0 D	„
25	m1132	11.5 D	„
25	m1132	12.0 D	„
25	m1132	13.0 D	„
25	m1143	9.0 D	Chairman Brown
50	m1143	9.5 D	„
50	m1143	10.0 D	„
50	m1143	10.5 D	„
50	m1143	11.0 D	„
25	m1143	11.5 D	„
25	m1143	12.0 D	„
25	m1143	13.0 D	„

Paid

Condition:
Excellent

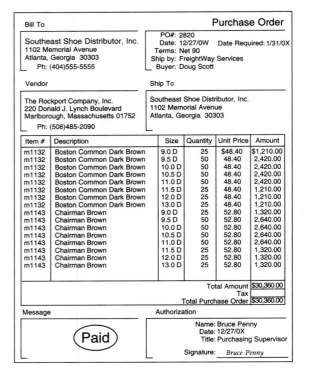

Purchase Order

Bill To

Southeast Shoe Distributor, Inc.
1102 Memorial Avenue
Atlanta, Georgia 30303
Ph: (404)555-5555

PO#: 2820
Date: 12/27/0W Date Required: 1/31/0X
Terms: Net 90
Ship by: FreightWay Services
Buyer: Doug Scott

Vendor

The Rockport Company, Inc.
220 Donald J. Lynch Boulevard
Marlborough, Massachusetts 01752
Ph: (508)485-2090

Ship To

Southeast Shoe Distributor, Inc.
1102 Memorial Avenue
Atlanta, Georgia 30303

Item #	Description	Size	Quantity	Unit Price	Amount
m1132	Boston Common Dark Brown	9.0 D	25	$48.40	$1,210.00
m1132	Boston Common Dark Brown	9.5 D	50	48.40	2,420.00
m1132	Boston Common Dark Brown	10.0 D	50	48.40	2,420.00
m1132	Boston Common Dark Brown	10.5 D	50	48.40	2,420.00
m1132	Boston Common Dark Brown	11.0 D	50	48.40	2,420.00
m1132	Boston Common Dark Brown	11.5 D	25	48.40	1,210.00
m1132	Boston Common Dark Brown	12.0 D	25	48.40	1,210.00
m1132	Boston Common Dark Brown	13.0 D	25	48.40	1,210.00
m1143	Chairman Brown	9.0 D	25	52.80	1,320.00
m1143	Chairman Brown	9.5 D	50	52.80	2,640.00
m1143	Chairman Brown	10.0 D	50	52.80	2,640.00
m1143	Chairman Brown	10.5 D	50	52.80	2,640.00
m1143	Chairman Brown	11.0 D	50	52.80	2,640.00
m1143	Chairman Brown	11.5 D	25	52.80	1,320.00
m1143	Chairman Brown	12.0 D	25	52.80	1,320.00
m1143	Chairman Brown	13.0 D	25	52.80	1,320.00

Total Amount	$30,360.00
Tax	
Total Purchase Order	$30,360.00

Message Authorization

Paid

Name: Bruce Penny
Date: 12/27/0X
Title: Purchasing Supervisor
Signature: _Bruce Penny_

SSD
Documents for Audits Procedure 4 (continued)

Receiving Report

Southeast Shoe Distributor, Inc.   Date Received: 02/15/0X
1102 Memorial Avenue   Receiving Report #: **2409**
Atlanta, Georgia 30303

Received from	**Purchase Order #:**
Esprit de Corp.	2844

Freight carrier	**Received by**
Express Transit Company	Sue Ravens

Quantity	Item #	Size	Description
12	w3288	8.0 M	Tribeca Jave
12	w3288	8.5 M	

Condition:
Excellent

Purchase Order

Bill To

Southeast Shoe Distributor, Inc.
1102 Memorial Avenue
Atlanta, Georgia 30303
  Ph: (404)555-5555

PO#: 2844
  Date: 02/06/0X   Date Required: 02/15/0X
Terms: Net 30
Ship by: Express Transit Company
  Buyer: Mary West

Vendor

Esprit de Crop.
900 Minnesota St.
San Francisco, CA 94107
  Ph: (415)648-6900

Ship To

Southeast Shoe Distributor, Inc.
1102 Memorial Avenue
Atlanta, Georgia 30303

Item #	Description	Size	Quantity	Unit Price	Amount
w3288	Tribeca Jave	8.0 M	12	$20.58	$246.96
w3288	Tribeca Jave	8.5 M	12	20.58	246.96

	Total Amount	$493.92
	Tax	
	Total Purchase Order	$493.92

Message

Authorization

Name: Bruce Penny
Date: 04/18/0X
Title: Purchasing Supervisor
Signature: Bruce Penny

Voucher

Check #:	6618	Approval:	JS
Payee:	Kenneth Cole Productions, Inc.	Voucher #:	7930
Amount:	$ 10,471.68	Account #:	12000
Due Date:	05/05/0X	Preparation Date:	03/14/0X
Description	Purchase of Women's Shoes		

Paid

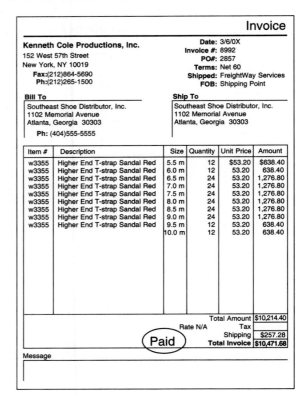

Invoice

Kenneth Cole Productions, Inc.
152 West 57th Street
New York, NY 10019
Fax:(212)864-5690
Ph:(212)265-1500

Date: 3/6/0X
Invoice #: 8992
PO#: 2857
Terms: Net 60
Shipped: FreightWay Services
FOB: Shipping Point

Bill To
Southeast Shoe Distributor, Inc.
1102 Memorial Avenue
Atlanta, Georgia 30303
Ph: (404)555-5555

Ship To
Southeast Shoe Distributor, Inc.
1102 Memorial Avenue
Atlanta, Georgia 30303

Item #	Description	Size	Quantity	Unit Price	Amount
w3355	Higher End T-strap Sandal Red	5.5 m	12	$53.20	$638.40
w3355	Higher End T-strap Sandal Red	6.0 m	12	53.20	638.40
w3355	Higher End T-strap Sandal Red	6.5 m	24	53.20	1,276.80
w3355	Higher End T-strap Sandal Red	7.0 m	24	53.20	1,276.80
w3355	Higher End T-strap Sandal Red	7.5 m	24	53.20	1,276.80
w3355	Higher End T-strap Sandal Red	8.0 m	24	53.20	1,276.80
w3355	Higher End T-strap Sandal Red	8.5 m	24	53.20	1,276.80
w3355	Higher End T-strap Sandal Red	9.0 m	24	53.20	1,276.80
w3355	Higher End T-strap Sandal Red	9.5 m	12	53.20	638.40
		10.0 m	12	53.20	638.40

Total Amount	$10,214.40
Rate N/A Tax	
Shipping	$257.28
Total Invoice	$10,471.68

Paid

Message

Receiving Report

Southeast Shoe Distributor, Inc.   Date Received: 03/09/0X
1102 Memorial Avenue   Receiving Report #: **2419**
Atlanta, Georgia 30303

Received from   **Purchase Order #:**
Jones Apparel Group, Inc.   2857

Freight carrier   **Received by**
FreightWay Services   Sue Ravens

Quantity	Item #	Size	Description
12	w3355	5.5 M	Higher End T-Strap Red Sandal
12	w3355	6.0 M	"
24	w3355	6.5 M	"
24	w3355	7.0 M	"
24	w3355	7.5 M	"
24	w3355	8.0 M	"
24	w3355	8.5 M	"
24	w3355	9.0 M	"
12	w3355	9.5 M	"
12	w3355	10.0 M	"

Paid

Condition:
Excellent

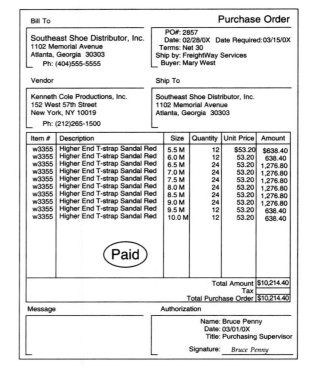

Purchase Order

Bill To

Southeast Shoe Distributor, Inc.
1102 Memorial Avenue
Atlanta, Georgia 30303
Ph: (404)555-5555

PO#: 2857
Date: 02/28/0X   Date Required: 03/15/0X
Terms: Net 30
Ship by: FreightWay Services
Buyer: Mary West

Vendor

Kenneth Cole Productions, Inc.
152 West 57th Street
New York, NY 10019
Ph: (212)265-1500

Ship To

Southeast Shoe Distributor, Inc.
1102 Memorial Avenue
Atlanta, Georgia 30303

Item #	Description	Size	Quantity	Unit Price	Amount
w3355	Higher End T-strap Sandal Red	5.5 M	12	$53.20	$638.40
w3355	Higher End T-strap Sandal Red	6.0 M	12	53.20	638.40
w3355	Higher End T-strap Sandal Red	6.5 M	24	53.20	1,276.80
w3355	Higher End T-strap Sandal Red	7.0 M	24	53.20	1,276.80
w3355	Higher End T-strap Sandal Red	7.5 M	24	53.20	1,276.80
w3355	Higher End T-strap Sandal Red	8.0 M	24	53.20	1,276.80
w3355	Higher End T-strap Sandal Red	8.5 M	24	53.20	1,276.80
w3355	Higher End T-strap Sandal Red	9.0 M	24	53.20	1,276.80
w3355	Higher End T-strap Sandal Red	9.5 M	12	53.20	638.40
w3355	Higher End T-strap Sandal Red	10.0 M	12	53.20	638.40

Paid

Total Amount	$10,214.40
Tax	
Total Purchase Order	$10,214.40

Message   **Authorization**

Name: Bruce Penny
Date: 03/01/0X
Title: Purchasing Supervisor
Signature: Bruce Penny

Voucher

Check #:	6771	Approval:	JS
Payee:	Florsheim Group Inc.	Voucher #:	8065
Amount:	$ 25,900.20	Account #:	12000
Due Date:	06/19/0X	Preparation Date:	04/24/0X

Paid

Description *Purchase of Men's Shoes*

Invoice

Florsheim Group Inc.
200 N. LaSalle St.
Chicago, IL 60601-1014
Fax:(312)458-2500
Ph:(312)458-7470

Date: 4/20/0X
Invoice #: 15622
PO#: 2948
Terms: Net 60
Shipped: Transit Freight Company
FOB: Shipping Point

Bill To
Southeast Shoe Distributor, Inc.
1102 Memorial Avenue
Atlanta, Georgia 30303
Ph: (404)555-5555

Ship To
Southeast Shoe Distributor, Inc.
1102 Memorial Avenue
Atlanta, Georgia 30303

Item #	Description	Size	Quantity	Unit Price	Amount
m2231	Trail Brown	7.0 D	30	$27.98	$839.40
m2231	Trail Brown	7.5 D	30	27.98	839.40
m2231	Trail Brown	8.0 D	30	27.98	839.40
m2231	Trail Brown	8.5 D	30	27.98	839.40
m2231	Trail Brown	9.0 D	30	27.98	839.40
m2231	Trail Brown	9.5 D	60	27.98	1,678.80
m2231	Trail Brown	10.0 D	60	27.98	1,678.80
m2231	Trail Brown	10.5 D	60	27.98	1,678.80
m2231	Trail Brown	11.0 D	60	27.98	1,678.80
m2231	Trail Brown	11.5 D	60	27.98	1,678.80
m2231	Trail Brown	12.0 D	60	27.98	1,678.80
m2231	Trail Brown	12.5 D	30	27.98	839.40
m2231	Trail Brown	13.0 D	30	27.98	839.40
m2231	Trail Brown	14.0 D	30	27.98	839.40
m2023	Newport Wine	9.0 D	20	30.78	615.60
m2023	Newport Wine	9.5 D	40	30.78	1,231.20
m2023	Newport Wine	10.0 D	40	30.78	1,231.20
m2023	Newport Wine	10.5 D	40	30.78	1,231.20
m2023	Newport Wine	11.0 D	40	30.78	1,231.20
m2023	Newport Wine	11.5 D	40	30.78	1,231.20
m2023	Newport Wine	12.0 D	20	30.78	615.60
m2023	Newport Wine	13.0 D	20	30.78	615.60

Paid

	Total Amount	$24,790.80
Rate N/A	Tax	
	Shipping	$1,109.40
	Total Invoice	**$25,900.20**

Message

Receiving Report

Southeast Shoe Distributor, Inc.   Date Received: *04/22/0X*
1102 Memorial Avenue   Receiving Report #: **2463**
Atlanta, Georgia 30303

Received from   **Purchase Order #:**
Florsheim Group Inc.   2948

Freight carrier   **Received by**
Transit Freight Company   *Sue Ravens*

Quantity	Item #	Size	Description
20	m2023	9.0 D	Newport Wine
40	m2023	9.5 D	"
40	m2023	10.0 D	"
40	m2023	10.5 D	"
40	m2023	11.0 D	"
40	m2023	11.5 D	"
20	m2023	12.0 D	"
20	m2023	13.0 D	"
30	m2231	7.0 D	Trail Brown
30	m2231	7.5 D	"
30	m2231	8.0 D	"
30	m2231	8.5 D	"
30	m2231	9.0 D	"
60	m2231	9.5 D	"
60	m2231	10.0 D	"
60	m2231	10.5 D	"
60	m2231	11.0 D	"
60	m2231	11.5 D	"
60	m2231	12.0 D	"
30	m2231	12.5 D	"
30	m2231	13.0 D	"
30	m2231	14.0 D	Trail Brown

Paid

Condition:
          Excellent

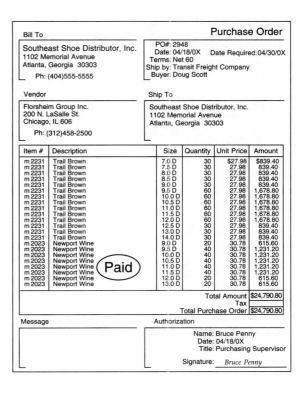

Purchase Order

Bill To
Southeast Shoe Distributor, Inc.
1102 Memorial Avenue
Atlanta, Georgia 30303
Ph: (404)555-5555

PO#: 2948
Date: 04/18/0X   Date Required: 04/30/0X
Terms: Net 60
Ship by: Transit Freight Company
Buyer: Doug Scott

Vendor
Florsheim Group Inc.
200 N. LaSalle St.
Chicago, IL 606
Ph: (312)458-2500

Ship To
Southeast Shoe Distributor, Inc.
1102 Memorial Avenue
Atlanta, Georgia 30303

Item #	Description	Size	Quantity	Unit Price	Amount
m 2231	Trail Brown	7.0 D	30	$27.98	$839.40
m 2231	Trail Brown	7.5 D	30	27.98	839.40
m 2231	Trail Brown	8.0 D	30	27.98	839.40
m 2231	Trail Brown	8.5 D	30	27.98	839.40
m 2231	Trail Brown	9.0 D	30	27.98	839.40
m 2231	Trail Brown	9.5 D	60	27.98	1,678.80
m 2231	Trail Brown	10.0 D	60	27.98	1,678.80
m 2231	Trail Brown	10.5 D	60	27.98	1,678.80
m 2231	Trail Brown	11.0 D	60	27.98	1,678.80
m 2231	Trail Brown	11.5 D	60	27.98	1,678.80
m 2231	Trail Brown	12.0 D	60	27.98	1,678.80
m 2231	Trail Brown	12.5 D	30	27.98	839.40
m 2231	Trail Brown	13.0 D	30	27.98	839.40
m 2231	Trail Brown	14.0 D	30	27.98	839.40
m 2023	Newport Wine	9.0 D	20	30.78	615.60
m 2023	Newport Wine	9.5 D	40	30.78	1,231.20
m 2023	Newport Wine	10.0 D	40	30.78	1,231.20
m 2023	Newport Wine	10.5 D	40	30.78	1,231.20
m 2023	Newport Wine	11.0 D	40	30.78	1,231.20
m 2023	Newport Wine	11.5 D	40	30.78	1,231.20
m 2023	Newport Wine	12.0 D	20	30.78	615.60
m 2023	Newport Wine	13.0 D	20	30.78	615.60

Paid

	Total Amount	$24,790.80
	Tax	
	Total Purchase Order	$24,790.80

Message   Authorization

Name: Bruce Penny
Date: 04/18/0X
Title: Purchasing Supervisor

Signature: *Bruce Penny*

Voucher

Check #:	7031	Approval:	JS
Payee:	Nine West Group Inc.	Voucher #:	8522
Amount:	$ 1,097.52	Account #:	12000
Due Date:	09/07/0X	Preparation Date:	08/11/0X

Paid

Description *Purchase of Women's Shoes*

Invoice

Nine West Group Inc.
9 West Plaza
1129 Westchester Ave.
White Plains, NY 10604
  Fax: (914)640-6013
  Ph: (914)640-6400

Date: 8/8/0X
Invoice #: 32501
PO#: 3102
Terms: Net 30
Shipped: United Parcel Service
FOB: Shipping Point

Bill To
Southeast Shoe Distributor, Inc.
1102 Memorial Avenue
Atlanta, Georgia 30303
  Ph: (404)555-5555

Ship To
Southeast Shoe Distributor, Inc.
1102 Memorial Avenue
Atlanta, Georgia 30303

Item #	Description	Size	Quantity	Unit Price	Amount
w369c	Amita White Leather	8.5m	24	$21.00	$504.00
w369c	Amita White Leather	9.5m	24	21.00	504.00

Paid

	Total Amount	$1,008.00
Rate N/A	Tax	
	Shipping	$71.52
	Total Invoice	**$1,079.52**

Message

Receiving Report

Southeast Shoe Distributor, Inc.   **Date Received:** *08/07/0X*
1102 Memorial Avenue   **Receiving Report #: 2610**
Atlanta, Georgia 30303

Received from	**Purchase Order #:**
Nine West Group, Inc.	3102

Freight carrier	**Received by**
United Parcel Service	*Sue Ravens*

Quantity	Item #	Size	Description
24	w369c	8.5 M	
24	w369c	9.5 M	

Condition:
Excellent

Paid

Purchase Order

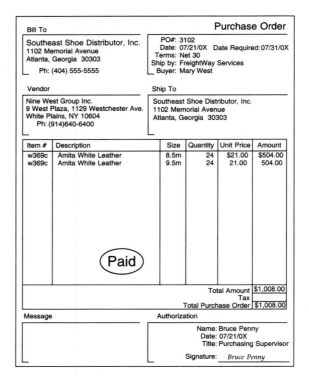

Bill To
Southeast Shoe Distributor, Inc.
1102 Memorial Avenue
Atlanta, Georgia 30303
  Ph: (404) 555-5555

PO#: 3102
Date: 07/21/0X   **Date Required:** 07/31/0X
Terms: Net 30
Ship by: FreightWay Services
Buyer: Mary West

Vendor
Nine West Group Inc.
9 West Plaza, 1129 Westchester Ave.
White Plains, NY 10604
  Ph: (914)640-6400

Ship To
Southeast Shoe Distributor, Inc.
1102 Memorial Avenue
Atlanta, Georgia 30303

Item #	Description	Size	Quantity	Unit Price	Amount
w369c	Amita White Leather	8.5m	24	$21.00	$504.00
w369c	Amita White Leather	9.5m	24	21.00	504.00

Paid

	Total Amount	$1,008.00
	Tax	
	Total Purchase Order	**$1,008.00**

Message   Authorization

Name: Bruce Penny
Date: 07/21/0X
Title: Purchasing Supervisor
Signature: *Bruce Penny*

Southeast Shoe Distributor, Inc.: Performance of Tests of Balances for the Expenditure Cycle (Acquisitions and Cash Disbursements)

Frank A. Buckless, Mark S. Beasley,
Steven M. Glover, and Douglas F. Prawitt

LEARNING OBJECTIVES

After completing and discussing this case you should be able to

- Recognize common documents and records used in the expenditure cycle
- Recognize common tests of balances for accounts payable
- Perform tests of balances for accounts payable
- Evaluate the results of tests of balances for accounts payable using a nonstatistical approach
- Recognize the linkage of substantive tests of balances to management assertions

INTRODUCTION

Southeast Shoe Distributor (SSD) is a closely-owned business that was founded 10 years ago by Stewart Green and Paul Williams. SSD is a distributor that purchases and resells men's, women's, and children's shoes to retail shoe stores located in small to midsize communities. The company's basic strategy is to obtain a broad selection of designer-label and name-brand footwear at low prices for resell to small, one-location, retail stores. SSD targets stores that have a difficult time obtaining reasonable quantities of designer and name-brand footwear. The company is able to keep the cost of footwear low by (1) selectively purchasing large blocks of production overruns, overorders, mid- and late-season deliveries and previous season's stock from manufacturers and other

This case was prepared by Frank A. Buckless, Ph.D. and Mark S. Beasley, Ph.D. of North Carolina State University and Steven M. Glover, Ph.D. and Douglas F. Prawitt, Ph.D. of Brigham Young University, as a basis for class discussion. It is not intended to illustrate either effective or ineffective handling of an administrative situation.

retailers at significant discounts, (2) sourcing in-season name-brand and branded designer footwear directly from factories in Brazil, Italy, and Spain, and (3) negotiating favorable prices with manufacturers by ordering footwear during off-peak production periods and taking delivery at one central warehouse.

During the year, the company purchased merchandise from more than 50 domestic and international vendors, independent resellers, manufacturers, and other retailers that have frequent excess inventory. Designer and name-brand footwear sold by the company include the following: Amalfi, Clarks, Dexter, Fila, Florsheim, Naturalizer, and Rockport. At the current time, SSD has one warehouse located in Atlanta, Georgia. Last year, SSD had net sales of $7,311,214. Sales are strongest in the second and fourth calendar-year quarters, with the first calendar-year quarter substantially weaker than the rest.

BACKGROUND INFORMATION ABOUT THE AUDIT

SSD is required to have an audit of its annual financial statements to fulfill requirements of loan agreements with financial institutions. The audit senior for this engagement is Jorge Hernandez. The two audit staff assigned to this engagement are Joy Avery and you. The two of you are responsible for performing the tests of balances and analytical tests outlined in the expenditure cycle audit program (referenced in the top right-hand corner as *E 2*).

The general ledger accounts related to purchasing and cash disbursement activities at SSD include the following:

- Inventory Purchases
- Purchase Discounts
- Purchase Returns and Allowances
- Freight In
- Administrative Expenses
- Warehousing Expenses
- Selling Expenses
- Prepaid Assets
- Accounts Payable

Joy Avery has already performed audit procedures 1 and 2 listed on working paper *E 2*. Her work is documented on working papers *E 2, E 10, E 50,* and *E 51*. Additionally, Joy has selected the audit sample for audit procedure 3 as noted on working paper *E 52*.

REQUIREMENTS

You are assigned responsibility for completing audit procedure 3a listed on audit program *E 2*. The supporting documents to be examined for this audit procedure are voucher, vendor invoice, receiving report, and purchase order. Assume that you have already tested 35 of the selected sample items, observing no misstatements. The documents and record for the remaining five sample items are provided behind the audit working papers. SSD's polices only require the generation of receiving reports for purchases of inventory and fixed assets. Additionally, purchase orders are not required to be generated for recurring services, such as utilities and cleaning. The results from performing audit procedure 3a should be documented on working paper *E 53*. Adjusting entries for any observed misstatements should be proposed on schedule *E 11*. Finally, assume that there was no systematic pattern or intent to commit a fraud based on a review and discussion with client personnel concerning observed misstatements.

Buckless / Beasley / Glover / Prawitt

Reference: _E 2_
Prepared by: _JA_
Date: _2/28/0Y_
Reviewed by: _____

Southeast Shoe Distributor
Expenditure Cycle Audit Program for
Year-End Analytical Procedures and Tests of Balances
Year Ended: December 31, 200X

Audit Procedures	Initial	Date	Ref.
1. Obtain a lead schedule for Accounts Payable and perform the following:	JA	2/14/0Y	E 10
a. Agree the prior-year balance to prior-year working papers.	JA	2/14/0Y	E 10
b. Agree current-year balance to the general ledger.	JA	2/14/0Y	E 10
2. Obtain a printout of the accounts payable vendor ledgers as of the end of the year and perform the following:	JA	2/17/0Y	N/A
a. Foot the year-end vendor ledgers and agree it to the lead schedule.	JA	2/17/0Y	E 10
b. Scan the year-end vendor ledgers for unusual, related-party, or debit balances and perform follow-up procedures for each one identified.	JA	2/17/0Y	E 50
c. Obtain the last five receiving reports issued before year-end and determine if they were properly included in the year-end vendor ledgers.	JA	2/18/0Y	E 51
d. Obtain the first five receiving reports issued after year-end and determine if they were properly excluded from the year-end vendor ledgers.	JA	2/18/0Y	E 51
3. Select a sample of checks issued after year-end and perform the following:	JA	2/28/0Y	E 52
a. Examine the voucher package and determine if the related payable was properly included or excluded from the year-end vendor ledgers.			E 53

Reference: _E 10_

Prepared by: _JA_

Date: _2/14/0Y_

Reviewed by: _____

Southeast Shoe Distributor
Accounts Payable—Lead Schedule
For the Year Ended December 31, 200X

Account	Audited Balance 12/31/0W	Unaudited Balance 12/31/0X	Adjustments		Adjusted Balance 12/31/0X
			Debit	Credit	
Accounts Payable	$453,370 ✓	$742,704 f, GL			

Tickmark Legend

✓ — *Agreed to prior-year working papers without exception (audit step 1a).*

GL — *Agreed to 12/31/200X general ledger without exception (audit step 1b).*

f — *Agreed to the footed balance of the 12/31/200X accounts payable vendor ledgers without exception (audit step 2a).*

Reference: _E 11_

Prepared by: _____

Date: _____

Reviewed by: _____

Southeast Shoe Distributor
Expenditure Cycle—Proposed Adjusting Entries Schedule
For the Year Ended December 31, 200X

Account	Debit	Credit
Explanation:		
Explanation:		
Explanation:		
Explanation:		

Reference: _E 50_____
Prepared by: _JA_____
Date: __2/17/0Y_____
Reviewed by: _____

Southeast Shoe Distributor
Unusual Balances—Expenditure Cycle Accounts Payable
For the Year Ended December 31, 200X

Vendor	Balance
No unusual or related-party balances were noted. See conclusion below.	

Follow-up procedures performed:
No unusual or related-party accounts payable balances were identified as a result of scanning the year-end vendor ledgers (audit step 2b). Thus, no follow-up procedures are needed.

Reference: _E 51_____

Prepared by: _JA_____

Date: _2/18/0Y_____

Reviewed by: _____

Southeast Shoe Distributor
Nonsampling Tests of Transactions—Expenditure Cycle Accounts Payable
For the Year Ended December 31, 200X

Procedure:

The last receiving report issued before December 31, 200X, was 2814. The vouchers, vendor invoices, and purchase orders supporting the last five receiving reports issued before year-end and first five receiving reports issued after year-end were examined and traced to proper inclusion/exclusion in/ from the December 31, 200X, vendor ledgers (audit steps 2c and d).

Exceptions/Misstatements:

No misstatements were noted.

Conclusion:

The results of audit steps 2c and d support that there were no material cutoff misstatements for purchase transactions occurring just before and after year-end.

Reference: _E 52_
Prepared by: _JA_
Date: _2/28/0Y_
Reviewed by: _____

Southeast Shoe Distributor
Nonstatistical Tests of Transactions Sample Plan—Expenditure Cycle
For the Year Ended December 31, 200X

Sampling Frame	Beg. Doc. # or Page #	End. Doc. # or Page #	Sample Size
Checks issued subsequent to year-end up through 2/28/0Y	7,431	7,584	40

Sample Selection Method:
The sample of checks issued subsequent to year-end were selected using the haphazard selection method.

Sample: _Check Number_

Sample Item	Sample Ref.	Sample Item	Sample Ref.	Sample Item	Sample Ref.
1	7,434	16	7,488	31	7,531
2	7,441	17	7,496	32	7,536
3	7,442	18	7,498	33	7,541
4	7,444	19	7,501	34	7,546
5	7,452	20	7,502	35	7,552
6	7,453	21	7,503	36	7,553
7	7,456	22	7,505	37	7,565
8	7,459	23	7,506	38	7,573
9	7,466	24	7,514	39	7,579
10	7,467	25	7,515	40	7,581
11	7,468	26	7,518		
12	7,473	27	7,520		
13	7,476	28	7,521		
14	7,479	29	7,523		
15	7,486	30	7,527		

Southeast Shoe Distributor
Nonstatistical Tests of Balance Evaluation—Expenditure Cycle Accounts Payable
For the Year Ended December 31, 200X

Misstatements:	Recorded Amount	Audited Amount	Misstatement Amount
Total Sample Misstatement			

Projected Misstatement:		
Total Sample Misstatement		
Dollar Value of Sample	÷	$184,583.10
Percentage Sample Dollar Misstatement	=	
Dollar Value of Accounts Payable per G/L	×	$742,704.11
Projected Dollar Misstatement for Accounts Payable	=	

Allowance for Sampling Risk		
Tolerable Misstatement		$ 40,000.00
Projected Dollar Misstatement for Accounts Payble	−	
Recorded Adjustments	+	
Allowance for Sampling Risk	=	

Conclusions:

Southeast Shoe Distributor, Inc.
Vendor Ledgers for Audit Procedure 3a*
For the Period from December 1, 200X to December 31, 200X

Vendor	Date	Trans. Ref.	Type	Debit Amount	Credit Amount	Balance
Brown Group, Inc.	12/01/0X	Balance Fwd				12,366.94
	12/10/0X	7357	CDJ	12,366.94		0
	12/16/0X	47314	PJ		1,952.64	1,952.64
	12/27/0X	49524	PJ		25,883.00	27,835.64
Georgia Natural Gas Service	12/01/0X	Balance Fwd				446.10
	12/11/0X	7358	CDJ	446.10		0
	12/23/0X	359052-002-08	PJ		553.86	553.86
Metro Cleaning	12/01/0X	Balance Fwd				0
	12/03/0X	18777	PJ		350.00	350.00
	12/27/0X	7415	CDJ	350.00		0
Vargo Rack & Shelving	12/01/0X	Balance Fwd				0
	12/30/0X	2077-45	PJ		717.47	717.47
Weyco Group, Inc.	12/01/0X	Balance Fwd				9,649.56
	12/05/0X	24715	PJ		7,111.88	16,761.44

*Abstracted from the printout of vendor ledgers using exact format of the printout (Note: Trans. Ref. refers to the corresponding check number or vendor invoice number and Type refers to the corresponding Cash Disbursement Journal—CDJ or Purchase Journal—PJ).

Voucher

Check #: 7453   **Paid**   Approval: _JS_

Payee: _Brown Group, Inc._   Voucher #: _9049_

Amount: _$ 1,952.64_   Account #: _12000_

Due Date: _1/10/0Y_   Preparation Date: _12/16/0X_

Description _Purchase of Women's Shoes_

Invoice

Brown Group, Inc.
8300 Maryland Avenue
St. Louis, MO 63105

Fax: (314)854-4000
Ph: (314)7854-4274

Date: 11/4/0X
Invoice #: 47314
PO#: 3336
Terms: Net 30
Shipped: United Parcel Service
FOB: Shipping Point

Bill To
Southeast Shoe Distributor, Inc.
1102 Memorial Avenue
Atlanta, Georgia 30303
Ph: (404)555-5555

Ship To
Southeast Shoe Distributor, Inc.
1102 Memorial Avenue
Atlanta, Georgia 30303

Item #	Description	Size	Quantity	Unit Price	Amount
45623	Naturalizer Royal Pumps Bone	6.5 M	36	$16.79	$604.44
45623	Naturalizer Royal Pumps Bone	7.0 M	36	16.79	604.44
45623	Naturalizer Royal Pumps Bone	7.5 M	36	16.79	604.44

Total Amount	$1,813.32
Rate N/A Tax	
Shipping	$139.32
Total Invoice	**$1,952.64**

Message

Paid

Receiving Report

Southeast Shoe Distributor, Inc.   Date Received: _12/11/0X_
1102 Memorial Avenue   Receiving Report #: **2780**
Atlanta, Georgia 30303

Received from	**Purchase Order #:**
Brown Group, Inc.	_3336_

Freight carrier	**Received by**
United Parcel Service	_Sue Ravens_

Quantity	Item #	Size	Description
_36_	_45623_	_6.5 M_	_Naturalizer Royal Pumps Bone_
_36_	_45623_	_7.0 M_	_''_
_36_	_45623_	_7.5 M_	_''_

Paid

Condition:
Excellent

Purchase Order

Bill To
Southeast Shoe Distributor, Inc.
1102 Memorial Avenue
Atlanta, Georgia 30303
Ph: (404)555-5555

PO#: 3336
Date: 12/05/0X   Date Required: 12/15/0X
Terms: Net 30
Ship by: United Parcel Service
Buyer: Mary West

Vendor
Brown Group, Inc.
8300 Maryland Drive
St. Louis, MO 63105
Ph: (314)854-4000

Ship To
Southeast Shoe Distributor, Inc.
1102 Memorial Avenue
Atlanta, Georgia 30303

Item #	Description	Size	Quantity	Unit Price	Amount
45623	Naturalizer Royal Pumps Bone	6.5 M	36	$16.79	$604.44
45623	Naturalizer Royal Pumps Bone	7.0 M	36	16.79	604.44
45623	Naturalizer Royal Pumps Bone	7.5 M	36	16.79	604.44

Total Amount	$1,813.32
Tax	
Total Purchase Order	**$1,813.32**

Message   Authorization

Paid   Name: Bruce Penny
Date: 12/05/0X
Title: Purchasing Supervisor

Signature: _Bruce Penny_

SSD
Documents for Audit Procedure 3 (continued)

Voucher

Check #: 7473	Approval: JS
Payee: Georgia Natural Gas Service	Voucher #: 9081
Amount: $ 553.86 **(Paid)**	Account #: 75000
Due Date: 1/15/0Y	Preparation Date: 12/23/0X
Description: Monthly Gas Service	

Service For:	Southeast Shoe Distributor, Inc. 1102 Memorial Avenue Atlanta, Georgia 30303	Your Account Number 359052-002-08	Rate - Type of Service 305 - Commercial	Billing Date 12/21/0X

(Paid)   *KT*

	GAS
Previous Balance	446.10
Payment - Thank You	(446.10)
Remaining Balance	0.00
Current Bill	553.86
Total	553.86

Current Bill Past Due After **January 15, 200Y**	Total Amount Due 553.86

HOW YOUR CURRENT GAS CHARGES ARE CALCULATED

Meter Number	Service Period	Days	Type of Reading	Meter Readings Current	Meter Readings Past	CCF Used	BTU Factor	Therms Used
159756	11/18/0X - 12/20/0X	32	Actual	15297	15985	688	1.049	722

Total Therms Billed	Energy Charge Therms X Rate (.73928)	WNA Therms X Factor (-.00558)	Facilities Charge	Taxable Amount	Sales Tax (3.00%)	Current Gas Charges
722	533.76	-4.03	8.00	537.73	16.13	553.86

SEE THE BACK OF THIS BILL FOR ADDITIONAL INFORMATION

GEORGIA NATURAL GAS SERVICES
5605 GLENRIDGE DR NE, ATLANTA, GA 30342
(404) 257-4000

Voucher

Check #: 7523	Approval: JS
Payee: Vargo Rack & Shelving	Voucher #: 9113
Amount: $ 717.47 (Paid)	Account #: 15000
Due Date: 01/27/0Y	Preparation Date: 12/30/0X

Description: Purchase of storage shelving

Invoice

VARGO RACK & SHELVING
6400 Hillandale Drive
Lithonia, GA 30058

Phone: (404)482-4000

Date: 12/28/0X
Invoice #: 2077-45
Customer Order #: 3348
Payment Terms: Net 30
Shipped: Our Truck
FOB: Destination

Bill To
Southeast Shoe Distributor, Inc.
1102 Memorial Avenue
Atlanta, Georgia 30303
Phone: 404-555-555

Ship To
Southeast Shoe Distributor, Inc.
1102 Memorial Avenue
Atlanta, Georgia 30303

Item #	Description	Quantity	Unit Price	Amount
H51118	Penco Erectomatic Shelving, beige	6	121.30	727.80

(Paid)

	Total Amount	$727.80
Rate 6.00% Tax		$43.67
	Shipping	
	Total Invoice	**$771.47**

Receiving Report

Southeast Shoe Distributor, Inc.   Date Received: 12/28/0X
1102 Memorial Avenue   Receiving Report #: **2805**
Atlanta, Georgia 30303

Received from	**Purchase Order #:**
Vargo Rack & Shelving	3348

Freight carrier	**Received by**
Their Truck	Sue Ravens

Quantity	Item #	Size	Description
6	H51118		Penco Erectomatic Shelving

(Paid)

Condition:
Excellent

Purchase Order

Bill To

Southeast Shoe Distributor, Inc.
1102 Memorial Avenue
Atlanta, Georgia 30303
Ph: (404)555-5555

PO#: 3348
Date: 12/26/0X   Date Required: 12/28/0X
Terms: Net 30
Ship by: Your Truck
Buyer: Mary Tally

Vendor

Vargo Rack & Shelving
6400 Hillandale Drive
Lithonia, GA 30058
Ph: (404)555-1212

Ship To

Southeast Shoe Distributor, Inc.
1102 Memorial Avenue
Atlanta, Georgia 30303

Item #	Description	Size	Quantity	Unit Price	Amount
H51118	Beige Penco Erectomatic Shelving		6	$121.30	$727.80

	Total Amount	$727.80
	Tax	$43.67
	Total Purchase Order	$771.47

Message   Authorization

(Paid)

Name: Bruce Penny
Date: 12/2/0X
Title: Purchasing Supervisor
Signature: Bruce Penny

Voucher

Check #:	7573	Approval:	JS
Payee:	Weyco Group, Inc.	Voucher #:	9138
Amount:	$19,656.00 **Paid**	Account #:	12000
Due Date:	02/23/0Y	Preparation Date:	1/13/OY

Description Purchase of Men's Shoes

Invoice

Weyco Group, Inc.
234 East Reservoir Avenue, P.O. Box 1188
Milwaukee, WI 53201

Fax: (414)263-8800
Ph: (414)263-8808

Date: 01/09/0X
Invoice #: 26171
PO#: 3349
Terms: Net 45
Shipped: Transit Freight Company
FOB: Shipping Point

Bill To
Southeast Shoe Distributor, Inc.
1102 Memorial Avenue
Atlanta, Georgia 30303
Ph: 404-555-5555

Ship To
Southeast Shoe Distributor, Inc.
1102 Memorial Avenue
Atlanta, Georgia 30303

Item #	Description	Size	Quantity	Unit Price	Amount
1617	Stacy Adams Low Top Tie Black	9.0 D	25	$31.50	$787.50
1617	Stacy Adams Low Top Tie Black	9.5 D	50	31.50	1,575.00
1617	Stacy Adams Low Top Tie Black	10.0 D	50	31.50	1,575.00
1617	Stacy Adams Low Top Tie Black	10.5 D	50	31.50	1,575.00
1617	Stacy Adams Low Top Tie Black	11.0 D	50	31.50	1,575.00
1617	Stacy Adams Low Top Tie Black	11.5 D	25	31.50	787.50
1617	Stacy Adams Low Top Tie Black	12.0 D	25	31.50	787.50
1617	Stacy Adams Low Top Tie Black	13.0 D	25	31.50	787.50
1618	Stacy Adams Low Top Tie Brown	9.0 D	25	31.50	787.50
1618	Stacy Adams Low Top Tie Brown	9.5 D	50	31.50	1,575.00
1618	Stacy Adams Low Top Tie Brown	10.0 D	50	31.50	1,575.00
1618	Stacy Adams Low Top Tie Brown	10.5 D	50	31.50	1,575.00
1618	Stacy Adams Low Top Tie Brown	11.0 D	50	31.50	1,575.00
1618	Stacy Adams Low Top Tie Brown	11.5 D	25	31.50	787.50
1618	Stacy Adams Low Top Tie Brown	12.0 D	25	31.50	787.50
1618	Stacy Adams Low Top Tie Brown	13.0 D	25	31.50	787.50

Total Amount		$18,900.00
Rate N/A	Tax	
	Shipping	$756.00
	Total Invoice	$19,656.00

Message **Paid**

Receiving Report

Southeast Shoe Distributor, Inc. **Date Received:** 01/09/OY
1102 Memorial Avenue **Receiving Report #:** **2814**
Atlanta, Georgia 30303

Received from **Purchase Order #:**
Weyco Group, Inc. 3349

Freight carrier **Received by**
Transit Frieght Company Sue Ravens

Quantity	Item #	Size	Description
25	m1132	9.0 D	Stacy Adams Low Top Tie Black
50	m1132	9.5 D	"
50	m1132	10.0 D	"
50	m1132	10.5 D	"
50	m1132	11.0 D	"
25	m1132	11.5 D	"
25	m1132	12.0 D	"
25	m1132	13.0 D	"
25	m1143	9.0 D	Stacy Adams Low Top Tie Brown
50	m1143	9.5 D	"
50	m1143	10.0 D	"
50	m1143	10.5 D	"
50	m1143	11.0 D	"
25	m1143	11.5 D	"
25	m1143	12.0 D	"
25	m1143	13.0 D	"

Paid

Condition:
Excellent

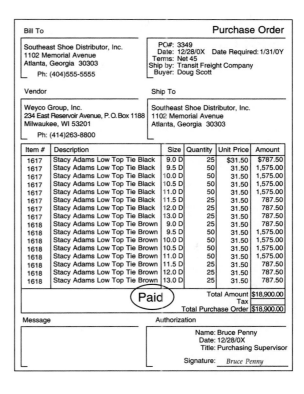

Purchase Order

Bill To
Southeast Shoe Distributor, Inc.
1102 Memorial Avenue
Atlanta, Georgia 30303
Ph: (404)555-5555

PO#: 3349
Date: 12/28/0X **Date Required:** 1/31/0Y
Terms: Net 45
Ship by: Transit Freight Company
Buyer: Doug Scott

Vendor
Weyco Group, Inc.
234 East Reservoir Avenue, P.O. Box 1188
Milwaukee, WI 53201
Ph: (414)263-8800

Ship To
Southeast Shoe Distributor, Inc.
1102 Memorial Avenue
Atlanta, Georgia 30303

Item #	Description	Size	Quantity	Unit Price	Amount
1617	Stacy Adams Low Top Tie Black	9.0 D	25	$31.50	$787.50
1617	Stacy Adams Low Top Tie Black	9.5 D	50	31.50	1,575.00
1617	Stacy Adams Low Top Tie Black	10.0 D	50	31.50	1,575.00
1617	Stacy Adams Low Top Tie Black	10.5 D	50	31.50	1,575.00
1617	Stacy Adams Low Top Tie Black	11.0 D	50	31.50	1,575.00
1617	Stacy Adams Low Top Tie Black	11.5 D	25	31.50	787.50
1617	Stacy Adams Low Top Tie Black	12.0 D	25	31.50	787.50
1617	Stacy Adams Low Top Tie Black	13.0 D	25	31.50	787.50
1618	Stacy Adams Low Top Tie Brown	9.0 D	25	31.50	787.50
1618	Stacy Adams Low Top Tie Brown	9.5 D	50	31.50	1,575.00
1618	Stacy Adams Low Top Tie Brown	10.0 D	50	31.50	1,575.00
1618	Stacy Adams Low Top Tie Brown	10.5 D	50	31.50	1,575.00
1618	Stacy Adams Low Top Tie Brown	11.0 D	50	31.50	1,575.00
1618	Stacy Adams Low Top Tie Brown	11.5 D	25	31.50	787.50
1618	Stacy Adams Low Top Tie Brown	12.0 D	25	31.50	787.50
1618	Stacy Adams Low Top Tie Brown	13.0 D	25	31.50	787.50

Paid	Total Amount	$18,900.00
	Tax	
	Total Purchase Order	$18,900.00

Message Authorization

Name: Bruce Penny
Date: 12/28/0X
Title: Purchasing Supervisor

Signature: Bruce Penny

SSD
Documents for Audit Procedure 3 (continued)

	Voucher
Check #: _7579_ (Paid)	Approval: __JS__
Payee: _Metro Cleaning Service_	Voucher #: _9170_
Amount: _$ 350.00_	Account #: _62000_
Due Date: _02/28/0Y_	Preparation Date: _02/01/0Y_
Description _Monthly Cleaning Service_	

Invoice

Metro Cleaning Service
600 10th Street NW
Atlanta, GA 30318
(404) 999-1818

Invoice #:   19483

Bill To:

Southeast Shoe Distributor, Inc.
1102 Memorial Avenue
Atlanta, Georgia 30303

Date Due: 02/28/0Y

Date	Description	Amount
01/31/0Y	January 200Y Cleaning Service	350.00

KT

(Paid)

	Total Amount Due	$350.00

EyeMax Corporation:
Evaluation of Audit Differences

Frank A. Buckless, Mark S. Beasley,
Steven M. Glover, and Douglas F. Prawitt

LEARNING OBJECTIVES

After completing and discussing this case you should be able to

- Evaluate proposed adjustments to client financial statements
- Appreciate the degree of judgment involved in determining a minimum adjustment, particularly when the client's preference is to not adjust
- Know how to support your decision to either book or pass adjustments

INTRODUCTION

The information below relates to the audit of EyeMax Corporation, a client with a calendar year-end. EyeMax has debt agreements associated with publicly traded bonds that require audited financial statements. The company is currently, and historically has been, in compliance with the covenants in the debt agreements. Further, management believes that having audited financial statements prepared in accordance with GAAP is important to shareholders and is "simply a good business practice."

Assume that audit fieldwork has been completed. At this point you are considering several items that have been posted to a "Summary of Audit Differences." The Summary of Audit Differences is a listing auditors compile during an audit as they uncover potential or proposed corrections to the client's financial statements. Additional detailed information about the items posted to the Summary of Audit Differences is provided on the following pages. Based on the information provided, you will be asked to decide the minimum adjustment (if any) to the financial statements that would be necessary before issuing a "clean opinion."

Make sure you carefully consider materiality as you evaluate the misstatements because auditors do not require their clients to book immaterial adjustments. Therefore, even if, for example, a client has followed a non-GAAP procedure, no adjustment would be required unless the impact is material (i.e., an individual adjustment(s) is

This case was prepared by Frank A. Buckless, Ph.D. and Mark S. Beasley, Ph.D. of North Carolina State University and Steven M. Glover, Ph.D. and Douglas F. Prawitt, Ph.D. of Brigham Young University, as a basis for class discussion. It is not intended to illustrate either effective or ineffective handling of an administrative situation.

greater than tolerable misstatement or aggregated sum of all misstatements are greater than overall materiality). At the end of this case you will also be asked several questions related to your decisions. Please carefully consider the following information before you answer the questions.

BACKGROUND

Nature of client's business. EyeMax is engaged in research and development, manufacture and sale of medical devices used by ophthalmologists during eye surgeries. Customers of the product lines are primarily doctors of ophthalmology and laser-eye clinics. The company was founded in 1982 by Wayne Carruth, MD, to produce and market a line of devices used in optic surgery that he designed. Several years ago, Eye-Max began to exploit the future prospects of laser technology in optic surgery. EyeMax has grown rapidly, especially in recent years, and has made significant strides in market share. EyeMax is currently the third-largest supplier of optical equipment, with a 25% market share, and employs 425 people, up from only 285 employees just two years ago. Thirty percent of the stock in EyeMax is owned by Wayne Carruth and his immediate family. Approximately 40 percent of the stock is owned by company employees, with the largest individual holding equal to about 10 percent of the company's shares. Venture capitalists and a few outside investors hold the remaining shares. The company's shares currently trade on the over-the-counter bulletin-board market.[1]

Accounting environment, risk assessments, and audit approach. The accounting department employs eight people: The controller is a CPA, the accounting supervisor and payroll supervisor each have college degrees in business, and the remaining five clerks have limited training and experience. Although the company has no material weaknesses in internal controls, the accounting department has not kept pace with the demands created by growth in production and sales. The department is overworked. Key controls appear to be functioning but are not always performed on a timely basis. In the planning phase of the audit, both inherent risk and control risk were assessed at less than the maximum, but the audit plan specifies an audit approach that relies primarily on substantive testing.

Management's position regarding audit adjustments. EyeMax has been an audit client for five years. Prior audits have generally detected accounting misstatements, and EyeMax's management has readily made the recommended adjustments. As the client has booked all identified prior-year differences, there are no "turn-around" effects to be considered from the prior year. However, in the past, audit reports have been dated before the end of February. This year, because of deadlines imposed by other clients and staffing problems at your audit firm, fieldwork at EyeMax was not completed by the end of February. Nonetheless, the president of EyeMax, without prior consultation with your firm, provided shareholders and creditors with preliminary earnings information in the last week of February. It is now the middle of March, and the president strongly prefers to minimize adjustments to the financial statements because he believes that such adjustments will unduly reduce shareholder and creditor confidence. In

---

[1]The OTC Bulletin Board (OTCBB) is a regulated quotation service that displays real-time quotes, last-sale prices, and volume information in over-the-counter (OTC) equity securities. An OTC equity security generally is any equity that is not listed or traded on NASDAQ or a national securities exchange. OTCBB securities include national, regional, and foreign equity issues, warrants, units, American Depositary Receipts, and Direct Participation Programs. For more information see www.otcbb.com.

his opinion, no adjustment should be made unless it is absolutely essential for fair presentation. The managing partner of your office has been notified of the situation and the client's request. She has not yet reviewed the supporting detail presented below, but at this point she agrees that the audit team should not require adjustments be made unless the firm has no choice based on firm audit-practice standards.

Materiality. For purposes of planning and conducting the audit, total financial statement materiality was set at $625,000. This amount is equal to approximately 5% of earnings before taxes. (Note that because materiality is stated on a before-tax basis, all of the information below is also presented on a before-tax basis.) According to firm policy, tolerable misstatement for any one financial statement account cannot exceed 75% of overall materiality.

MISSTATEMENTS POSTED TO THE SUMMARY OF AUDIT DIFFERENCES

Four proposed adjustments are posted to the Summary of Audit Differences. These differences are related to warranty expense, repair and maintenance expense, litigation expense, and accounts receivable. All items posted to the Summary of Audit Differences have been discussed with the client and the client agrees with our (the auditors') position on each item. However, for the reasons discussed above, the client would prefer not to book any of the items in the fiscal year under audit. The first three adjustments have been calculated/estimated based on nonsampling procedures. Information about the last difference is based on audit sampling. A sample was selected from accounts receivables. The sample size was determined based on the tolerable misstatement for the account, the expected misstatement in the population tested, and the acceptable level of risk.

Warranty expense. Warranty expense in the current year is estimated to be understated by $130,000 based on the following information: EyeMax grants a written one-year warranty for all products, and estimates of warranty expense based on current-year sales have been properly recorded. However, during the last two years, the company has been making verbal commitments to repair or replace all products for a two-year period. The company has been complying with its verbal commitments and intends to continue the practice to improve customer relations. Because of this change in warranty policy, analysis of warranty repair and replacement data supports a $130,000 addition to the warranty expense estimate for the current year.

Repair and maintenance expense. Repair expense in the current year is understated by $200,000. The client inappropriately capitalized $240,000 of cost related to modifications to its production process. Because the modifications were unsuccessful, the full amount should be written off in the current year. The client has included one-sixth of the capitalized amount in depreciation expense for the year, therefore, net of the amount included in depreciation expense for the current year, overall expense in the current year is understated by $200,000.

Litigation expense. Product liability expense is overstated by $50,000 based on the following information: The client maintains product liability insurance with a $50,000 per occurrence deductible. The client has an excellent record relating to product liability. One liability case was pending at year-end, and the client had conservatively accrued $50,000 at year-end to provide for the potential loss even though the likelihood of loss was remote. A judge ruled the case was without merit shortly after year-end.

Accounts Receivable. The major audit work in the accounts receivable area was confirmation of customer balances. At year-end, EyeMax had receivables from 1,545 customers with a book value of approximately $12,600,000. Based on preliminary estimates, a random sample of 40 accounts was selected for positive confirmation. Customer-reported differences and alternative audit procedures applied to nonreplies revealed misstatements in four accounts that are detailed in Exhibit 1. The misstatements all appeared to be unintentional (e.g., using an incorrect price in billing). The net effect of the misstatements is an overstatement of Accounts Receivable (and Sales) at year-end.

Exhibit 1

Item Number	Customer Number	Customer Name	Balance Per Client	Balance Per Audit	Difference
1	998	Clear Vision Clinic	14,226	10,562	3,664
2	1963	South Cleveland Ophthalmologists	6,871	4,332	2,539
3	1133	Saint Luke's Medical Center	1,955	1,551	404
4	2479	Speedy Eye Center	25,587	23,532	2,055
5 to 40		All other receivables in sample	277,457	277,457	0
		Totals	326,096	317,434	8,662

SUMMARY OF AUDIT DIFFERENCES

The following items have been recorded on the Summary of Audit Differences:

	Known Misstatement
Warranty expense	$130,000
Repair and maintenance expense	200,000
Litigation expense	(50,000)
Accounts Receivables (Sales)	8,662
Net overstatement of earnings	$288,662

REQUIREMENTS

Assume that you are the auditor responsible for the EyeMax audit. It is now March 30, and all planned fieldwork has been completed. Recall that total financial statement materiality has been set at $625,000. Taking into account information provided, please answer the following questions.

1. Which of the following three alternatives best describes the conditions under which you would issue a clean opinion for EyeMax? (select one)

    _____ a. I would not be willing to issue a clean opinion even if EyeMax is willing to make adjustments for items on the Summary of Audit Differences.

    _____ b. I would be willing to issue a clean opinion without any adjustments.

_____ c. I would be willing to issue a clean opinion only if EyeMax is willing to make some adjustments to their financial statements for items on the Summary of Audit Differences.

Briefly explain your choice:

2. If you selected options **"a"** or **"b"** in question 1, assume now that the client has decided that they will make an adjustment of up to $250,000 to their financial statements. Please decompose the total adjustment you would recommend into the individual account classifications included on the Summary of Audit Differences in the space provided below (e.g., what adjustment would you require for warranty expense, repair and maintenance expense, etc? The dollar values of your individual account adjustments should sum to no more than $250,000).

If you selected item **"c"** in question 1, continue to assume that the client prefers to make no adjustments. What is the minimum dollar value of the total adjustment to net income that you would require before issuing a clean opinion? $ _____. Please decompose this total adjustment into the individual account classifications included on the Summary of Audit Differences in the space provided below (e.g., what adjustment, if any, would you require for warranty expense, repair and maintenance expense, etc? The dollar values of your individual account adjustments should sum to your required minimum adjustment).

Warranty expense	_____
Repair and maintenance expense	_____
Litigation expense	_____
Accounts Receivables/Sales	_____
Total	_____

Please briefly explain your decisions:

Auto Parts, Inc.: Considering Materiality When Evaluating Accounting Policies and Footnote Disclosures

Frank A. Buckless, Mark S. Beasley,
Steven M. Glover, and Douglas F. Prawitt

LEARNING OBJECTIVES

After completing and discussing this case you should be able to

- Understand audit and footnote-disclosure issues associated with changes in accounting principles
- Develop a reasonable estimate for financial statement materiality and identify qualitative issues that may affect materiality estimates
- Evaluate the reasonableness of a client's proposed accounting and disclosure preference

BACKGROUND

Auto Parts, Inc. ("the Company") manufactures automobile subassemblies marketed primarily to the "big three" U.S. automakers. The publicly-held Company's unaudited financial statements for the year ended December 31, 200X, reflect total assets of $56 million, total revenues of approximately $73 million, and pretax income of $6 million. The Company's audited financial statements for the year ended December 31, 200W, reflected total assets of $47 million, total revenues of approximately $60 million, and pretax income of $5 million. Earnings per share have increased steadily during the past five years, with a cumulative return of 140% over that period.

During 200X, the Company significantly expanded its plant and fixed-asset spending to accommodate increased orders received by its brake valve division. The company also accumulated significant levels of tooling inventory, which primarily consists of drill

This case was prepared by Frank A. Buckless, Ph.D. and Mark S. Beasley, Ph.D. of North Carolina State University and Steven M. Glover, Ph.D. and Douglas F. Prawitt, Ph.D. of Brigham Young University, as a basis for class discussion. It is not intended to illustrate either effective or ineffective handling of an administrative situation.

bits and machine parts utilized in the manufacturing process. The nature of the tooling inventory is such that the parts are worn out in a relatively short period of time, requiring continual replacement.

In prior years, the Company expensed tooling supplies as they were purchased. However, in 200X the controller and chief financial officer determined that capitalization of the tooling inventory would be the preferable method of accounting. The Company changed its accounting policy accordingly and began to include the tooling supplies inventory in "other current assets" until the inventory is placed into service, at which time they transfer the inventory to expense.

During the prior year, 200W, the Company incurred roughly $650,000 of tooling expense and held approximately $175,000 of the inventory on hand at year-end (the on-hand inventory was not included in assets on Auto Parts' balance sheet at 12/31/0W). The unaudited financial statements for the year ended December 31, 200X, reflect $1,000,000 of tooling expense on the income statement and $300,000 of tooling inventory as current assets on the balance sheet. Because your accounting firm serves as external auditor for Auto Parts, the chief financial officer and the controller asked your firm for advice on whether the Company would be required to account for and disclose the accounting policy change as a change in accounting principle. In the client's opinion, the change is not material to the financial statements and, therefore, would not require disclosure in the 200X financial statements. The client strongly prefers to not make any disclosure related to the policy change.

REQUIREMENTS

1. Do you agree that capitalization of the tooling inventory is the preferable method of accounting at this company? Why or why not?

2. Assuming the policy change is considered material, how should it be reported and disclosed in the financial statements and what effect, if any, would the accounting change have on the auditor's report?

3. In general, how do auditors develop an estimate of planning materiality? For Auto Parts, Inc., what is your preliminary estimate of financial statement materiality? Are there qualitative factors that might impact your decision about the materiality of the accounting treatment and the related disclosure?

4. Do you concur with management's assessment that the accounting change is immaterial and, therefore, requires no disclosure? Why or why not?

K&K, Inc.:
Leveraging Audit Insights to
Provide Value-Added Services

Frank A Buckless, Mark S. Beasley,
Steven M. Glover, and Douglas F. Prawitt

LEARNING OBJECTIVES

After completing and discussing this case you should be able to

- List key issues to consider when auditing the production process and inventory balances for a manufacturing firm
- Understand the role of a manufacturing client's costing system in the context of a financial statement audit
- Understand how insights gained through the conduct of a financial statement audit can be used as a foundation to add additional value to auditing services provided for a client
- Leverage knowledge of concepts from many different disciplines to generate useful business insights for audit clients

INTRODUCTION

Spencer and Loveland, LLP, is a medium-sized, regional accounting firm based in the western part of the United States. A new client of the firm, K&K, Inc., which manufactures a variety of picture frames, recently contracted with Spencer and Loveland to perform an audit of the company's financial statements for the year ended December 31, 200X. K&K expects to use the audited financial statements to obtain a more favorable line of credit with their bank.

Spencer and Loveland has a reputation for providing value to their clients above and beyond the high-quality auditing services they perform. They successfully look for opportunities to leverage insights obtained during the audit as a basis for offering advice to their clients as a business adviser. K&K management is eager to receive Spencer

This case was prepared by Frank A. Buckless, Ph.D. and Mark S. Beasley, Ph.D. of North Carolina State University and Steven M. Glover, Ph.D. and Douglas F. Prawitt, Ph.D. of Brigham Young University, as a basis for class discussion. It is not intended to illustrate either effective or ineffective handling of an administrative situation.

and Loveland's financial advice, given that the company's current accounting personnel primarily have clerical backgrounds. Thus, the audit engagement team has been instructed to generate suggestions that might help improve the growth and profitability of K&K, which has taken a turn for the worse during the past year.

K&K's original, labor-intensive, custom-frame line appears to be struggling. Given rising costs for skilled labor over the past few years, K&K's production manager believes that it is only a matter of time before the company's older custom-frame line will begin to lose the long-term profitability it has enjoyed. He believes the custom line's declining profitability over the past year vindicates the decision to expand the company's product line into new areas. At the beginning of last year, K&K invested in the RX-1000 system to mass-produce plastic frames. Internal cost accounting reports indicate that the new plastic-frame line has been quite profitable, despite operating at low volume levels relative to its capacity. The production manager recently recommended to K&K's president that the company consider discontinuing the labor-intensive custom-frame line to focus on expanding the less labor-intensive, higher-volume, higher-margin line of plastic frames.

You are a second-year audit senior at Spencer and Loveland. You and your audit staff are currently auditing the inventory and production costing systems at K&K. You and the junior staff auditor on the team have performed most of the audit procedures outlined on the audit program and have documented your findings in the audit papers.

As audit senior, you are responsible for reviewing the working papers and reporting to the audit engagement manager any areas of concern with respect to the audit. In addition, the manager asked you to analyze the client's inventory and production situation to indicate any areas in which you believe the firm can provide value-added constructive suggestions to the client.

BACKGROUND ABOUT K&K, INC.

K&K, Inc. was founded 25 years ago when brothers Kent and Kevin Shaw started making custom-made picture frames for local artists using their father's workshop. They soon realized there was profit to be made in building large frames for use by painting and portrait studios. Over the years, K&K has become a well-known picture frame manufacturer in the western part of the United States and has distinguished itself as a company that produces and sells high-quality, made-to-order picture frames. K&K manufactures and sells three basic sizes of frames, which are relatively large and ornate. K&K sells wholesale to portrait studios, retailers, and other users of large, hardwood picture frames.

Due to the nature of the frames produced, the production process for custom frames at K&K is labor intensive. Most of the work is done by hand, with the aid of specialized carving and shaping tools. Skilled workers use these tools to craft the wood pieces used in making the picture frames. K&K uses a traditional job-order costing system and allocates overhead costs to the frames on the basis of direct labor hours. K&K's custom frames can be categorized into three basic sizes (small, medium, and large) that use a variety of designs and materials.

K&K has grown slowly over the past 25 years, generating reasonable profits along the way. Early last year, management decided to accelerate its growth by entering the market for smaller, mass-produced picture frames of the type sold in most craft and department stores. The company first experimented with inexpensive metal frames. They purchased two used machines to produce these frames, which manufactured a large quantity of metal frames in a relatively short time. However, the frames produced were of varying quality and did not sell well. Thus, the machines remained idle through the second half of last year, and the company does not plan to produce any more of this type of frame.

K&K currently produces about 4,000 custom hardwood frames a month, or 48,000 a year. After the failed experiment with mass-produced metal frames, K&K invested in new machinery called the RX-1000 system. This new system is capable of producing standard-sized (5 × 7, 8 × 10, and 11 × 14 inch) plastic picture frames at a rate of up to 60,000 frames a month, with little variation in quality. The new machinery fits easily into K&K's existing plant facilities.

Even though the machinery was quite expensive, the plastic frame line is much less labor-intensive to produce than the custom hardwood frame line. Based on the past year's cost data, the production manager is convinced that the new machinery will pay for itself in a matter of two or three years as production and sales volumes for the new frame line increase. Production volumes for the new frames averaged about 24,000 frames a month over the past year, which is close to the production level of 288,000 K&K had budgeted.

Sale prices on these mass-produced plastic frames are obviously much lower than those for the custom frames, but management expected to generate a reasonable profit through high-volume production and higher percentage profit margins. So far, K&K's internal data indicates that the new line is far more profitable than had been hoped even at current production volumes, with gross margins just below 50%. By contrast, the gross margin percentage for the custom frame line dropped from its usual average of 9% to 10% to an anemic 5.6% over the past year. The production foreman prepared a cost summary for the company's two product lines, which is provided on the pages that follow (see Exhibits 1 and 2).

The RX-1000 system consists of three machines integrated into a single system. The first machine mixes appropriate quantities of the resins and other liquid and powder materials needed to produce a molded plastic frame. The second machine injects the mixed raw materials into a large sheet of molds of a particular size, depending on the production run. When the material is cool, the machine breaks the hardened frames free of the molds, and the molds are then manually fed into the third stage. Here, the third machine polishes the frames and inserts a clear, hard plastic sheet, which serves as a picture protector. Workers manually place a glossy paper picture of an attractive young couple behind the clear plastic in each frame (for marketing purposes), and the frames are then packaged for sale and shipment.

The RX-1000 system initially cost $380,000. Management estimates each of the three machines will have a useful life of six years. K&K depreciates the machinery using the straight-line method. These new machines do not require nearly as much direct labor as the custom frame line, but in addition to the manual labor needed to package the frames, a specially trained employee is required to operate and monitor the system.

The system is also costly to maintain, requiring regular maintenance every two weeks to keep it running effectively. Each regular maintenance cycle requires replacement of parts and lubricants, costing approximately $2,450 a month for labor and parts that must be replaced regularly. A breakdown of expected maintenance and other costs is found in the production foreman's analysis of production costs in the following pages.

Early on, the RX-1000 was so effective at mass-producing defect-free frames that management rented out an additional storage facility to hold the finished inventory produced by the new machinery. Later in the year, production rates had to be scaled back, and the system periodically sat idle until plastic frame inventories shrank to more reasonable levels. Management wants to be in a position to fill orders on a timely basis and is content to have a considerable amount of both finished goods and raw material inventories on hand.

Inventory costs consist of direct materials, direct labor, and overhead. Overhead continues to be allocated to both product lines from a common, companywide cost pool using direct labor hours as the activity base. Further detail on K&K's production costs are found in the following exhibits.

REQUIREMENTS

1. Briefly list and explain the primary audit risks in the production and inventory segment of the K&K audit.

2. Identify any accounting or auditing issues in the way K&K handles its product costs, including overhead allocation, that need to be addressed in the current audit.

3. Review the analysis performed by K&K on the two product lines. K&K's management is debating the elimination of the manual line given that it is no longer profitable. Should K&K discontinue the labor-intensive custom-frame product line? Why or why not?

4. Based on your analysis, prepare a memo to the audit manager suggesting areas in K&K's inventory and production-costing systems where your firm could provide advice and value-added services to the client. In addition, suggest any areas in which your firm might be able to provide consulting services that would be of value to the client.

Exhibit 1—Cost Breakdown

Direct Materials

Custom (cost per foot)[1]		Plastic (cost per oz.)[2]	
Maple	$1.85	Tan	$0.05
Oak	$2.55	Brown	$0.05
Cherry	$3.30	Black	$0.05

Glass or Plastic Sheeting (per unit)—Regular

Custom		Plastic	
Size Small	$4.50	Size 5 × 7	$0.06
Size Medium	$5.00	Size 8 × 10	$0.09
Size Large	$6.00	Size 11 × 14	$0.11

Glass or Plastic Sheeting (per unit)—Nonglare

Custom		Plastic	
Size Small	$5.00	Size 5 × 7	$0.08
Size Medium	$5.75	Size 8 × 10	$0.11
Size Large	$7.10	Size 11 × 14	$0.14

Direct Labor

Custom			Plastic		
DL Rate / hour:		$16.00	DL Rate / hour:		$12.00
	Hrs./unit	Unit Labor Cost		Hrs./unit	Unit Labor Cost
Size Small	1.0	$16.00	Size 5 × 7	0.015	$ 0.18
Size Medium	1.5	$24.00	Size 8 × 10	0.015	$ 0.18
Size Large	2.0	$32.00	Size 11 × 14	0.015	$ 0.18

Overhead per Direct Labor Hour

Budgeted Direct Labor Hours:[3]	76,320
Overhead Rate per Direct Labor Hour:[4]	$2.36 ($180,333 ÷ 76,320)

Breakdown of Overhead Costs

Warehouse Rent	$5,250 /month
Warehouse Utilities	$750 /month
Misc. Indirect Materials	$350 /month[5]
Sales Bonuses	$275 /month
Maintenance on RX-1000 system	$1,650 /month
Replacement Parts for RX-1000 system	$800 /month
Depreciation for RX-1000 system	$5,278 /month[6]
Depreciation for Custom Frame Machinery	$675 /month
Total **Annual** Overhead Costs	$180,333 /year

[1]Size Small requires 5 feet, Size Medium requires 8 feet, and Size Large requires 10 feet.
[2]Size 5 × 7 requires 2 ozs., Size 8 × 10 requires 3 ozs., and Size 11 × 14 requires 4.5 ozs.
[3]Based on a production level of 48,000 custom frames and 288,000 plastic frames. K&K produces approximately equal proportions of the three frame sizes in both product lines.
[4]Overhead rate per DLH equals total annual overhead costs divided by budgeted total direct labor hours. Assume for simplicity that budgeted direct labor hours equal actual direct labor hours, and that budgeted costs equal actual costs. Thus, there is no over/under applied overhead for the year.
[5]Assume approximately $\frac{1}{2}$ of indirect materials costs are attributable to each product line.
[6]$5,278 = $380,000 ÷ 72 mos.

Exhibit 2—Comparison Cost Breakdown

Custom / Plastic

Total Costs	Size Small	Size Medium	Size Large	Total Costs	Size 5 × 7	Size 8 × 10	Size 11 × 14
Maple w/ regular	$ 32.11	$ 47.34	$ 61.23	Tan w/ regular	$ 0.38	$ 0.45	$ 0.55
Maple w/ nonglare	$ 32.61	$ 48.09	$ 62.33	Tan w/ nonglare	$ 0.39	$ 0.47	$ 0.58
Oak w/ regular	$ 35.61	$ 52.94	$ 68.23	Brown w/ regular	$ 0.38	$ 0.45	$ 0.55
Oak w/ nonglare	$ 36.11	$ 53.69	$ 69.33	Brown w/ nonglare	$ 0.39	$ 0.47	$ 0.58
Cherry w/ regular	$ 39.36	$ 58.94	$ 75.73	Black w/ regular	$ 0.38	$ 0.45	$ 0.55
Cherry w/ nonglare	$ 39.86	$ 59.69	$ 76.83	Black w/ nonglare	$ 0.39	$ 0.47	$ 0.58

Sales Price (Wholesale) / Sales Price (Wholesale)

	Size Small	Size Medium	Size Large		Size 5 × 7	Size 8 × 10	Size 11 × 14
Maple w/ regular	$ 32.50	$ 49.50	$ 66.00	Tan w/ regular	$ 0.70	$ 0.85	$ 1.00
Maple w/ nonglare	$ 33.50	$ 50.75	$ 68.00	Tan w/ nonglare	$ 0.75	$ 0.90	$ 1.07
Oak w/ regular	$ 35.00	$ 55.50	$ 73.00	Brown w/ regular	$ 0.70	$ 0.85	$ 1.00
Oak w/ nonglare	$ 36.00	$ 56.50	$ 75.00	Brown w/ nonglare	$ 0.75	$ 0.90	$ 1.07
Cherry w/ regular	$ 42.75	$ 62.00	$ 81.00	Black w/ regular	$ 0.70	$ 0.85	$ 1.00
Cherry w/ nonglare	$ 43.75	$ 63.00	$ 83.00	Black w/ nonglare	$ 0.75	$ 0.90	$ 1.07

Margin / Margin

	Size Small	Size Medium	Size Large		Size 5 × 7	Size 8 × 10	Size 11 × 14
Maple w/ regular	$ 0.39	$ 2.16	$ 4.77	Tan w/ regular	$ 0.32	$ 0.40	$ 0.45
Maple w/ nonglare	$ 0.89	$ 2.66	$ 5.67	Tan w/ nonglare	$ 0.36	$ 0.43	$ 0.49
Oak w/ regular	$ (0.61)	$ 2.56	$ 4.77	Brown w/ regular	$ 0.32	$ 0.40	$ 0.45
Oak w/ nonglare	$ (0.11)	$ 2.81	$ 5.67	Brown w/ nonglare	$ 0.36	$ 0.43	$ 0.49
Cherry w/ regular	$ 3.39	$ 3.06	$ 5.27	Black w/ regular	$ 0.32	$ 0.40	$ 0.45
Cherry w/ nonglare	$ 3.89	$ 3.31	$ 6.17	Black w/ nonglare	$ 0.36	$ 0.43	$ 0.49

K&K arrived at the per unit margin numbers by using the following summarized unit cost data:

Custom / Plastic

Wood	Size Small	Size Medium	Size Large	Plastic	Size 5 × 7	Size 8 × 10	Size 11 × 14
Maple	$ 9.25	$ 14.80	$ 18.50	Tan	$ 0.10	$ 0.15	$ 0.23
Oak	$ 12.75	$ 20.40	$ 25.50	Brown	$ 0.10	$ 0.15	$ 0.23
Cherry	$ 16.50	$ 26.40	$ 33.00	Black	$ 0.10	$ 0.15	$ 0.23

Glass				Glass			
Regular	$ 4.50	$ 5.00	$ 6.00	Regular	$ 0.06	$ 0.09	$ 0.11
Nonglare	$ 5.00	$ 5.75	$ 7.10	Nonglare	$ 0.08	$ 0.11	$ 0.14
Labor	$ 16.00	$ 24.00	$ 32.00	Labor	$ 0.18	$ 0.18	$ 0.18
Overhead per unit[1]	$ 2.36	$ 3.54	$ 4.73	Overhead[1]	$ 0.04	$ 0.04	$ 0.04

[1]Overhead is allocated based on Direct Labor Hours from a common cost pool.

Surfer Dude Duds, Inc.: Considering the Going-Concern Assumption

Frank A. Buckless, Mark S. Beasley,
Steven M. Glover, and Douglas F. Prawitt

LEARNING OBJECTIVES

After completing and discussing this case you should be able to

- Understand the difficulty of assessing the client's going-concern assumption
- Describe the "self-fulfilling prophecy" aspect of a going-concern opinion
- Identify factors that encourage objective auditor judgments despite the presence of friendly client-auditor relationships

BACKGROUND

Mark glanced up at the clock on his office wall. It read 2:30 P.M. He had a scheduled 3:00 P.M. meeting with George "Hang-ten" Baldwin, chief executive officer of Surfer Dude Duds, Inc. Surfer Dude specialized in selling clothing and accessories popularized by the California "surfer" culture. Mark had served as audit partner on the Surfer Dude Duds audit for the past six years and was about ready to wrap up this year's audit.

He enjoyed a strong client relationship with George Baldwin, who was ordinarily a relaxed and easygoing man, now going on 50 years of age. For several years, Mark had received a personal invitation from George to attend a special Christmas party held only for George's employees and close associates. Mark considered George a good friend.

In his six years on the audit, Mark never had any reason to give anything but a clean audit opinion for Surfer Dude Duds, Inc. But this year was different. The economy was in a mild recession, and given the faddishness of clothing trends, Surfer Dude's retail chain was hurting. As sales decreased, Surfer Dude was struggling to meet all its financial obligations. Retail analysts foresaw continuing hard times for clothing retailers in general, and current fashion trends did not seem to be moving in Surfer Dude's direction.

This case was prepared by Frank A. Buckless, Ph.D. and Mark S. Beasley, Ph.D. of North Carolina State University and Steven M. Glover, Ph.D. and Douglas F. Prawitt, Ph.D. of Brigham Young University, as a basis for class discussion. It is not intended to illustrate either effective or ineffective handling of an administrative situation.

As a result, Mark was beginning to doubt Surfer Dude's ability to stay in business through the next year. In fact, after conferring with the concurring partner on the audit, Mark was reluctantly considering the addition of a going-concern explanatory paragraph to the audit report. When Mark broached this possibility with George several weeks ago, George brushed him off.

The purpose of the scheduled 3:00 meeting was to inform George of the decision to issue a going-concern report and to discuss the footnote disclosure of the issue. Mark rehearsed what he was going to say several times, but he remained uneasy about the task before him.

When Mark arrived at George Baldwin's office, a secretary greeted him and told Mr. Baldwin of Mark's arrival. When Mark heard George say, "Send him in," he took a deep breath and headed into George's office with a smile on his face. George was sprawled out in a large executive chair, with his ever-present smile. Mark always marveled at how a person could invariably seem so relaxed and happy. "Hey Mark, what's up? You know I don't like meetings on Friday afternoons," George yawned.

"Well George, I'll get right to the point. As you well know, the retail clothing market has really gone south the past few months. I know I don't need to tell you that Surfer Dude is struggling right now."

"I know, but we'll pull out of it," George insisted. "When you fall off, you've got to climb right back on to ride the next monster, right? We always manage to come out on top. We just need to ride this one out, just like the other times we've struggled."

"George, I know you have high hopes that things will get better soon, but this time things are a little different," Mark sighed. "I know that you might just be able to pull the company out of this. But given the circumstances, I think we're going to have to look at including a going-concern explanatory paragraph in the audit report. I substantially doubt that Surfer Dude will be able to continue as a going concern for the next year. I also recommend that you include a footnote in your financial statements to the same effect."

"What? Mark, you can't go slapping a going-concern report on me! Surfer Dude will go belly-up for sure. No one will be willing to loan us any money. Shoot, nobody will even be willing to sell us anything on account—all our inventory purchases and everything else will be C.O.D. It'll be cash-and-carry only. And what about our customers? Will they buy if they're not sure we'll be there to stand behind our return policy? It'll be your report that puts us under, not the ripples we're hitting now. I've got a feeling things are going to get better soon. We just need a little more time."

"George, you've got to consider the consequences if…."

"Mark, if you slap me with a going-concern report, there is no way we'll be able to pull out of this. Think of all the people who will lose their jobs if Surfer Dude shuts down. Please, I'm asking you to at least think about it." George's ever-present smile was gone.

Mark was silent for what seemed like an eternity. "Okay George, let's both think about it over the weekend. I'll drop by on Monday morning so we can work this out. Thanks for your time."

Mark walked slowly out of the building and to his car. This was not going to be a relaxing weekend.

REQUIREMENTS

1. What are Mark's options?
2. How might a going-concern explanatory paragraph become a "self-fulfilling prophecy" for Surfer Dude?

3. What potential implications arise for the accounting firm if they issue an unqualified report without the going-concern explanatory paragraph?

4. Discuss the importance of full and accurate auditor reporting to the public, and describe possible consequences for both parties if the going-concern explanatory paragraph and footnote are excluded. How might Mark convince George that a going-concern report is in the best interests of all parties involved?

5. How appropriate is it for an audit partner to have a friendly personal relationship with a client?

6. What factors should motivate Mark to be objective in his decision, despite his personal concern for his friend?

7. In your opinion, what should Mark do?

Murchison Technologies, Inc.: Evaluating Attorney's Response and Identifying Proper Audit Report

Frank A. Buckless, Mark S. Beasley,
Steven M. Glover, and Douglas F. Prawitt

LEARNING OBJECTIVES

After completing and discussing this case you should be able to

- Understand the role and timing of client attorney responses to the auditor
- Interpret information contained in an attorney's response letter
- Evaluate proper accounting treatment for material uncertainties
- Identify the correct audit report in light of varying circumstances

INTRODUCTION

Murchison Technologies, Inc., recently developed a patient-billing software system that they market to physicians and dentists. Jim Archer and Janice Johnson founded the company in Austin, Texas, five years ago after working at IBM for more than 15 years. Jim worked as a software programmer and Janice worked as a sales representative, frequently calling on stand-alone medical practices. Together, they identified a need for software to help physician and dental offices track charges for patient services provided by doctors and their staff. With the initial backing of three local venture capitalists, they left IBM, created Murchison Technologies, and devoted their full-time efforts to the development of the billing system software.

For more than three years, they worked on developing the software. After extensive pilot testing, the company shipped its first product to customers in early 200V, just more than three years ago. Sales have been surprisingly strong for the product, which is marketed as MEDTECH Software. Feedback from physicians and dentists has been extremely positive. Most note that billing clerks and office staff find the system quite flexible in tracking numerous types of services for large numbers of patients. Most are

This case was prepared by Frank A. Buckless, Ph.D. and Mark S. Beasley, Ph.D. of North Carolina State University and Steven M. Glover, Ph.D. and Douglas F. Prawitt, Ph.D. of Brigham Young University, as a basis for class discussion. It is not intended to illustrate either effective or ineffective handling of an administrative situation.

pleased with the ability to customize system features for their unique practice needs. Another key to the product's success is the relative cost of the software and the minimal upgrades required of office microcomputers and networks to operate the software.

The company has gradually added employees to their staff. Currently, Murchison employs about 60 people, including software programmers who continually update the software for emerging technological developments. Janice serves as chief executive officer (CEO), and Jim serves as president. Although both serve on the board of directors, they ultimately are accountable to the board, which also includes representatives from the three venture capitalists and two local bankers who financed company expansions through commercial loans issued three years ago.

Your firm, Custer & Custer, LLP, was first engaged by Murchison four years ago to perform a review of their December 31, 200U financial statements. In the subsequent year, the company engaged your firm to conduct the audit of its December 31, 200V financial statements to fulfill requirements of the loan agreements. Custer & Custer issued standard, unqualified reports on both the 200V and 200W annual financial statements.

BACKGROUND ABOUT THE AUDIT

Your firm is in the process of completing the audit of the December 31, 200X financial statements. Currently it is February 17, 200Y and most of the detailed audit testing is complete. As audit senior, you are wrapping up the review of staff working papers. The partner anticipates performing the review and signing off on working papers tomorrow. This should allow fieldwork to be completed in the next day or two.

In preparation for completion of fieldwork, you recently worked with the client to send requests to outside legal counsel asking them to provide the standard attorney-letter response regarding material outstanding claims against the company. You sent requests for attorney confirmations to three law firms providing legal representation for the company.

Based on all the audit work performed, you do not expect any substantive issues related to outstanding litigation claims against Murchison. Your only concern relates to an alleged copyright infringement claim against Murchison that apparently was filed in October 200X. You learned about this case during your review of the November 200X minutes of the board of directors' meeting. The minutes made reference to the case being filed; however, based on notations about the board's discussion it appeared to you that the probability of an unsuccessful outcome related to this case is extremely doubtful. Apparently, another software development company, Physicians Software, Inc., claims that Murchison's MEDTECH software violates a copyright held by Physicians Software. They are suing Murchison for $220,000.

Your subsequent inquiries of management about the case confirmed your expectation of a very low likelihood of unfavorable outcome. In addition, management believes the claim is immaterial relative to the December 31, 200X financial statements. Those financial statements indicate that Murchison's total assets as of December 31, 200X were $7 million, with revenues of $22 million and pretax income of $1.8 million, respectively, for the year then ended.

You received two of the attorney confirmation letters in the mail yesterday. Your review of the attorney responses produced no surprises. Most of the issues being handled by those attorneys relate to collection efforts on delinquent receivables. Those same firms also helped management develop contracts for special sales agreements with two new customers.

One of your audit staff members just delivered mail from the office after running by the office during lunch to pick up a few supplies. You are pleased to see that today's mail includes the attorney confirmation from the third law firm. You quickly open the envelope to make sure all is OK. You begin reading the letter, which is presented in the pages that follow.

You are a little surprised to read the attorney's assessment of the case, and some of the language referencing American Bar Association (ABA) policies puzzles you. You quickly link to professional standards stored on your laptop to review the relevant ABA policy statements. An excerpt of those statements, which are presented as an appendix to Statement on Auditing Standards No. 47, *Inquiry of a Client's Lawyer Concerning Litigation, Claims, and Assessments,* is presented in Exhibit 1 on the pages that follow.

You want to closely evaluate the information contained in the letter in order to have ideas about possible accounting treatment and audit reporting issues so that you can discuss those intelligently with the partner tomorrow. It is also likely that the partner will want to discuss those issues with Murchison's management. In order to properly prepare, please complete the following items noted below.

REQUIREMENTS

1. Review the requirements of Statement of Financial Accounting Standards (SFAS) No. 5, *Accounting for Contingencies.* Describe the three ranges of loss contingencies outlined in SFAS No. 5 and summarize briefly the accounting and disclosure requirements for each of the three ranges.

2. Based on your review of the attorney's confirmation, in which of the three ranges of probability of loss do you think the Physicians Software, Inc., claim falls? How does that assessment differ from management's assessment of the loss probability?

3. Assuming that management and the attorney's assessments differ, how would you resolve such differences when assessing the potential for an unfavorable outcome associated with the claim? What are the pros and cons of relying on the attorney's assessment versus management's assessment?

4. In preparation for tomorrow's meeting with the partner and a likely subsequent meeting with Murchison management, develop recommended responses to the following possible scenarios. In developing your responses, assume that each scenario is independent of the others:

   a. If generally accepted accounting principles require disclosure of this contingency, how would you respond to management's decision against disclosure because they view the claim as immaterial to the December 31, 200X financial statements? Do you believe the potential loss is material? Why or why not?

   b. Assume that even though you convince management that the claim is material, they refuse to provide any disclosure that might be required. Prepare a draft of the auditor's report that would be issued in that scenario.

   c. Assume that you determine, through subsequent discussions with the attorney, that a more likely estimate of the range of loss falls between $30,000 to $45,000. What type of financial statement disclosure do you believe is required in that case? Prepare a draft of the auditor's report that you would issue in that scenario.

d. What if you learn that management has pertinent information available about the case (and the case is deemed material) but refuses to share that information with you? Prepare a draft of the auditor's report that you would issue in that scenario.

e. Assume that you convinced management to disclose the contingency in the footnotes to the December 31, 200X financial statements and that your audit report on those financial statements was a standard, unqualified audit report. What would your responsibilities be if you learned two months after the issuance of the report that Murchison settled the case for $190,000?

f. Assume that the settlement of the litigation prohibits future sales of MEDTECH software. What implication would that have on the auditor's report on the December 31, 200X financial statements?

5. Discuss why the attorney's letter is being received so close to the completion of the audit. Was the request for the attorney's response an oversight that should have been taken care of closer to December 31, 200X, or was Custer & Custer appropriate in not requesting the response until close to the end of fieldwork?

6. Assume that Custer & Custer was delayed a month in completing fieldwork. What actions would be appropriate relating to gathering evidence about potential contingencies?

7. Review the ABA policy statement excerpts in Exhibit 1. What limitations exist as it relates to the attorney's response? To what extent should auditors rely solely on attorney responses to identify outstanding claims against audit clients?

Dunn & King, PLLC
First National Tower, Suite 2300
200 Church Street
Austin, Texas 78701

February 15, 200Y

Custer & Custer, LLP
City National Plaza
16th Floor
435 Seventh Avenue, South
Austin, Texas 78702

Dear Sirs:

By letter dated February 4, 200Y, Mr. James Archer, President of Murchison Technologies, Inc., (the "Company") has requested us to furnish you with certain information in connection with your examination of the accounts of the Company as of December 31, 200X.

Subject to the foregoing and to the last paragraph of this letter, we advise you that since January 1, 200X, we have not been engaged to give substantive attention to, or represent the Company in connection with material-loss contingencies coming within the scope of clause (a) of Paragraph 5 of the ABA Statement of Policy referred to in the last paragraph of this letter, except as follows:

On October 16, 200X, a suit was filed naming Murchison Technologies, Inc., as defendant in an alleged copyright infringement claim. The plaintiff, Physicians Software, Inc., ("Physicians") alleges that Murchison's MEDTECH software violates Physicians' copyright registered for Physicians' PHYSITRACK software. The PHYSITRACK software also is marketed as a medical-practice billing system software and is a direct competitor of Murchison. The pending litigation claim alleges that Murchison violated Physicians' copyright protection in the development of the MEDTECH software. Allegedly, a former software development programmer of Physicians was hired away by Murchison four years ago when Murchison was in the development phase of the MEDTECH software. Physicians claims that trade secrets on its PHYSITRACK software were pirated from Physicians and incorporated into the design of the MEDTECH software. The plaintiff is seeking damages of $220,000.

In preparation of providing this letter to you, we have reviewed the merits of the claim against Murchison, which is currently in the deposition phase. At this time, our assessment of the likelihood of a negative future outcome occurring against Murchison in this case is more than remote but less than likely. The possible ranges of costs and damages are estimated to extend from $150,000 to $200,000.

The information set forth herein is as of February 15, 200Y, the date on which we commenced our internal review procedures for purposes of preparing this letter, and we disclaim any undertaking to advise you of changes which thereafter may be brought to your attention.

This response is limited by, and in accordance with, the ABA Statement of Policy Regarding Lawyer's Responses to Auditor's Requests for Information (December 1975); without limiting the generality of the foregoing, the limitations set forth in such Statement on the scope and use of this response (Paragraphs 2 and 7) are specifically incorporated herein by reference, and any description herein of any "loss contingencies" is qualified in its entirety by Paragraph 5 of the Statement and the accompanying Commentary (which is an integral part of the Statement). Consistent with the sentence of Paragraph 6 of the ABA Statement of Policy and pursuant to the Company's request, this will confirm as correct the Company's understanding as set forth in its audit inquiry letter to us that whenever, in the course of performing legal services for the Company with respect to a matter recognized to involve an unasserted possible claim or assessment that may call for financial statement disclosure, we have formed a professional conclusion that the Company must disclose or consider disclosure concerning such possible claim or assessment, we, as a matter of professional responsibility to the Company, will so advise the Company and will consult with the Company concerning the question of such disclosure and the applicable requirements of Statement of Financial Accounting Standards No. 5.

Very truly yours,

Dunn & King, PLLC

Austin, Texas

Exhibit 1
Excerpts from Exhibit II of AU Section 337C
American Bar Association Statement on Policy Regarding Lawyers' Responses to Auditor's Requests for Information[1]

Paragraph 2—Limitations of Scope of Response

"It is appropriate for the lawyer to set forth in his response, by way of limitation, the scope of his engagement by the client. It is also appropriate for the lawyer to indicate the date as of which information is furnished and to disclaim any undertaking to advise the auditor of changes which may thereafter be brought to the lawyer's attention. Unless the lawyer's response indicates otherwise, (a) it is properly limited to matters which have been given substantive attention by the lawyer in the form of legal consultation and, where appropriate, legal representation since the beginning of the period or periods being reported upon, and (b) if a law firm or a law department, the auditor may assume that the firm or department has endeavored, to the extent believed necessary by the firm or department, to determine from lawyers currently in the firm or department who have performed services for the client since the beginning of the fiscal period under audit whether such services involved substantive attention in the form of legal consultation concerning those contingencies referred to in Paragraph 5(a) below, but beyond that, no review has been made of any of the client's transactions or other matters for the purpose of identifying loss contingencies to be described in the response."

Paragraph 5—Loss Contingencies

"When properly requested by the client, it is appropriate for the lawyer to furnish to the auditor information concerning the following matters if the lawyer has been engaged by the client to represent or advise the client professionally with respect thereto and he has devoted substantive attention to them in the form of legal representation or consultation:

    a.   overtly threatened or pending litigation, whether or not specified by the client;

    b.   a contractually assumed obligation which the client has specifically identified and upon which the client has specifically requested, in the inquiry letter or a supplement thereto, comment to the auditor;

    c.   an unasserted possible claim or assessment which the client has specifically identified and upon which the client has specifically requested, in the inquiry letter or a supplement thereto, comment to the auditor...."

Paragraph 6—Lawyer's Professional Responsibility

"Independent of the scope of his response to the auditor's request for information, the lawyer, depending upon the nature of the matters as to which he is engaged, may have as part of his professional responsibility to his client an obligation to advise the client concerning the need for or advisability of public disclosure of a wide range of events and circumstances. The lawyer has an obligation not knowingly to participate in any violation by the client of the disclosure requirements of the securities laws. In appropriate circumstances, the lawyer also may be required under the Code of Professional Responsibility to resign his engagement if his advice concerning disclosures is disregarded by the client. The auditor may properly assume that whenever, in the course of performing legal services for the client with respect to a matter recognized to involve an unasserted possible claim or assessment which may call for financial statement disclosure, the lawyer has formed a professional conclusion that the client must disclose or consider disclosure concerning such possible claim or assessment, the lawyer, as a matter of professional responsibility to the client, will so advise the client and will consult with the client concerning the question of such disclosure and the applicable requirements of FAS 5."

Paragraph 7—Limitation on Use of Response

"Unless otherwise stated in the lawyer's response, it shall be solely for the auditor's information in connection with his audit of the financial condition of the client and is not to be quoted in whole or in part or otherwise referred to in any financial statements of the client or related documents, nor is it to be filed with any governmental agency or other person, without the lawyer's prior written consent. Notwithstanding such limitation, the response can be furnished to others in compliance with court process or when necessary to defend the auditor against a challenge of the audit by the client or a regulatory agency, provided that the lawyer is given written notice of the circumstances at least twenty days before the response is so to be furnished to others, or as long in advance as possible if the situation does not permit such period of notice."

[1]Source: Statement on Auditing Standards No. 12, *Inquiry of a Client's Lawyer Concerning Litigation, Claims, and Assessments,* AU Section 337, *AICPA Professional Standards* Volume 1.

Index